THE BROADVIEW
INTRODUCTION TO
BOOK HISTORY

THE BROADVIEW INTRODUCTION TO BOOK HISTORY

MICHELLE LEVY & TOM MOLE

broadview press

BROADVIEW PRESS — www.broadviewpress.com
Peterborough, Ontario, Canada

Founded in 1985, Broadview Press remains a wholly independent publishing house. Broadview's focus is on academic publishing; our titles are accessible to university and college students as well as scholars and general readers. With over 600 titles in print, Broadview has become a leading international publisher in the humanities, with world-wide distribution. Broadview is committed to environmentally responsible publishing and fair business practices.

© 2017 Michelle Levy and Tom Mole

All rights reserved. No part of this book may be reproduced, kept in an information storage and retrieval system, or transmitted in any form or by any means, electronic or mechanical, including photocopying, recording, or otherwise, except as expressly permitted by the applicable copyright laws or through written permission from the publisher.

LIBRARY AND ARCHIVES CANADA CATALOGUING IN PUBLICATION

Levy, Michelle Nancy, 1968–, author
    The Broadview introduction to book history / Michelle Levy & Tom Mole.

Includes bibliographical references and index.
ISBN 978-1-55481-087-1 (softcover)

    1. Books—History. I. Mole, Tom, 1976–, author II. Title.

Z4.L584 2017   002.09   C2017-900528-6

Broadview Press handles its own distribution in North America
PO Box 1243, Peterborough, Ontario K9J 7H5, Canada
555 Riverwalk Parkway, Tonawanda, NY 14150, USA
Tel: (705) 743-8990; Fax: (705) 743-8353
email: customerservice@broadviewpress.com

Distribution is handled by Eurospan Group in the UK, Europe, Central Asia, Middle East, Africa, India, Southeast Asia, Central America, South America, and the Caribbean. Distribution is handled by Footprint Books in Australia and New Zealand.

Canada

Broadview Press acknowledges the financial support of the Government of Canada through the Canada Book Fund for our publishing activities.

Copy edited by Martin R. Boyne
Cover design by Michel Vrana
Typesetting by Jennifer Blais

*For Ethan and Nate,
and for Freya.*

Contents

List of Figures   ix
Acknowledgements   xi
Introduction   xiii

Chapter 1: Materiality   1

Reading Books   3
Bibliography   10
Making Printed Books   17
Typography   22

Chapter 2: Textuality   29

Who's Been Tampering with My Text?   31
Copy-Text   38
Variants   41
Authorial Intentions   45
Textual Pluralism   54

Chapter 3: Printing and Reading   63

Print and the Book   66
The Impact of Print   70
Models for Book History   74
Print Economies   77
Controlling Print / Controlling Reading   81
Methods for a History of Reading   89

Chapter 4: Intermediality   99

Models of Intermediality   103
Orality and Writing   105
Manuscript and Print   112
Text and Image   123

Chapter 5: Remediating   133

New Media, New Materiality   135
(Hyper)Textuality   141
Digital Printing and Screen Reading   145
Reading, Knowledge, and the Digital Turn   153
Computer-Assisted Reading   156

Conclusion   163

The History of the Book: A Brief Chronology   171
Glossary   179
Further Reading   205
Permissions Acknowledgements   215
Index   217

List of Figures

1.1: The First Folio, frontispiece and facing page   15
1.2: Basic anatomy of the roman letterform   23
3.1: Copy of one of Gutenberg's 1454 indulgences   68
3.2: Darnton, "Communications Circuit"   75
3.3: Adams and Barker, "A New Model for the Study of the Book"   76
3.4: Messrs. Lackington, Allen & Co., Temple of the Muses, Finsbury Square (1809)   81
3.5: Thomas Bowdler, *The Family Shakspeare* (1861)   88
3.6: Men reading newspapers in Chicago, outside the *Chicago Daily News* offices   93
4.1: Emily Dickinson, "We talked with each other about each other," c. 1879, Amherst Manuscript #514   120
4.2: Emily Dickinson, "We talked with each other about each other," in *Bolts of Melody: New Poems of Emily Dickinson*   121
4.3: Thomas Bewick, "The Great Bustard," *A History of British Birds* (1787–1804)   127
5.1: *New York Times* Subscription Plans, 21 January 2016   147
5.2: Jane Austen, *Pride and Prejudice*, Interactive Edition (2014)   149

Acknowledgements

We are grateful to the students who have taken our courses on book history over the last several years; they have helped us to understand the field and to articulate our explanations of it. Some of them will recognize ideas and examples from their classes in this book. We have been fortunate to benefit from the scholarship, collegiality, and intelligence of exceptional colleagues in the Print Culture program at Simon Fraser University, the Centre for the History of the Book at the University of Edinburgh, and the Interacting with Print Research Group. We'd like to acknowledge the work of everyone at Broadview Press, especially Marjorie Mather, who commissioned the book, Martin Boyne, who offered valuable advice, and Tara Trueman, who oversaw the production process. Like its companion volume, *The Broadview Reader in Book History*, this book emerged from extended periods of long-distance collaborative writing, punctuated by short and intense bursts of writing and editing together in person. We've each been grateful for the other's support, dedication, and good humour throughout the process. We are also thankful for the love and support of our families, which made the writing of this book possible.

Introduction

Book history is the study of books as physical objects: as devices for storing and circulating knowledge and ideas. It is also, therefore, the study of how books are produced, circulated, and received at different historical times and places. It is interested in every aspect of books: how they are made; how they are promoted and sold; how they are purchased, used, kept, organized, and re-circulated; and by whom. The books it studies can take many forms. They may be manuscript, printed, or electronic, produced on vellum, paper, or computer chips. They may be ornate luxuries made as gifts for kings or mass-market commodities for everyday consumers. They may be books of scripture read aloud in services of worship or pornographic ones viewed in private, slim volumes of avant-garde poetry printed by hand, or graphic novels viewed on an e-reader. Book history is also interested in material that was not bound into volumes—printed broadsides, pamphlets, periodicals, engravings; loose sheets of handwriting, such as letters; and even inscriptions, such as one might find on a gravestone. We use "books," then, as a capacious term, standing in a much broader field that studies both material artefacts and the cultural practices of their creation and use. For much of our recorded history, books—understood expansively—have been a key technology for conveying information, ideas, and entertainment. As a result, book history is a wide-ranging and important area of study.

Book history emerged as a distinctive and dynamic field of inquiry in the 1980s and 1990s by bringing together a variety of existing intellectual activities and setting them into new relationships with one another. It drew on existing core humanities subjects such as history, literature, and art history, as well as areas of specialization that had previously been seen as marginal within these disciplines, such as economic and publishing history (within history), bibliography and textual criticism (within literary studies), and reproductive prints (within art history). It has generated new areas of study, such as the history of authorship and reading. In the last two decades, the study of books has been invigorated by the rise of digital media: as material artefacts have migrated into new electronic formats, they have raised profound questions about the nature of materiality and textuality. The result has been not just a new sub-specialization within an existing subject but also a disruptive new way of thinking. Book history has helped to produce new accounts of major historical events and movements, fostered a new kind of attention to material culture, and challenged some of the core assumptions of literary and intellectual history.

Book history emerged in different ways in different contexts and places. In France (as *histoire du livre*), its early focus was on the circulation of books in society and their effect on large historical events. In Germany (as *Buchwissenschaft* or *Geschichte des Buchwesens*), its focus was on the history of how books are published and distributed. In Great Britain, it has been connected to bibliography or textual editing, which studies the different versions of a work, usually in order to produce a new edition of it. In literary studies, it emphasizes the material circulation of literary texts in manuscript, print, or digital media and the ways in which they become meaningful in historical contexts. In history departments, book history has been allied with the *Annales* school, which tends to focus on long historical durations, quantitative evidence, and the history of ordinary people; it has also been practised as micro-history, which uses narrow case studies to illuminate broader historical mentalities. In economic history, the focus has been on the operation of the book trades, the system of copyright, or the marketing of books. Art historians consider the production and circulation of printed images, or the role of books in circulating early photographs. Students of information studies may focus on how books were collected, organized, stored, and preserved in the past by collectors and libraries. The history of reading has emerged as a specialization in its own right. Among scholars of digital humanities, media archaeology, and new media studies, book history has taken still other forms.

The aim of this introductory guide is not to provide a comprehensive overview. It tries not to privilege any one disciplinary perspective or historical period, although it undoubtedly bears the marks of our training in literary studies and of our background as scholars of the eighteenth and nineteenth centuries. No short introduction of this kind could take account of the increasingly global range of book history, as scholars investigate the history of the book in South Asia, New Zealand, Canada, colonial America, and elsewhere. Nor could it hope to offer anything like a satisfying survey of the millennia-long history of books, from their earliest appearance to their current transformation by electronic media. Rather, this guide and its accompanying Reader aim to help you to find your bearings within the field, and to provide a map that will help you navigate as you explore book history more widely and identify your own particular interests within it.

To get started, we might think about four epochs in the history of the book, to help clarify the story that unfolds in this Introduction and its accompanying Reader. The first is the appearance of one particular form of the book, called the codex, and its slow adoption in the first centuries of the Common Era. A codex consists of a number of sheets (of paper or papyrus or vellum), folded and/or stacked on top of one another, fixed together along a spine, and usually surrounded by a cover of some kind. Almost all of the books we're familiar with today are codices (the plural of codex). Before codices, books took the form of scrolls, where the reader rolled a long piece of papyrus or vellum from the bottom to the top, reading downwards, or from one side to the other, reading in columns. The codex took quite a long time to replace the scroll as the default form of the book. It was first described by the Roman poet Martial in the first century CE, but it didn't come to dominate book production until about the fifth or sixth century. The codex's rise in popularity coincided with the spread of Christianity throughout the Roman Empire. During those centuries, Christians were early adopters of the codex form; they used it especially for their scriptures and pioneered some of the techniques for making codices. The codex was portable, resistant to wear and tear, and it allowed you to flip back and forth between pages and to move more easily between different sections of the text.

The second important epoch in our story is Johannes Gutenberg's invention of moveable type and the printing press around 1439, and its subsequent adoption throughout Europe and beyond. Printing with moveable type is described in more detail in Chapter 1. Whereas previously texts had to be laboriously copied by hand, printing made it possible to produce large numbers of (reasonably) accurate copies much faster. Scholars debate the nature and speed of print's impact (see Chapter 3) but there's no debate about the massive significance of printing for Western science and culture. It became possible to copy text faster, to produce large numbers of copies, and to disseminate them widely. Much time that had previously been spent by scientists and scholars in copying was now freed up for research, and where scholars had previously travelled to look at books, books now increasingly travelled to their readers. New ideas could reach larger audiences more rapidly. The literature and knowledge of previous centuries could increasingly be encountered first hand rather than mediated through oral tradition, and the scriptures could be read by believers rather than mediated to them through sermons and other kinds of oral teaching. Nor was print used only for books: a wide range of other printed matter, like song-sheets, posters, and proclamations also appeared. Print did not immediately displace manuscript books, which continued to circulate alongside printed volumes. But with the invention of print, the history of the book moved into a new epoch.

Although printed books were produced in quite large numbers throughout the sixteenth and seventeenth centuries in Europe, they remained fairly expensive and their circulation was confined to a literate elite, usually concentrated geographically around the court and/or major centres of learning. The third important epoch in the history of the book occurred over the course of at least a century, beginning in the late eighteenth century, as the amount of printed matter that was produced increased dramatically and the cost of print gradually decreased. There are a number of reasons for this: changes in copyright law, rising literacy rates, improvements in technology that industrialized print production (discussed in Chapter 1), and the opening of non-local markets, among others. In several waves that began at the end of the eighteenth century and continued to the end of the nineteenth, print saturated European culture. The default assumption became that most people would engage with print. From around 1800 onwards, it makes sense to speak of the West (and, in due course, most of its colonial territories) as a "print culture."

For a long time, then, print was the default method for publicly circulating knowledge, information, and entertainment. Printed books and other print matter played an important role in studying, working, and relaxing. Print had always co-existed with manuscript and oral forms of transmitting information, but from the mid-nineteenth century onward, print increasingly co-existed with a wider range of media. This is our fourth (and current) epoch, when print faces competition from an array of new media. The photograph, telegraph, typewriter, phonograph, telephone, cinema, radio, and eventually television are just some of the new media that emerged as other important means of communication, displacing the centrality of print. The story continues with the introduction of personal computing in the late twentieth century and with the rise of digital technology in the last 30 years, which has once again shifted the media ecology in which the book exists. Some people have been prompted to produce gloomy elegies about the death of the book, the demise of print, or the end of serious reading. Others have worried about the differences between reading on the page and reading on the screen, suggesting that screens—especially when they belong to Internet-enabled devices—make us worse readers. For a long time, these assertions had little hard data to back them up. Now, however, studies are starting to emerge about e-book sales, reading patterns, and the effect of screen reading on how well people understand what they read and how much they retain. Digital technologies are revolutionizing how we interact with, and think about, books. We discuss these developments in more detail in Chapter 5.

Just as the book has taken many forms, so has reading: silently or aloud, perusing many books or repeatedly returning to the same one, paying close attention or skimming. When exactly the practice of silent reading began is a matter of dispute. In St Augustine's *Confessions*, written at the end of the fourth century CE (just as the codex form was starting to gain ground over the scroll), Augustine describes Ambrose, his teacher, reading silently. He recalls how "[w]hen [Ambrose] read, his eyes scanned the page and his heart sought out the meaning, but his voice was silent and his tongue was still." Augustine seems to have found silent reading unusual enough to be worth commenting on. Before this, he implies, most people vocalized the text when they read, even if they were reading to themselves. Children learning to read still say words out loud as they read them today. There is some evidence of silent reading as far back as classical Greece: Plutarch tells a story in the first century CE about Alexander the Great reading silently. Many historians argue, however, that silent reading took a long time to become widespread. Even when silent reading became more common, reading aloud continued to be practised in a variety of settings. People read aloud in university lectures, in services of worship, and to their families; monks read aloud to their communities during shared meals; and servants read to their employers. Reading aloud has always been how written texts are disseminated to the illiterate, but literate people have often chosen to be read aloud to as well. Since the twentieth century, audiobooks have provided a new version of reading aloud.

Historians of reading sometimes distinguish between "intensive" and "extensive" reading. Reading "intensively" means returning to a small number of books again and again, whereas reading "extensively" involves reading a much larger number of books (or other printed matter), and often reading them only once. There are several reasons why you might read intensively. When books were very expensive and labour-intensive to produce (especially when they had to be copied by hand), most people had access to very few books. People often read these books intensively because they didn't have access to any other reading matter. As a result, they came to know their books well and invested significant emotional energy in them. Another reason why people read intensively has to do with the content of the written material. Sacred books may be read repeatedly as part of devotional practice, while a textbook might be read intensively to prepare for an exam. Children often read (or are read to) in this way, asking for the same story over and over again. (They also consume other media "intensively," watching the same movie repeatedly.) Many of us have favourite books that we return to regularly. Extensive reading is a response to easy access to reading matter and has often been associated with the proliferation of print. Historians of reading have at times suggested that the history of reading can be told as a transition from intensive to extensive reading. With more printed matter in circulation, most people's reading experience shifted from conditions of scarcity to conditions of relative plenty. By the end of the eighteenth century, the sense of information overload—already experienced by scholars in the early modern period—became a generalized concern. But historians of reading have also identified a whole range of problems with and exceptions to this narrative. We prefer to think about intensive and extensive reading as describing a set of practices that have long co-existed, and that also co-exist in the lives of individual readers.

The history of reading also raises questions about the nature or quality of attention itself. One form of reading may be described as "attentive" reading—an immersive, long-form, and linear practice, such as reading a novel from beginning to end, with care and thought. This kind of reading might be supported by annotation, note taking, highlighting, or copying, all of which manifest a certain level of intellectual engagement with a text. Alternatively, immersive reading might mean that you are incapable of stopping to add a note, and even that you are able to read without being distracted by your environment. This kind of reading seems qualitatively different from what has been described as "hyperreading," which includes searching, filtering, skimming, and hyperlinking, all ways in which we might read a newspaper, magazine, or website (Hayles, *Broadview Reader in Book History* [hereafter *BRBH*] 491–510; see below for this referencing format). Studies using eye-tracking software have shown that we tend to scan web pages in an F pattern, our eyes moving quickly down the left-hand side and flicking occasionally across the screen as we skim efficiently to pull out the information we need. Canny web designers capitalize on this, putting the most important information (or the most lucrative advertisements) where we're most likely to look. These different modes of reading suggest that the ways in which we read are not always the choice of the reader but are rather cued by the different material forms our reading material takes. Although "hyperreading" might sound like an inferior version of reading, we think of it as a strategy, a positive set of skills that we use to negotiate information overload.

This survey of different reading practices tells us that people read in different ways for different reasons, and that they have always done so. Someone might read a thriller to relax before going to bed, a textbook to become more knowledgeable, a magazine to pass the time in an airport, a bible in search of spiritual edification, and an erotic story because they hope it will be sexually arousing. One person can switch between intensive reading and extensive reading, as well as between reading on the screen and reading on the page. Book history can study all these modes of reading and the books that make them possible. Book historians sometimes have strong attachments to the printed codex or to particular kinds of reading. But book history as a field of study isn't committed to any one form of the book, or any particular kind of reading. Its methods can be applied to manuscripts and electronic texts, to the most intensive kind of devotional reading and the most cursory skimming, to the most expensive books and the cheapest, the oldest and the newest.

Although you can certainly read it on its own, we have designed this book to be read alongside the *Broadview Reader in Book History*. As mentioned above, we refer to the essays in that book using the abbreviation *BRBH*. Like that book, this one is divided into five sections. Chapter 1, "Materiality," considers how our understanding of books is transformed when we think of them not simply as "transparent" vehicles for the texts they contain but as material artefacts. It introduces the idea that books convey messages not only through the texts they contain but also through their material features, which book historians call the "bibliographic code." In order to decipher this code, we have to understand something about bibliography—the study of books as material objects—and about how books were made on the handpress, as well as about how the features we're familiar with, such as the title page, took shape historically. This chapter introduces those topics. Chapter 2, "Textuality," is about how, when the same work appears in different books (or magazines, manuscripts, and so on), one text often varies in small but important ways from another. Scholarly editors try to reconstruct why those variants appear and to produce the best new edition of the work that they can. This chapter explains how they do that, and, since editors don't always agree about how best to proceed, it outlines some of the ways in which they disagree. Chapter 3, "Printing and Reading," examines the conceptual models and historical narratives that have been developed to help us understand some of the social, economic, religious, and political impacts of print. This chapter also explores the history of reading, focusing on long-standing attempts to control reading, and the methodological challenges presented by studying practices that often leave no trace. Chapter 4, "Intermediality," considers the book as one medium within a much larger media ecology. Drawing upon the fields of new media studies and communication theory, this chapter argues for the need to understand the book intermedially, that is, to situate it among other forms of communication technology, such as oral, manuscript, and visual culture. Chapter 5, "Remediating," considers how digital media are transforming the aspects of book history and book culture covered in the first four chapters. Many new digital innovations might prompt us to think not only about whether digital media are displacing print media but also about how the printed book has interacted historically with other media. In this chapter, we also think about how digital media offer new possibilities for studying books from the past. The book concludes with a chronology, glossary, and guide to further reading; words that appear in the glossary are **bolded** in the text.

Partly as a result of the media shifts examined in Chapter 5, now is a great time to study book history. For over 500 years in the West, a particular form of the book—the printed codex—has been woven into the very fabric of our lives. It has been the default medium for publicly circulating information and entertainment and has structured the work, leisure, and religious devotion of countless people. When anything becomes as ubiquitous as this—a discourse, a medium, a technology, or a set of ideas—it becomes difficult to make it an object of inquiry. It's so pervasive that we can't really step back and see it clearly. Now, as the cultural centrality of the printed codex is challenged, we are prompted to reassess its value. We are also gaining a new perspective on the printed codex as a material form, which allows us better to analyse its merits and shortcomings as a technology for information storage, circulation, and retrieval, to situate it in the long history of media change, to think about how it differed from the forms of the book that came before, and to contemplate how it might differ from what is to come.

CHAPTER I

MATERIALITY

Reading Books

Book history involves paying careful attention to the material form of the book and how it was made, circulated, and used. Some people think that this is exactly the wrong way to approach a book. The most important thing about a book, they say, is the text it contains. The material form of the book—the paper, the binding, the typeface, the format, the dust jacket—is just the vehicle that allows words to reach their readers. It's the words, not the vehicle, that should command our attention. This view, which dismisses the materiality of the book, has a long heritage. It stretches back at least to the eighteenth century—not coincidentally, the period when books first became cheap enough to circulate widely. In one of Alexander Pope's poetic **epistles**, from 1731, he introduces a rich fool who wastes his money on a flashy but tasteless house and its contents, including a study lined with beautiful and expensive books that their owner hasn't read. Pope writes: "In books, not authors, curious is my Lord."[1] The mark of an idiot, Pope said, was to pay too much attention to the physical form of the book and not enough to its contents. Lord Chesterfield advised his son in 1749 that "[d]ue attention to the inside of books, and due contempt for the outside, is the proper relation between a man of sense and his books."[2]

This attitude extends into modern academic discussions of the book. The Belgian literary critic Georges Poulet wrote in 1972 that "[b]ooks are objects. On a table, on shelves, in store windows, they wait for someone to come and deliver them from their materiality, from their immobility."[3] Even as Poulet acknowledges the physical form taken by the book ("books are objects"), he is keen to leave that material dimension behind in order to get to an experience of the text (and, through the text, the mind of the author). Poulet imagines us "deliver[ing]" the book from its physical existence, as Christians pray "deliver us from evil" in the Lord's Prayer. The body of the book is cast aside in order that the soul of the text may be experienced in a realm of pure language, or a space of thought unsullied by contact with the world of things. The desire to look *through* the book, rather than *at* the book, is a common one. It's a desire that book history resists. Book historians linger over the physical form of the book—its thingness—in order to learn what it can tell us.

And it can tell us quite a lot. The physical form of a book sends us messages about how it might be or have been circulated, used, and valued.

When we talk about the *meaning* of, say, *Jane Eyre*, we're normally talking about the meaning of the work written by Charlotte Brontë; but the material form of the book in which we read that work is also part of how meaning is constructed. The literary critic Jerome McGann makes this point by distinguishing two kinds of semiotic system, or two codes, that combine in a book. "Every literary work that descends to us," he writes, "operates through the deployment of a double helix of perceptual codes: the linguistic codes, on one hand, and the bibliographic codes on the other."[4] The "linguistic code" is composed of the words in the text. The "bibliographic code" is composed of the messages sent by the paper the book is printed on, the way it's bound, its size, the appearance of the dust jacket, and so on.

Most of us are actually quite adept at deciphering these bibliographic codes, even if we don't realize we're doing it. Imagine you've got three books in front of you: one is a cheap popular thriller, another is an academic **monograph**, and the third is a prayer book. Now imagine, for a moment, that these books are all written in a language you can't read. You can still understand a lot about them by paying attention to their physical format. The first one is printed on cheap, off-white paper. It's a paperback. The spine has been glued rather than stitched. The cover is brightly coloured and has big silver lettering on it. It's light and small enough to fit in a coat pocket. What do these facts tell us about the book? We can tell that it's portable and not meant to endure: the pages would start to fall out after only a few re-readings. It's basically disposable: the cheap, acidic paper will become brittle and crumble over time. When you read the book you will damage the spine, producing visible creases (and so, incidentally, you can usually tell if someone else has read this book before you). The bright, shiny cover is designed to catch your eye in a shop display, which tells you that this might well be an impulse buy rather than a book you would seek out. You could read the book anywhere, because it's designed to be easy to read on the go. You could certainly take it on a journey with you, or read it on the bus. In fact, you know from your experience of seeing similar books that this is the kind of mass-market paperback often sold in airports for people to read on planes. You probably wouldn't give it as a gift on a significant occasion, take it with you when moving house, or display it on your shelves with any special pride. Without reading a word of the text, then, you know quite a lot from the physical format of the book about where this book is sold, how it is valued, and how it is supposed to be used.

Now examine the second book. It's printed on bright white paper, which is comparatively thick. It's a hardback. The spine is sturdy and has been stitched. It has either no dust jacket or a comparatively plain one. It's significantly larger than the first book. This is obviously a more expensive book than the first one. It's made to last: the paper is probably acid-free and will not deteriorate over time. The binding will stand up to multiple readings, so the book can either be read by one person many times or by many people once. If you open it up, it will probably lie flat on the desk, allowing you to take notes from it or put it aside while you consult another volume. You know from your experience of seeing books like this one that you might find it in a university library. This is one reason why it doesn't need an eye-catching dust jacket: most libraries discard dust jackets, and in any case, this book doesn't need to attract attention from a traveller in an airport bookstore: its intended purchaser is a professional scholar or a librarian, who will likely learn about it through other channels, such as publishers' **catalogues** or reviews in scholarly journals. At the bottom of the spine this book bears the name of a university press, a sign of its academic prestige. The physical format of this book tells you that the text it contains should be taken seriously. It makes possible certain kinds of use, such as taking notes, comparing, and checking citations, and it ensures that the text the book contains can be read by many people and will be accessible for many years. It also discourages other kinds of use. You're more likely to read this book at a desk or in a study than on an airplane.

Finally, consider the prayer book. It's a very small book that easily fits into your hand. It's printed on very thin paper (actually known as "Bible-paper" in the book trade). It's a hardback, and the spine is sturdy. It has no dust jacket, but it has gilt lettering on the front cover. The edges of the pages have also been gilded, making them shine gold. On one hand, then, this is a portable book—you're supposed to keep it with you. On the other hand, the book has comparatively high status: it comes with some of the trappings of authority, such as a hardback cover and gilt lettering and edging. These features also make it more expensive. It is durable and would last a lifetime if you looked after it. In the front it has a presentation plate with spaces for the names of the giver and the recipient, to allow it to be given as a gift. If you inhabit the religious tradition this prayer book belongs to, you will almost certainly have seen similar books. The physical form of the book, in this case, tells you that the texts it contains are at the same time highly valued and intended for regular use.

As well as taking on a particular physical form, these books also come with textual elements that don't form part of the main body of the text. These elements may be written by the book's author or by someone else: an editor, reviewer, or another author, for example. The critic Gérard Genette notes that the text is "rarely presented in an unadorned state, unreinforced and unaccompanied by a certain number of verbal or other productions, such as an author's name, a title, a **preface**, illustrations."[5] He calls these elements of the book "**paratexts**." The popular thriller will probably have quotations from reviews on the back cover, or endorsements from other thriller writers. The academic monograph will have endnotes documenting the research its author undertook. These paratexts can send messages even if you don't read their text. The presence of a long section of endnotes displays the scholar's erudition even before you start to read them. The *absence* of paratexts can also be significant. The fact that the prayer book has no blurb or introduction might suggest that its authority can stand without any reinforcement from others.

We're all able to read these bibliographic codes because we're familiar with the conventions that the publishing industry has developed to distinguish different kinds of books from one another. Most of the time you don't notice that you're reading the bibliographic code, but you would notice it if the conventions were broken. You'd think it strange if you were browsing in an airport bookstore and suddenly, among all the small-format paperbacks with their shiny covers, you came across a large, academic-looking hardback with a sober dust-jacket. And you'd also find it strange if you were looking along a shelf of academic books in a university library and came across one packaged like the latest novel by a popular thriller writer. Although they are familiar to us now, these bibliographic and paratextual codes took a long time to become established. Lucien Febvre and Henri-Jean Martin have shown in detail how the basic conventions of the printed book emerged in early-modern Europe (*BRBH* 15–36). For example, they note how, in the earliest printed books, no **title pages** existed. Details about the production of a book would appear at the end of the text in what is known as the **colophon**. The colophon, they observe, was "a residue from the manuscript," and it took some time for the title page to replace it (21). Paratextual conventions have thus evolved over time. Just as we sometimes have difficulty reading the unfamiliar language of older texts, we have to make an effort to learn the bibliographic codes of older books.

Book historians, then, think of the book as a complex artefact that constructs and conveys meanings through both its physical form and its linguistic contents, rather than simply as a container or vehicle for the meaning of the text. This leads them to think about the other people besides the author who are involved in the production of the material book. Authors, after all, don't write books. They write novels, poems, plays, political treatises, religious tracts, histories, memoirs, and so on, and these are then turned into books—into material artefacts made of paper, ink, and so forth—by other people, usually many other people. In some cases, authors exercise quite a lot of control over the physical production of their work: the eighteenth-century novelist Laurence Sterne, for example, paid minute attention to the punctuation of his novel *Tristram Shandy*, making the printer change the length of dashes on some pages.[6] But in most cases, recognizing that the material form of the book shapes how it is read means acknowledging that people besides the author are involved in making meaning.

It also means that, when a work is reprinted in different books, the relationship between the linguistic code and the bibliographic code changes. If a piece of writing is republished in a new **edition**, included in an **anthology**, or embedded in a school textbook, then McGann's "double helix of perceptual codes" is untwisted: the linguistic code is detached from its bibliographic code and attached to a new one. When you read a classic novel in a modern edition, with the paratexts of an introduction and notes, you have an experience of that novel that is different from that of its first readers. Even before you read the introduction or notes (or even if you skip them), the fact that an editor and a publisher thought it was worthwhile to edit and publish the text in this format tells you at least two things. First, they must have thought the novel worth studying and analysing in detail. Second, they believed it to be sufficiently difficult that modern readers would need some help to understand it. The novel's first edition would have appeared without these paratexts, or with different ones. By encouraging us to pay attention to these details, book history can sensitize us to the distance between our own reading experiences and those of readers in the past, including those reading the same words.

If some of the information we can glean from the material form of a book originates with the **publisher**, other aspects of a book's physical appearance may originate with the purchaser or reader. Book historians call this "copy-specific information," because it appears in only one copy of the book, not in every copy of an edition. Often this information tells us who has owned the book in the past. Many people write their names in their books. Books given as gifts often have inscriptions in the front pages naming the giver and receiver, and the occasion for the gift. Libraries often stamp their books to indicate ownership. Book collectors may also use stamps or paste decorative labels (known as bookplates) into their books. Bookplates may also appear in books given as prizes—a practice very common in schools in the late nineteenth and early twentieth centuries. M.O. Grenby, who has studied children's books from the eighteenth and nineteenth centuries, discovered that some children not only wrote their names in their books but also wrote threats to beat up children who might steal them.[7]

Books often bear traces not only of the people who owned them but also of how they were used and valued. Many people write in the margins of their books, entering into dialogue with the printed text and sometimes with other readers of the same book in a process of social annotation. Samuel Taylor Coleridge wrote extensive **marginalia**, weaving his words around the text block until the white space at the edges of some pages was almost covered. His marginalia often reveal his thought processes while reading, and scholars have collected, transcribed, and published them.[8] All kinds of people wrote in their books, and not only in order to engage intellectually with the work, as Coleridge did. When paper was in short supply, people sometimes used the blank pages at the beginning and end of the book (the **endpapers**) to write things that had no relation to the text in the book. In extreme cases, they might overwrite the printed text altogether. The booktraces project (www.booktraces.org) collects examples of signs of use in nineteenth-century books, including, for example, books in which people have traced around their hands on the endpapers.

Even when previous owners did not write in their books, they sometimes left physical traces that allow us to discover something about how they used them. Until the mid-nineteenth century, most books were sold with unopened pages—that is, readers often had to use a paper-knife to cut along the edges of the **leaves**, allowing the pages to be read. When the leaves of a book like this were left untouched, we know that it wasn't read. A story from the history of science gives us a good example of this kind of evidence. Charles Darwin had a persistent problem in his evolutionary theory: his discovery of natural selection couldn't explain how, for example, two brown-eyed parents could have a blue-eyed child. To solve this problem he needed the theory of genetics (which showed, to simplify a little, that the allele for blue eyes was recessive and therefore could be carried by both brown-eyed parents without being expressed). Gregor Mendel developed this theory in Darwin's lifetime, and Darwin actually owned a copy of a book that described it. But after Darwin's death, the pages of the book in his library were found to be unopened. It would seem that Darwin never read of Mendel's discovery.[9]

Finally, the binding of a book *may* offer copy-specific information. In some cases, books were sold in paper wrappers and bound according to the specifications of their owners. Sometimes these bindings were fairly generic, but the choice of materials—and their price—can tell us something about how the owner valued the book. And the fact that the book was bound at all was usually a sign that the owner intended to keep it. Books that were thought of as ephemeral could be read in paper wrappers and then passed on, thrown away, or taken apart and used as wrapping paper or toilet paper. In some cases, owners chose to add illustrations to their books when they had them bound: by binding in single leaves of **engravings**, they made their copy of the book unique. This is known as extra-illustration, and it was particularly popular in the eighteenth and early nineteenth centuries, when an extra-illustrated book might swell the original printed book from one volume to many. The meaning of copy-specific information can also depend on historical context. If an early nineteenth-century reader left a book in its original paper wrappers, it may indicate that he or she didn't value the book enough to have it bound. If a twenty-first-century collector leaves the same book in the same wrappers, it may indicate that he or she values the book too much to alter its original condition.

The material form of the book, then, is both a rich source of information about the past and a meaningful component in how texts construct literary, historical, political, and social meanings. The paper, **type**, format, size, binding, dust jacket, and so on offer evidence about how and when the book was made, as well as how it was intended to be sold, circulated, used, and valued. The traces left by past users, such as cuts made with a paper-knife, ownership inscriptions, book plates, marginalia, ink-blots, and tear stains, tell us something about how the book was in fact used. Once we learn how to read books from the past—and not only the texts they contain—we can learn a lot about the place of books in society and the significance of particular books to their producers and users.

Bibliography

The academic name for the kind of detailed attention to the material form of books that we've been talking about is **bibliography**. This word literally means "writing about books," and because it's quite a general term, people use it to refer to several different things. A list of works cited or consulted at the end of a book or essay can be called a bibliography. So can a comprehensive list of writings about a particular topic, or by a particular author, or issued from a particular press. Compiling these lists is sometimes called enumerative bibliography. Bibliographers sometimes count books published over a period of time to show statistically, for example, how rapidly the total output of printed books rose, or how literary books expanded their market share at the expense of religious books. This quantitative approach is called **bibliometry**. Other bibliographers examine books in order to reconstruct the process by which they were printed and so to learn about how the printing house worked in the past. This approach is sometimes called historical or **analytical bibliography**. Relatedly, others attend to the material form of the book in order to trace variants between different editions or states of a text and so to reconstruct the process by which it was transmitted. This approach is sometimes called textual bibliography or **critical bibliography**. It is useful to scholarly editors trying to produce a new edition of a work, and we will discuss it in more detail in Chapter 2. For now, however, we're really concerned with **descriptive bibliography**—that is, the branch of bibliography that describes in more or less detail the format of the book, how it is constructed, the paper, binding, and type, the illustrations, and, where appropriate, any copy-specific information it may contain. Descriptive bibliographers have developed rigorous shorthand formulas for recording these features of the book.

This kind of close attention to the material form of the book, and the protocols for describing its physical condition, has been one important strand of book history. Some scholars have seen book history as two interwoven traditions of enquiry: on the one hand an "anglo-American" tradition grounded in bibliography, which privileges attention to the material aspects of particular books; on the other hand a "Continental" tradition sometimes distinguished by its French name *histoire du livre*, which focuses on the **circulation** of books in society. The terms "anglo-American" and "Continental" can be misleading here. Some leading exponents of the

"Continental" approach actually work in America, and some scholars working in Continental Europe take an "anglo-American" approach, so the labels distinguish two intellectual tendencies that aren't limited to the geographical or linguistic contexts in which they emerged. Book history has taken shape as a powerful field of interdisciplinary study, in part, by combining and developing these two approaches into a unified and multi-faceted intellectual agenda.[10]

Sir Walter Wilson Greg (1875–1959) was a key figure in establishing the foundations of modern bibliography (and also modern scholarly editing; we'll hear from him again in the next chapter). In his essay "What Is Bibliography?" (*BRBH* 3–14), he set out a severe ideal of how bibliography should be defined and practised. Greg saw bibliography's potential as a quasi-scientific discipline whose methods were rigorous and repeatable (he would have liked to call it "bibliology" to emphasize this scientific nature, but the term didn't catch on [4]). He wanted to accelerate the shift that he thought was in progress, from an old style of bibliographer who wrote "elegant essays on individual points . . . more or less accidentally . . . connected with books" to a new "science by which we co-ordinate facts and trace the operation of constant causes" (3–4). Greg saw bibliography as one of the foundational disciplines of the humanities, one that provided, borrowing W.A. Copinger's phrase, "the grammar of literary investigation" (9). By this, we think, he meant that bibliography didn't offer a set of statements about the meaning of a text; rather, it provided the preliminary structure that made such statements possible, just as the grammar of a language makes it possible to form meaningful sentences in that language, although the grammar doesn't signify anything by itself. Bibliography was the bedrock on which other investigations could build.

Since he wanted to cultivate scientific rigour, Greg aimed to develop a technical vocabulary for describing books so that any competent bibliographer who tackled the same book would arrive at the same descriptive formulation. This would remove subjectivity and interpretation from bibliographical description and so reduce it to recording matters of fact and elevate bibliography to the level of a science. He saw that a properly rigorous bibliography could provide essential evidence to support investigations into how texts were transmitted. It would become, he wrote, "the science of the material transmission of literary texts." Bibliographical training would be invaluable to editors, because bibliography, Greg wrote, "aims at the construction of a calculus for the determination of textual problems" (9).

Greg's choice of words here—"grammar," "science," "calculus"—shows his ambition for a kind of bibliography that was closer to the hard sciences than to the interpretative work of the humanities.

In pursuit of this ambition, Greg tried to quarantine bibliography from interpretation. The description of a book was one thing, the interpretation of the text it contained was another, and in Greg's view the two were best kept apart. He went so far as to say that "bibliography has nothing to do with the subject matter of books."[11] The bibliographer should pay attention to the words on the page "merely as arbitrary marks; their meaning is no business of his."[12] Greg was trying to unravel the double helix of perceptual codes (to use McGann's terms again) and to separate the bibliographic code from the linguistic one. While he thought the two were intimately related, he thought that the only sure way to elevate bibliography to the status of a science was to distance it from the fallible and controversial work of interpretation. Greg's approach to bibliography also tended to focus on evidence of the book's production rather than on evidence of the history of its use. This approach, which Greg himself acknowledged was a "severely ideal method," did much to set bibliography on a sound intellectual footing. But in many humanities departments in the twentieth century, the work of bibliographical description came to seem unconnected to the work of interpreting historical events or literary texts. By trying to make bibliography more scientific and less humanistic, Greg may also have made it seem a little less human.

Donald Francis McKenzie (1931–99) tried to put social and cultural context back into bibliography by reimagining it as "the sociology of texts." He helped to put bibliography back on the radar of historians, literary scholars, and other humanists and to make it seem—at least for people concerned with material culture—integral to our understanding of history, literature, and culture. McKenzie claimed that Greg's attempt to limit bibliography to the marks on the page prevented bibliographers from making their most valuable contributions. For Greg, the key to bibliography had been the encounter between a scholar and a particular object. While historical and literary concerns were interesting and important, they were not properly part of bibliography. For McKenzie, by contrast, bibliography was interesting and valuable precisely because studying the physical book revealed a whole network of social actors, each with their own motives and interests, who contributed to the production of the book and shaped its meaning. Publishers' archives provided another source of information about these individuals. "What writers thought they were doing in writing texts, or **printers** and **booksellers** in designing and publishing them, or readers in making sense of them are issues which no history of the book can evade," he wrote.[13]

The human contexts uncovered by bibliography turn out to be messy and resistant to generalizations, difficult to reduce to a formula. In a famous essay, McKenzie showed through a detailed study of printing-house practices that printers worked concurrently on several books at once, as well as a variety of other printing jobs, such as posters, handbills, blank receipts, and so on. They didn't tend to work through a single book from beginning to end, as historians had assumed.[14] By studying physical books alongside publishers' archives, we can reconstruct the efforts of all those involved in their production, from the authors who wrote the text to the **compositors** who set the type. This interest in the personal, social, and historical dimensions revealed by bibliographical investigation led McKenzie to say that we should think of bibliography as the sociology of texts. "In the ubiquity and variety of its evidence," he claimed, "bibliography as a sociology of texts has an unrivalled power to resurrect authors in their own time and their readers at any time."[15] McKenzie also thought bibliography could be applied to non-book texts. He wanted the methods of bibliography to be used to study historical documents, films, television, radio, and electronic text, as well as books. He demonstrated how this might be done in an extended analysis of the film *Citizen Kane* (BRBH 52–56), as well as in a detailed bibliographic account of a controversial document of New Zealand history, the Treaty of Waitangi, "signed" in 1840 between non-literate indigenous peoples and the representatives of Queen Victoria.

The burgeoning of critical theory from the late 1960s to the 1980s influenced McKenzie in conflicted ways. He was sympathetic to some of its insights. Writing in the wake of Marshall McLuhan's 1964 slogan "the medium is the message," McKenzie sought to re-establish the connection between the physical form of the book (the medium) and the message it contained, insisting (against Greg) that the two could not be separated. Following Frederick Jameson's 1981 injunction to "always historicize," McKenzie sought to re-embed the material book in the historical contexts from which it emerged. But McKenzie also hoped that, once bibliography had been reconceived as a sociology of texts, it would help to counter what he saw as an anti-humanistic tendency in literary and cultural theory. McKenzie quoted approvingly Edward Said's 1984 judgment that literary theory "isolated textuality from the circumstances, the events, the physical senses that made it possible and render it intelligible as the result of human work."[16] He controversially saw in bibliography "a massive authority with which to correct that tendency."[17] Bibliography could recover not only the author's intentions but also those of the many other people involved in the production of books. "It can, in short, show the human presence in any recorded text."[18]

In some cases, the double helix of perceptual codes identified by McGann is tightly woven. The book's material format supports and enhances its linguistic content, with the two complementing one another in the construction of meaning. The experimental novelist B.S. Johnson (1933–73) provides an extreme but revealing example. Johnson felt that the standard **codex** form was not being used to its full potential by writers. He wrote a series of avant-garde novels that deformed or rethought the material form of the printed codex. *Albert Angelo* (1964) has holes cut in some of the leaves, allowing readers glimpses into the narrative's future, on pages as yet unread. This material device sensitizes readers to the way the codex form, with a certain number of pages bound together on a spine, relates to the temporal extension of the story. Even though (unlike the **scroll**) the codex allows us to flip back and forth through its pages, we tend to read from beginning to end in a linear narrative sequence. The narrative moves towards its conclusion as the pile of pages between the fingers of your left hand grows and the one between those of your right hand shrinks. By disrupting this practice, Johnson made the material form in which his writing circulated integral to its meaning. He pushed this experiment even further in *The Unfortunates* (1969), which was printed on a set of loose cards contained in a box. Two of the cards are marked "First" and "Last," but the rest can be read in an order of the reader's choice—or selected at random by shuffling the pack. With this novel, Johnson abandoned the codex form altogether (although he later returned to it), insisting that an experimental piece of writing needed to appear in an experimental bibliographic format. For a writer like Johnson, then, the language in which a text is written and the form in which it circulates work closely together.

We can see this close alliance between material form and linguistic content especially clearly in the work of a modern, experimental writer like Johnson, but there are many examples from earlier historical periods. Compare one of the most famous of all books: the First Folio of

Shakespeare's plays, which was published in 1623, seven years after the playwright's death. In several ways, the First Folio mobilized its bibliographic code to assert that Shakespeare was a major writer whose plays were not just entertainments to watch in the theatre but literary works that would be re-read (as well as restaged) for generations to come. In his lifetime, as David Scott Kastan suggests (*BRBH* 353–74), Shakespeare took little interest in the printing of his plays, and many plays by other playwrights from this period were never printed at all. The First Folio, however, offers Shakespeare's plays to readers with all the trappings of prestige and authority. The book is printed in the large, folio format, usually reserved for high-status books. It includes a large title-page portrait of the author, known as the Droeshout portrait (the engraver was Martin Droeshout), of the kind more commonly found in classical works. Facing the title page is a poem "To the Reader," by Ben Jonson. The title page claims that the book is both comprehensive and authoritative. It advises readers that the book includes "Comedies, Histories, & Tragedies" and that the plays are "published according to the true Originall Copies." As a whole, then, the First Folio clearly signals in its bibliographic code that this is a book to be taken seriously, valued highly, and read attentively.

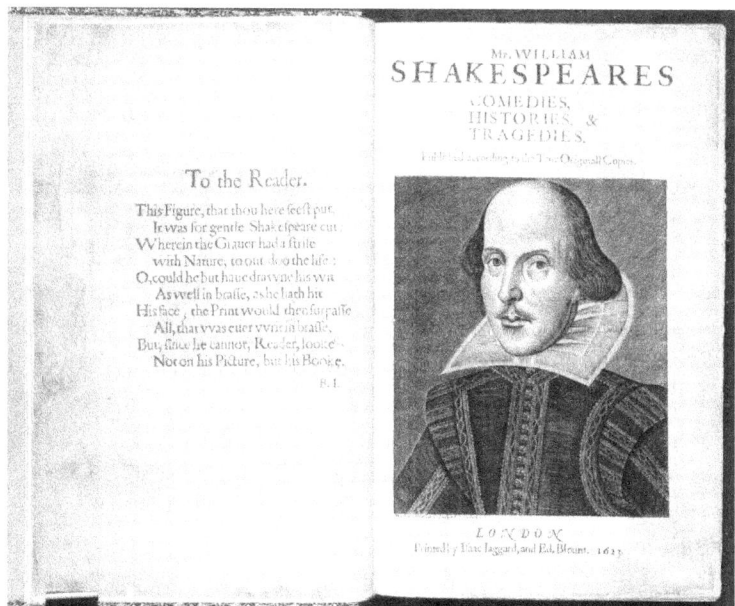

Figure 1.1: The First Folio, frontispiece and facing page (British Library copy).

In some books, however, the literary and bibliographic codes don't work together so harmoniously; sometimes they even seem to be pulling in opposite directions. Percy Shelley deliberately disguised his revolutionary poem *Queen Mab* (1813) as an innocuous tale in verse, in the hope that it would slip into the houses of the upper classes more easily. Shelley knew that if his poem was published as a cheap, flimsy **chapbook**, it might look like a radical political tract. If it was well printed in the larger quarto format, it might pass as a more respectable publication. He requested "[a] small neat Quarto, on fine paper & so as to catch the aristocrats." "They will not read it," he predicted, "but their sons & daughters may."[19] Shelley printed the volume privately, controlling almost every aspect of its physical appearance. Here the bibliographic code functions not as a material counterpart to the text's contents but as a kind of camouflage allowing Shelley to smuggle radical ideas in a respectable disguise.

Shelley intended the linguistic and bibliographic codes of *Queen Mab* to diverge, but when Lord Byron published the first two cantos of his controversial poem *Don Juan* in 1819, it was his publisher, John Murray, who wanted to protect the poem from attack by cloaking it in an innocuous form. Murray knew that the poem might be prosecuted for blasphemous **libel** because it contained a parody of the Ten Commandments. But he also knew that the courts tended not to convict on these charges if the book in question was clearly aimed at the upper classes, who were thought to be sufficiently educated and discerning not to be led astray by heterodox opinions. Murray therefore published the poem in an expensive large quarto format, with wide margins and fine printing, and sold it at the high price of 31 shillings. This placed it beyond the reach of the labouring classes and ensured that it would have only an upper-class audience. Murray omitted not only Byron's name from the title page but also his own. His strategy didn't stop the poem from being reprinted by others and sold in cheap editions—in fact it probably encouraged it—but at least it kept him out of court. The material format in which the first two cantos of *Don Juan* were published, then, sent the message that the poem was safe, refined, and suitable for inclusion in the best private libraries. In other words, the physical form of the book was at odds with the message of the text it contained. Whereas in Shelley's case the author engineered this divergence between form and content, in Byron's case the publisher made the decision to publish the poem in this format without the author's agreement.

So the physical format of a book sends messages to its purchasers and users about what kind of book it is and about how we're expected to circulate, use, and value it. We can think of these messages as forming a "bibliographic code" that operates alongside the "linguistic code" of the words in the book, and so we can "read" the material book as well as reading the text it contains. If we learn to read the bibliographic code of books from the past, we can understand something important about how their producers intended them to be received, even if their first readers did not always use the books as their producers intended. Bibliography is the academic discipline that has developed a technical vocabulary for describing the physical form of any book; bibliographical descriptions can help us to understand what the material form of a book was like even if we can't actually handle the book ourselves. In some cases, the bibliographic code works alongside the linguistic code, so that the material form of the book supports and enhances the meaning of the text. In other cases, however, the two codes diverge, so that the material book disguises or even undermines the meaning of the text it contains.

Making Printed Books

To understand why books take the material form that they do, we have to understand something about how they are made. Printing has been done differently in different times and different places, and using different technologies, but many aspects of the process didn't change that much between the fifteenth and the early nineteenth century, a time known as the "**handpress** period." Michael Twyman discusses the key processes (*BRBH* 37–44).[20] If you wanted to have your work published in the handpress period, you needed at least a printer, and probably a publisher and bookseller (sometimes the same person fulfilled all these roles, but they became increasingly separate over time). We'll call the workers in the print shop "he," because they were usually men. There were some women in the print trade, however, at most stages of the production process throughout the handpress period, though their levels of involvement fluctuated over time and place.

If you reached an agreement with a publisher to turn your **manuscript** into a book, he would decide how many copies of your book he was going to print, based on his estimate of how many he could sell. The printer would work out how much paper your book would require and make sure he had sufficient stock. Then your manuscript would be sent to the typesetter, also called a "compositor." The compositor would stand in front of a pair of **typecases**, arranged one above the other. The upper case contained pieces of type with capital letters on them, while the lower case contained small letters (that's where the terms "upper-" and "lower-case" come from). Each of these cases was divided into compartments, with one compartment for pieces of type showing each letter or typographical symbol. Just as the keys on a computer keyboard are arranged to make the ones we use most the easiest to reach, so were the compartments in the typecase arranged to make the most commonly used letters easy to reach. The compartment for the letter e, the most commonly used letter in the alphabet, was in the centre of the case. It was also the largest compartment. The compartments for t and h were nearby, allowing the compositor to set the most common word, "the," quickly. The compositor would read the manuscript and reach into the typecase for the letters needed to spell the words. Just as a proficient typist doesn't look at the keyboard, the compositor didn't need to look at each piece of type he set. He felt for a notch on the top of the type to make sure it was the right way up, and then slotted it into his composing stick, a hand-held metal tool set to the width of the page to be printed. Sometimes the compositor made mistakes, either because he misread the manuscript, or because he reached into the wrong compartment in the typecase, or because a piece of type got into the wrong compartment by mistake (a problem known as "foul case"). The letters were reversed (or "offset") in the process of printing, so letters that are mirror images of one another, like p and q, were easily confused. (Some people think this is where we get the phrase "mind your p's and q's.")

Once the compositor had set a few lines of type, he would slide them off the composing stick onto a metal tray called a **galley**, and then carry on working until the galley contained a full **page** of text set up in type. Each page of set type was then tied up with string and set aside. All printed books are made from printing several pages on a large **sheet** of paper and then folding the printed sheet up. After several pages had been set, then, they had to be arranged in the right order and the right orientation to make sure they came out correctly when the sheet of paper was folded. This process of arranging the typeset pages is called imposition. The number of pages printed on each sheet, and the number of times the sheet was folded, varied. There were four major **formats**, or ways of folding and **gathering** printed sheets to make a book. In **folio** books, the sheet was folded in half once, producing two leaves or four pages. In **quarto** books, the sheet was folded twice, producing four leaves or eight pages. In **octavo** books the sheet was folded three times, producing eight leaves or sixteen pages. **Duodecimo** books involved a more complex process of folding and cutting to produce twelve leaves or twenty-four pages from each sheet. In quarto, octavo, and duodecimo books there were folds along either the top (short) edge or the fore-edge (the long side that you open to read the book) of the book that had to be cut open before the text could be read, either by the binder or by a reader wielding a paper-knife. Once the type for a whole sheet had been set and imposed, it was locked into a wooden or metal frame called a "chase." The type and the chase together are called a **forme**. Once it was set up, the forme was carried to the press for printing.

 Johannes **Gutenberg**, a German goldsmith, invented **moveable type** and the hand printing press around 1439. (Printing from woodblocks on both **parchment** and textiles was known much earlier in China and elsewhere, including some reusable blocks for Chinese characters.) Gutenberg based his design for the printing press on existing presses used for making oil and wine, and all subsequent handpresses shared the same basic design. The forme was laid on the "bed" of the press, facing upwards. The printer then applied ink to the type, using a ball of leather or a roller. This was skilled work: too little ink and the type wouldn't print clearly, too much and the middles of letters like e, a, and o would fill up with ink. Once the type was inked, the printer placed a sheet of paper on top of it. The paper was usually dampened for printing and was often held in an apparatus hinged to the bed of the press called a tympan, which kept it in place. A frame called a frisket protected the margins from ink. Once the paper was sitting on top of the inked type, the printer turned a handle that moved the type and the paper into the press and pulled a lever, which turned a screw that pressed a flat weight onto the paper, pushing it down on the inked type and transferring the ink onto the paper. It usually took two pulls of the lever to print the whole sheet. Working the press was hard physical work, usually done by a team of two men.

 The presses used from the Western invention of the handpress until the end of the eighteenth century were made of wood. In the later eighteenth century, inventors began to make some parts of the press out of metal, and around 1800 the first press to be made completely of iron, the Stanhope Press, was produced. This made the press less laborious to work, faster, and less likely to break down, but it still used the same principles as the wooden handpress. The first printing press to be powered by steam was invented in 1814, and by the twentieth century most presses were powered by electricity. Newspapers were early adopters of new printing technologies, because they needed particularly fast printing. Book publishers tended to be slower to adopt new technologies. By the middle of the nineteenth century, however, steam presses were used widely for all kinds of printing.

After the pressmen had printed a sheet, it would be hung up to dry and they would re-ink the type and print the next sheet. Having printed as many sheets as were required, they would then move on to the next forme of type. Once the sheets were dry, they could be turned over and put back in the press to print the other side. As McKenzie discovered, books weren't necessarily printed in order, and sometimes pressmen printed something else—a poster or a sheet of blank receipts, for example—in between working on the sheets for a book. The first sheets to be printed were "proof" sheets, which were sent to the author or someone else to check for errors. The time allowed for correcting **proofs** was usually very limited, because publishers wanted to print the book, distribute the type back into the typecases, and get on with the next job. The type was their most valuable asset—it was more expensive than the presses—so printers wanted it to be in constant use, not standing in the chase waiting to be printed. Making changes at this stage was also difficult and time-consuming. Pressmen could correct one or two wrong letters by removing them from the forme with tweezers and inserting replacements, but anything more than that might mean the line endings of the text were affected, or even the page endings, requiring whole pages of type to be reset. Authors who had second thoughts at proof stage and asked for substantial changes or additions to their texts were therefore likely to be unpopular with their publishers.

Once the proofs had been corrected, the first edition could be printed. Sometimes further errors were spotted and the pressmen stopped work to correct them, and then continued. These changes are called stop-press corrections. In some cases, the printer would keep the uncorrected sheets for binding, so that variants could appear between copies of a single edition. Such is the case with the First Folio: there exist many variations between the 233 copies of the First Folio that survive (it is thought that 800 copies were originally printed). The reason for this is that the Folio, like many books of the period, was proofread and corrected whilst the printing was ongoing, with both uncorrected and corrected sheets bound together to make individual copies.[21] Interestingly, the engraving used in the title page was also retouched: in four surviving copies of the First Folio, the engraved portrait has subtle differences from the remaining copies, suggesting that Droeshout altered the plate after printing the first few test copies.

Once all the sheets of paper that made up the book had been printed and dried, they would be folded and stitched together. They might be roughly stitched into a temporary paper wrapper, or stitched into a temporary or incomplete binding, or bound by the publisher and sold in that form. Once the whole edition had been printed, the type in the formes was broken up and again and dispersed back into the typecases so that it could be set for the next job.

How many copies were printed depended on the publisher's estimate of how many would sell. Books offered for sale directly to the public by a publisher involved risk, and so a publisher had to gauge demand for a book carefully if he didn't want to be left with unsold copies on his hands. There were several ways that book publication could be financed and they varied at different times and places. A publisher might purchase the **copyright** directly from an author for a single payment. Or books could be published on **subscription**: in this case the author or publisher had already secured some promises to buy and/or payments before publication, so these books were lower risk. Another way publication was financed involved the author paying entirely for the costs of printing, a process that was sometimes mediated by a publisher and/or bookseller. Under this method, a publisher usually took a commission on each book sold. The publisher bore the least risk under this method, but it would still be in his best interest to ensure that the print run did not significantly exceed demand and cause the author a loss, as then the author would be less likely to return to the publisher in the future. Finally, publication could operate on a profit-sharing agreement, whereby the author and the publisher agreed to share the profits after all expenses were paid. This is the royalty system most often used today.

All of the copies of a book that were made from sheets printed from one setting of type are what book historians call an **edition**. If more copies were called for, a printer would have to reset the type. Given the high cost of paper during the handpress period, having unsold copies significantly cut into profits. As a result, most print runs were small, between 500 and 2000 copies per edition. Resetting the type for a new edition meant a considerable investment of time, effort, and money on the part of the publisher and/or printer. On the other hand, printing a second edition gave the author and publisher a chance to correct errors that had crept into the first edition, as well as to make any revisions that they wanted. Since the compositors had to set the type for the whole book again anyway, it was much easier to incorporate changes at this stage than when the book was in proof. The publisher might actually want to include revisions in the new edition, and new paratexts, in the hope that a new, improved, or updated version of the book would sell better and even be purchased by some people who had already bought the first edition. Including revisions or new material in the second edition might also encourage readers to purchase the new edition over a cheaper second-hand copy of the first edition. For these reasons, the text of later editions often varies in small or large ways from that of earlier editions. As we'll see in the next chapter, modern scholarly editors have to take these variants into account when producing new editions of a work.

Understanding the process of making books in the handpress era, then, gives us important historical information about the spread and circulation of texts and ideas. It helps us to reconstruct the elements of the bibliographic code that were current at different historical moments. It also allows us to understand the behaviour of authors and publishers once we grasp the technological constraints and affordances, the economic imperatives, and the commercial contexts within which they were working. Historians of the book trade use this knowledge to reconstruct the production, marketing, and circulation of books in the past. Literary scholars use it to understand the transmission of texts and the reasons why a work might exist in different versions. And bibliographers use it to help explain how and why the physical features of a particular book came into being. As Roger Chartier shows using the example of *Don Quixote* (BRBH 73–92), the processes of production often fascinated authors as well, and the print shop sometimes features in their texts in self-reflexive ways.

Typography

The choice of the **typeface** that the book is printed in is another important part of the bibliographic code, but one that we find easy to overlook. We tend to think of the type a book is printed in as irrelevant to its meaning. We're conditioned to look past type to get at the meaning of the words, and we tend to think that the same words in a different typeface would be identical in all meaningful ways. If you're applying for a job, you might be advised to format your application letter in a standard font such as Times New Roman, but you should probably spend more time thinking

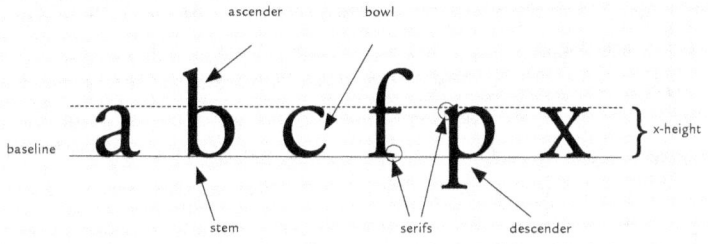

Figure 1.2: Basic anatomy of the roman letterform. Reprinted with the permission of Paul C. Gutjahr and Megan L. Benton.

about how to word your application letter than what font to print it in. We're taught to think of type as incidental to meaning, but seeing it as part of the bibliographic code means acknowledging the part it plays in shaping how we read.

A variety of factors affect how readable a page of type will appear. First is the shape of the letters themselves (see Figure 1.2). The look of a typeface will be determined by factors such as the balance of thicker and thinner parts of the letter form, the height of letters such as a, c, and x (known as the x-height), the relative height of ascenders (those parts of letters like h, f, d, and b that exceed the x-height) and length of descenders (those parts of letters like q, y, p, and g that extend below the baseline), and the presence or absence of serifs (those little bits at the ends of the main strokes of a letter where the line flares out slightly in some typefaces). The look and readability of the page will also be affected by how the type has been arranged on the page (sometimes referred to using the French term *mise en page*). Again, several elements contribute to the overall effect. One is the size of margins (the space between the edge of the text and the edge of the page), which are rarely all the same size in handpress books. The textblock is often slightly off-centre in these books, towards the top left of the page. Another element is the text's justification: whether it is arranged in a straight line on the left margin with a ragged edge down the right-hand side (left justified), or arranged to produce straight edges down both margins (fully justified; the text in this book is fully justified). A third is the amount of space between letters in a word (called kerning) and the space between lines (called leading, because this space was created in the handpress period by inserting thin pieces of lead between lines of type). These elements are the subject of sometimes-heated debates among professional typographers, but they are also familiar to anyone who uses word-processing software.²²

Typographers often think that we should look *through* type, rather than *at* it. Type that draws attention to itself, they sometimes say, is not doing its job properly. Instead, good type is "transparent" and doesn't distract readers from the matter of the text. Beatrice Warde expresses this ideal of type subordinating itself to meaning by comparing good type to a crystal goblet.²³ Given the choice between drinking wine out of an ornate gold chalice encrusted with jewels, or drinking it from a clear crystal glass, a wine connoisseur, Warde says, will choose the crystal glass. The chalice might be more ornate, more interesting to look at, and more valuable than the glass, but the wine connoisseur isn't really interested in the chalice or the glass: she's interested in the wine. She wants to enjoy the wine without distractions, and so she will prefer the drinking vessel that lets the colour and the flavour of the wine come through as fully and readily as possible. In the same way, according to Warde, a good reader should be interested in what the text says, so a good typeface will get out of the reader's way and let the message come through with minimal noise. Good type is easy to read and doesn't draw attention to itself: it serves the message that the words convey.

Johanna Drucker makes a distinction between "marked" and "unmarked" texts. Marked texts conspicuously manipulate **typography**, using bold or italic lettering and different sizing and spacing to draw attention to their own typographical form. Drucker's examples are drawn mostly from experimental works of the early twentieth century such as Wyndham Lewis's *Blast* magazine (1914). Unmarked texts, on the other hand, follow Warde's injunction not to draw attention to their typography but to make it the discreet vehicle of the author's message. As Paul Gutjahr and Megan Benton argue, however (*BRBH* 63–72), the decision not to draw attention to the typography is just as much an artistic choice as the decision to foreground it. Typography shapes the way we read, whether it whispers or shouts.

The meaning of typographical decisions, moreover, changes in different cultural and historical contexts. In the fifteenth century, **blackletter**, an elaborate gothic style of typeface, was widely used, at least for certain kinds of documents. But when a nineteenth-century publisher used a blackletter typeface for an edition of a medieval poem, the text took on a strong antiquarian flavour, drawing attention to the poem's historical distance from the present. When it was designed in the 1950s, the

Helvetica typeface looked striking, modern, and even countercultural. But now that it's become ubiquitous in signage (on the New York subway, for example), company logos (including those of American Airlines and Gap), and in word-processed documents, many designers find it too staid and too saturated with corporate connotations, and so they seek out alternatives. This story is told in Gary Hustwit's charming documentary film *Helvetica* (2007). Finally, typographical choices are not exempt from political concerns. A certain class of ornate typefaces known as Fraktur became associated with German nationalism in the twentieth century and was used on Nazi letterheads and posters. But in a remarkable U-turn in 1941, Nazi Germany declared Fraktur typefaces to be *Judenlettern* (Jewish letters) and therefore unsuitable for official documents (ironically, the declaration was printed on a letterhead that used a Fraktur typeface).[24] Earlier, in the late nineteenth century, William Morris, Theodore Low De Vinne, and others reacted against what they saw as the "feminine" appearance of Victorian mass-produced books, which used thin letter forms. Morris preferred thicker, more "robust" letter forms, deeply impressed into the paper, a style that De Vinne said "remasculated" the printed page.[25] As these episodes show, typography can also be gendered and racialized.

Book history, then, teaches us to read books, and not only the texts they contain. Some other intellectual traditions encourage us to ignore or disdain the material form of the book, seeing it as just the vehicle for a message that consists of language or ideas. But book history insists that we pay attention to the ways in which the material form of the book inflects our response to it. Printed books store and circulate texts, but the ways in which they do so are complicated by their material construction out of type, paper, ink, cardboard, leather, and so on, as well as the paratexts they contain. Those physical aspects of the book send their own messages, which we can think of as a bibliographic code. Most of us are quite adept at understanding those messages in the present, but we have to learn to decipher them in books from the past. Choices about the format of a book, its size, the kind of paper and type used, and so forth may have been made by the author of the text the book contains, but often several different people were involved in making the book, and they didn't always share common interests or a common vision. The decisions they made in producing the book mobilized culturally constructed codes and connotations—for example, the feeling that some typefaces looked "modern" or "feminine."

To understand how and why a book has its particular physical appearance, it's useful to know something about how it was produced, and so an important part of book history and bibliography has been reconstructing how books were printed on the handpress. While some aspects of the material book are evidence of its producers' intentions, others are evidence of how its earlier readers responded to it. Writing on endpapers or in the margins, bookplates, bindings, cut or uncut leaves, and stains from ink, tea or tears all show how a book was used and valued in the past. Once we learn how to crack the bibliographic code, we can start to see how the material form of a literary text or historical document is entwined with its linguistic content. Books don't speak to us only by using words but also through every aspect of their physical construction.

Notes

1. Alexander Pope, "Epistle to Burlington, On the Use of Riches," *The Twickenham Edition of the Poems of Alexander Pope*, vol. III.ii, *Epistles to Several Persons (Moral Essays)*, ed. F.W. Bateson (New Haven, CT: Yale UP, 1961), 150 (line 134).
2. Philip Dormer Stanhope Chesterfield, *The Letters of Philip Dormer Stanhope, 4th Earl of Chesterfield*, ed. Bonamy Dobrée (New York: AMS P, 1968), 1291.
3. Georges Poulet, "Criticism and the Experience of Interiority," *The Structuralist Controversy: The Languages of Criticism and the Sciences of Man*, ed. Richard Macksey and Eugenio Donato (Baltimore: Johns Hopkins UP, 1970), 56–73, 56.
4. Jerome McGann, "The Socialization of Texts," *The Textual Condition* (Princeton, NJ: Princeton UP, 1991), 69–87, 77.
5. Gérard Genette, *Paratexts: Thresholds of Interpretation*, trans. Jane E. Lewin (Cambridge: Cambridge UP, 1997), 1.
6. Peter J. De Voogd, "*Tristram Shandy* as Aesthetic Object," *Word and Image* 4.1 (1988): 383–92.
7. M.O. Grenby, *The Child Reader, 1700–1840* (Cambridge: Cambridge UP, 2011), 27.
8. The complete marginalia are included in Princeton University Press's multi-volume Bollingen edition, *The Collected Works of Samuel Taylor Coleridge*. For a selection, see Samuel Taylor Coleridge, *A Book I Value: Selected Marginalia*, ed. H.J. Jackson (Princeton, NJ: Princeton UP, 2003).
9. It is unclear whether the document in question was an offprint of one of Mendel's own papers or another work that mentioned Mendel. See Pablo Lorenzano, "What Would Have Happened if Darwin Had Known Mendel

(or Mendel's Work)?" *History and Philosophy of the Life Sciences* 33 (2011): 3–48.
10 Here we follow G. Thomas Tanselle, "The History of Books as a Field of Study" (1981), reprinted in Tanselle's *Literature and Artifacts* (Charlottesville: Bibliographical Society of the U of Virginia, 1998), 41–58.
11 W.W. Greg, "Bibliography—An Apologia," *Collected Papers*, ed. J.C. Maxwell (Oxford: Clarendon, 1966), 239–66, 240.
12 Greg 247.
13 D.F. McKenzie, *Bibliography and the Sociology of Texts* (Cambridge: Cambridge UP, 1999), 19.
14 D.F. McKenzie, "Printers of the Mind: Some Notes on Bibliographical Theories and Printing-House Practices," *Making Meaning: "Printers of the Mind" and Other Essays*, ed. Peter D. McDonald and Michael F. Suarez, S.J. (Boston: U of Massachusetts P, 2002), 13–85.
15 McKenzie, *Bibliography* 28–29.
16 Edward Said, *The World, the Text, and the Critic* (London: Faber and Faber, 1984), 4, qtd. in McKenzie, *Bibliography* 28.
17 McKenzie, *Bibliography* 28–29.
18 McKenzie, *Bibliography* 29.
19 P.B. Shelley, *The Letters of Percy Bysshe Shelley*, vol. 1, ed. Frederick L. Jones (Oxford: Clarendon, 1964), 361.
20 For a much fuller account, which we follow in this section, see Philip Gaskell's classic manual of bibliography, *A New Introduction to Bibliography* (New Castle, DE: Oak Knoll, 2009).
21 Through careful examination of the surviving copies, it is now known that 134 out of the total 900 pages were proofread and corrected in this way, with about 500 corrections made as a result.
22 Useful guides to typography include Jan Tschichold, *Treasury of Alphabets and Lettering* (London: Lund Humphries, 1992) and Robert Bringhurst, *The Elements of Typographic Style*, 4th ed. (Vancouver: Hartley & Marks, 2013).
23 Beatrice Warde, "The Crystal Goblet; or, Printing Should Be Invisible," *Typographers on Type*, ed. Ruari McLean (New York: Norton, 1995), 73–77.
24 The document is reproduced at http://www.ligaturix.de/bormann.htm.
25 See Megan L. Benton, "Typography and Gender: Remasculating the Modern Book," *Illuminating Letters: Typography and Literary Interpretation*, ed. Paul C. Gutjahr and Megan L. Benton (Amherst: U of Massachusetts P, 2001), 71–93.

CHAPTER 2

TEXTUALITY

Who's Been Tampering with My Text?

John Keats's poem "Ode on a Grecian Urn" is one of the best known in the English language, and most readers of this book have probably encountered it already. If so, you may remember its famous final lines with their ringing statement about truth and beauty. The urn is described as "a friend to man, to whom thou say'st"—but what, exactly, do those familiar lines say? Which of the following four versions is correct?

1. Beauty is truth,—Truth Beauty,—that is all
   Ye know on Earth, and all ye need to know.

2. Beauty is Truth, Truth Beauty. —That is all
   Ye know on Earth, and all ye need to know.

3. "Beauty is truth, truth beauty,"—that is all
   Ye know on earth, and all ye need to know.

4. "Beauty is truth, truth beauty, —that is all
   Ye know on earth, and all ye need to know."

In each case the words are the same, but the use of capital letters and punctuation marks is different. And the differences matter to the meaning of the lines. Do the abstractions of truth and beauty deserve the status conferred on them by writing "Truth" and "Beauty"? Are these lines one sentence or two? And where do the quotation marks belong, if they should be there at all? If the quotation marks don't close until the end of the second line, then both lines seem to be spoken by the urn (or attributed to it by the poem's speaker). But if the quotation marks close after "beauty," then it seems that the urn says only the bit about truth and beauty and that the rest is a comment, by the speaker of the poem, on the urn's utterance. Where the quotation closes also affects how we understand the addressee of the final lines: the "ye" in "that is all / Ye know on earth, and all ye need to know." If both lines are spoken by the urn, then these words are part of the urn's message to mankind. The statement about truth and beauty is all that any of us know or need to know. But if the urn says the bit about truth and beauty and the rest is a comment by the speaker, then the end of the poem reads very differently.

The speaker addresses the figures on the urn as "ye," possibly with sarcasm or even contempt. Truth and beauty may be identical in the world of the urn, but the rest of us, who are unable to inhabit the urn's unruffled world of silence and slow time, may have to grapple with the pain and suffering of mortality. The figures on the urn may not need to know anything else, but the rest of us may need to learn how to avoid being seduced by beautiful falsehoods, or how to face unpalatable truths, in order to live responsible lives. We won't be able to settle arguments about what the poem means until we know what the poem says. So which is the right version of the lines?

In fact, each of them has a strong claim to be "right." No **manuscript** of the poem in Keats's handwriting survives. His brother, George Keats, made a **transcript** of the poem, presumably working from a lost manuscript in the author's hand, which he dated 1819. In this text, the last lines appear in the first of the four versions above, with irregular capitalization and no quotation marks. The poem then appeared in the magazine *Annals of the Fine Arts* in January 1820, but we don't think Keats had a chance to correct any errors before publication. In this text, the last lines appear in the second version above, which uses capital letters for "Truth" and "Beauty" (but also for "Earth") and makes the lines into two sentences, but doesn't include any quotation marks. The poem was then printed in Keats's third volume of poetry, entitled *Lamia, Isabella, The Eve of St Agnes and Other Poems* in July 1820. We know that Keats was on hand during the printing of the volume, which prints the lines in the third version above, with quotation marks around the aphorism "Beauty is truth, truth beauty." The fourth version comes from a modern paperback edition of Keats's poetry, where the editor (the distinguished Keats scholar John Barnard) has chosen not to reprint any of the earliest versions of these lines, but to **emend** them, placing the quotation marks around both lines to make clear that both of them are part of the urn's message to mankind.[1]

So when you read "Ode on a Grecian Urn," it would be naïve to think that, in any straightforward way, you were reading exactly what the poet wrote or what his or her first readers read. (And in Keats's case the problem is compounded by the fact that he sometimes invited his friends to edit his poems for him as they circulated in manuscript and were printed.) The "Ode on a Grecian Urn" is not an exceptional case. Similar complexities can be found in many other pieces of writing in modern editions or **anthologies**. The kinds of variation that occur between texts of "Ode on a Grecian Urn" from Keats's lifetime are the rule, not the exception.

The scholarly editor's job is to research those texts, explain how they relate to each other and differ from one another, form opinions about which versions are the most authoritative (and what constitutes "authority") and, usually, to produce a new text that combines authoritative evidence from earlier witnesses without necessarily reprinting any of them exactly.

Textual scholars and scholarly **editors** distinguish between the **work** that is "Ode on a Grecian Urn" and the **texts** of that work that appear in particular manuscript or printed documents. Note that the terms "text" and "work" are here used in a specialist sense that's unlike the way we use the words in other discussions of writing. Textual scholars and scholarly editors often identify several texts of a work, which differ from each other in small or large ways. However, editors don't all agree on the definition of a work, or the relationship between a work and its texts. Whether it's a novel, a poem, a speech, a sermon, a proclamation or something else, many scholars would say that the work consists of a particular, motivated arrangement of words. It exists in language. The only access we have to the work, however, is through the media of its transmission in manuscript or print (or in certain cases performance, broadcast, carving on stone, and so on). These fallible media create historically specific, imperfect records of the work, which we call "texts." Although the work is a linguistic construct, and therefore immaterial, its texts are material, and so editors have to pay attention to their bibliographic features. It's a bit like different performances of a piece of music. Every time someone plays, say, Beethoven's "Moonlight" Sonata, a new iteration of that work is created, but the work is not simply identical with any of its iterations. The work that we call "Ode on a Grecian Urn," on this view, is a particular arrangement of words (and punctuation) intended by its author. The texts we quoted a moment ago are witnesses to that work, but none of the witnesses are entirely reliable. Like an investigator trying to reconstruct events based on witness statements, the scholarly editor tries to get as close as possible to the work based on the evidence of its texts. Different texts convey the work with varying degrees of reliability, but the work is not simply identical with any one text.

For some scholars, however, the material texts of a work don't simply witness its existence: they constitute it. Giving the words a material form *makes* the work. The ideal conception of the work we just described arguably reflects a post-Romantic conception of authority, in which a work is understood to express an individual's consciousness. This understanding was bolstered by developments in **copyright** law in the eighteenth and nineteenth centuries that gave an author property rights to his or her writing. Earlier descriptions of writing and publishing, however, sometimes depict the work coming into being through the efforts of many people. Confined in the Bastille in Paris, in 1785, the Marquis de Sade scribbled sexual fantasies on scraps of paper smuggled into the prison, gluing them together into a twelve-metre-long roll, which he hid in a crack in his cell wall. On the one hand Sade appears to have decided on a fixed structure for his writing, suggesting that he thought he was producing a "work." On the other hand, the writing is clearly unfinished, breaking into disjointed notes after the first part. The roll was transcribed and published as a book over a hundred years later, in 1904. When first published, these writings were treated as a document likely to interest medical practitioners involved in classifying sexual pathologies. Only later, as the book circulated more widely, did it begin to be treated as part of literary and intellectual history. So when did these words become a work? Arguably they were only the unhinged sexual ramblings of a madman until, fortified by the attention of an editor and given a new material form as a published book, they gained the dignity of a work, called *The 120 Days of Sodom*. In some cases, at least, a more pragmatic understanding of what makes a work may be appropriate. In these cases, rather than existing in an ideal realm of language to which material texts can point only imperfectly, the work may be best understood to exist in the material conditions of its transmission, and nowhere else.[2]

We use the title "editor" in everyday speech to refer to a number of different people involved in the overlapping worlds of writing, scholarship, and publishing. There are magazine editors, who decide what fills each issue of the magazine and commission articles from journalists. There are editors who work for publishing firms, who may be commissioning editors tasked with identifying new books for the press to publish, developmental editors responsible for working with authors to improve manuscripts that have potential but are not yet ready to be published, or copy editors who prepare a manuscript for publication by checking its grammar and formatting (and in some cases its factual accuracy) and making it conform to the house style of the **publisher**. There are also editors of anthologies and collections, who select (and in some cases commission) the pieces of writing to be included. These kinds of editors may play important roles in shaping the final version of a work. In 2009, newly published early versions of some of Raymond Carver's short stories made it clear that Carver's editor, Gordon Lish, had intervened dramatically in the manuscript versions, in some cases cutting over half the text and helping to produce the spare, minimalist, suggestive prose that most of Carver's readers think of as characteristically his own. This kind of editing is certainly important, then, but it's not the kind of **editing** that concerns us here.

The scholarly editor differs from these other kinds of editor. Scholarly editors usually deal with historical writing (it may be very ancient, or just a few decades old). They surround this writing with explanatory notes that help to make its meaning clear to modern readers. But more importantly, they identify and compare (or **collate**) all the texts of a work from the author's lifetime, plus any later texts that might reflect the author's intentions, and record how they differ from one another. Having brought this information together, scholarly editors use it in different ways to create a new **edition**. Some editors (working in the genetic editing tradition practised mostly in Continental Europe) represent on the page as much information as possible about the history of the work's development through multiple states. Others (working in the **eclectic** editing tradition practised mostly in the UK and North America) make tough choices to produce a clean reading text of the work in their new edition and corral information about textual variants into a "critical apparatus" at the bottom of the page or at the back of the book. The resulting editions can sometimes be a bit difficult for non-specialists to read, but it's well worth paying attention to them, because they tell us not just what one text of the work says, but what all the relevant texts of the work say. Editors thus catalogue all the "variants" between texts, or the places where they differ from one another, and form judgments about which texts best reflect the work the author intended.

To understand how editors make these judgments, we have to understand something about how writing from the past comes down to us in the present. This process of textual transmission, of course, differs in different geographical contexts and different historical periods. As a result, the kinds of evidence we have to draw on—the texts of a work that are still extant—differ too. In a manuscript culture, such as in Europe before the invention of printing in the 1430s, writing had to be copied by hand. It's almost impossible to produce an absolutely exact copy of a long text by hand, and so surviving manuscript copies of a given text often differ from one another. Copies may have been lost or destroyed, leaving the historical record incomplete. In early modern print culture, such as in Shakespeare's England, we often have limited pre-publication material, because the author's manuscripts were usually destroyed during the process of printing. None of the manuscripts of Shakespeare's plays have survived. Instead, we have a range of published versions whose connection to the lost manuscripts is notoriously difficult to establish. In more recent times, from the late eighteenth century onwards, far more pre-publication material survives, including rough drafts, **fair copies**, and proof copies (early printed versions sent to the author to be corrected), as well as first and subsequent editions. Authors sometimes also revised their works for later editions, or for collected editions of their works, introducing more textual variants after the first publication. The evidence available to scholarly editors about the textual history of a work, then, varies from case to case and from one historical period to another.

By examining this evidence, editors can reconstruct the textual history of a work. Think of a work's textual history as a kind of family tree showing the relationships between all the different early texts of a work. In a manuscript culture, when an existing text of a work (call it A) is copied to make a new text (B), the new text is like the daughter of the existing one. If text A is copied again to make another new text (C) then C would be the sister of B and daughter of A. Using sophisticated techniques of analysis pioneered by nineteenth-century scholars of the Bible and classical texts, textual scholars can reconstruct these family trees and represent them in "stemmatic diagrams." They can even hypothesize the existence of lost texts forming missing branches of the family tree. The most famous example comes from biblical criticism. The Gospels of Matthew and Luke share a significant amount of material with each other and with the Gospel of Mark. Textual scholars have shown that the authors of Matthew and Luke likely knew Mark's earlier gospel and drew on it. But what about the material that appears in both Matthew and Luke but not in Mark? Textual scholars argue that Matthew and Luke almost certainly derived some of their material from a shared written source, known as Q (from the German *Quelle*, meaning "source"), rather than one of them deriving material from the other. No copy of Q survives. While the gospels offer different versions of the same story, rather than different texts of the same work, the techniques used by scholars to reconstruct the process of transmission are comparable.

Traditionally, scholarly editors thought of the process of textual transmission as a process of **corruption**. As new texts of a work are produced, errors creep in. Bored scribes make mistakes. Tired typesetters lose concentration. Drunken pressmen make blunders (Benjamin Franklin recorded in his autobiography that the pressmen he worked with in London were "great Guzzlers of Beer").³ Deliberate changes are introduced to "improve" the text without the author's consent. As a result, editors often attempt to identify printer's errors, scribal mistakes, and all kinds of non-authorial interventions in order to strip them away and restore the work to the state it was in when it left the author's hands. This aspiration gets more complicated when the author has been closely involved in the process of publication or has revised the work after its first publication. In these cases, when later texts of the work vary from earlier ones, it will be necessary for editors to work out which of the variants reflect the author's revisions and which are errors or unauthorised interventions. Generally speaking, then, the scholarly editor will reconstruct the process of textual transmission and produce a full account of textual variants. He or she will do this in order to distinguish authorial revisions from non-authorial interventions and to preserve the former while purging the latter. Fredson Bowers, one of the pioneers in this field, set out this view clearly. "The recovery of the initial purity of an author's text and of its revision (insofar as this is possible from the preserved documents)," he wrote, "and the preservation of this purity despite the usual corrupting process of reprint transmission, is the aim of textual criticism."[4]

The apprentice boys who worked in the printer's shop were often called "printer's devils," partly because devils were usually depicted as black and the boys would often end up with blackened hands and faces from working with printers' inks, and partly because printing was sometimes seen as an infernal invention. The name also reflects the half-humorous and half-superstitious suggestion that the Devil assigned special demons to printing houses to introduce errors into the books, and the number of misprints that still creep into modern books, even with all the advantages of electronic typesetting, suggests how difficult it is to avoid such errors. Many books come with lists of **errata** showing misprints that were spotted too late to be corrected. The new editions produced by scholarly editors are, of course, subject to the same contingencies, and so they always risk introducing new errors, even as they correct the errors they discover in earlier texts. But scholarly editors try to offer their readers a text produced by angels, not printer's devils. Taking the utmost care in researching the new edition and seeing it through the press, they aim for a new text of the work that strips away the errors introduced in previous versions, records the variants between earlier texts of the work, and transmits the work effectively.

Copy-Text

Having surveyed all the relevant texts of a work, editors often find it helpful to select one of them as the basis of their new edition. The textual scholar R.B. McKerrow was the first to describe this practice, and he called the text on which he based his edition of Thomas Nashe's works the **copy-text**. The name has stuck, but it might be slightly misleading, because editors do not simply copy the copy-text. They use it as the basis of a new edition, but they emend it whenever there seem to be errors in it to correct, or when the author has revised a later text of the work. The term "copy-text" may refer to a manuscript or a printed edition, and it's the term we'll stick with here. But since printed books can vary from each other in small ways even within the same edition (as we saw in the case of Shakespeare's First Folio), some editors who are using an early printed edition as a copy-text also specify the particular copy they are using (for example, the one in the British Library in London). This individual copy is called the base-text.

Depending on the kind of edition being undertaken, editors may decide to modernize or regularize spellings and punctuation or update the text in other ways, for example by removing the long version of the letter s that was commonly used before about 1800. While some editions simply identify an early text of the work and reprint it, "eclectic" editions emend the copy-text in light of all the evidence about the work's textual history gathered by collating relevant early texts of the work. This is the effort that sets scholarly editions apart from other kinds of editions, and editors understandably pride themselves on the thoroughness of their research and the judiciousness of their choices. A few years ago, one of us heard a story from a colleague who was editing a paperback selection of a poet's works. This colleague told a respected scholarly editor that this new edition would just reprint earlier texts. "That's not editing," the older scholar spluttered, "that's photocopying!"

In working with a copy-text, editors have two issues to address: which text are they going to choose as their copy-text, and when are they going to depart from it? Some sophisticated theoretical debates have grown up around both of these questions, as textual scholars try to formulate a general theory of copy-text and ground rules for when to emend it. Let's take the first question first. Which early text of a work should an editor use as the basis for a new edition? McKerrow thought the answer was straightforward: you should use the earliest available complete text as the copy-text. McKerrow's approach was influenced by his research on early modern works, for which there is often no pre-publication material. His position rests on two assumptions, both of which have been challenged by other scholars, as we'll see below. First, he assumes that the composition of a work is finished before the process of transmission starts. Second, he assumes that the process of textual transmission, whether in manuscript or print, introduces errors into the text; he understands the transmission of a work as a falling-off from a state of original "purity." So if a fair-copy manuscript existed, McKerrow thought, the editor should use that, because it was the text that most closely approximated the author's conception of the work. If no such manuscript existed, he reasoned, we should choose the text that was closest to it. In the case of texts from before the age of print, which come down to us through a series of increasingly corrupt manuscript copies, the text closest to the author's lost manuscript would be the earliest available manuscript copy. In the case of printed texts, it would usually be the first edition. In both cases, if we can't get to the author's own manuscript, then McKerrow wants either the text copied directly from it or, if that has been lost, the text with the fewest intervening steps.[5]

There are cases, however, when the earliest text is not the best copy-text. If, for some reason, the author was not available to see his or her work through the press for the earliest printed version, then errors may have slipped in. If he or she was able to oversee a later edition, then it might be better to select the later text as the copy-text. In this case, the author could have corrected errors in the later text that he or she wouldn't have had the chance to correct in the earlier text. The later text would therefore come closer to the author's conception of the work. Keats's "Ode on a Grecian Urn" provides a good example. The poem was first printed in *Annals of the Fine Arts* in January 1820, but Keats probably did not oversee this publication. He probably *did* oversee the poem's second publication in his volume *Lamia, Isabella, The Eve of St Agnes and Other Poems*, which appeared six months later. In this case, then, the later text may be a better copy-text because it more closely follows what Keats wanted. We don't have the manuscript of "Ode on a Grecian Urn," but even if we did, it might not be the best choice of copy-text. As we'll see later, in some cases authors expected their manuscripts to be quite extensively edited—with spelling and punctuation standardized, for example—before they reached the reader. In these cases, to follow the manuscript too closely may mean including readings that the author thought of as errors to be corrected in the process of publication. Even a manuscript in the author's hand does not necessarily offer a perfect text of the work.

To help address these issues, the pioneering bibliographer and textual scholar W.W. Greg distinguished two kinds of variants between texts of a work: **accidentals** and **substantives** (*BRBH* 127–29). Accidentals are details of the text that do not affect the meaning of the work. They might include spellings (in works written before standardized spelling), changes from British to American spelling, different approaches to breaking words across a line-break using hyphens, the indentation of paragraphs, and the handling of dialogue. Despite their name, they do not necessarily arise from accidents. Substantives are details of the text that do affect the meaning of the work, such as variant words. In some cases, apparently minor details of punctuation or capitalization can actually be substantive variants, as we saw in the example of Keats's "Ode on a Grecian Urn." Consider these two texts:

> The professor says the student is an idiot

and

> The professor, says the student, is an idiot.

You can see that the commas here are substantive variants, not accidental ones, because they change the meaning of the sentence. Greg argued that editors should not change the accidentals of their copy-texts, but that where there were substantive variants between the copy-text and later texts they should consider substituting the later readings for the earlier ones if the author probably wanted the change, or if the earlier reading was clearly wrong. "Wherever there is more than one substantive text of comparable authority," Greg wrote, "then although it will still be necessary to choose one of them as copy-text, and to follow it in accidentals, this copy-text can be allowed no over-riding or even preponderant authority so far as substantive readings are concerned" (*BRBH* 132–33).

In some situations, however, an editor may choose not to select a copy-text. Sometimes, when an editor is sorting out the relationships between the texts of a work, he or she will find two or more texts that are equally close to a lost fair-copy manuscript but will not find any evidence for preferring one over the other(s). One example is the short stories of Stephen Crane, which were published simultaneously in a number of syndicated newspapers. The newspapers all independently typeset the story on the basis of a master copy provided by the syndicate office. The master copy derived directly from the manuscript. Neither the manuscript nor the master copy survives. Each newspaper that published the story, then, is as close to the lost manuscript as every other newspaper, and there's no compelling reason to choose one or other of them as the copy-text for a new edition. In this kind of case, the available texts of the work can't be arranged into a family tree, because they are all equidistant from the lost original. Editors call this a "radiating texts" situation.[6] In this situation, the editor can either choose one or other of the radiating texts as the copy-text more or less arbitrarily, or he or she can decide to edit without a copy-text. Working without a copy-text means that the editor starts with a blank page, as it were, and considers several texts of the work at every stage in producing a new edition. There is no default text on which to fall back. When working without a copy-text, then, the editor is not so much repairing the errors and corruptions that have crept into the text of a work as rebuilding the work's lost original on the basis of the traces it has left in the available texts.[7]

Variants

Where two texts of a work differ from one another, then, an editor must decide which one to follow, and whether to emend his or her copy-text. Deciding whether a substantive variant is the result of the author revising his or her work or the result of a mistake by the typesetter or copyist is an important part of the editor's task. Imagine a poem whose manuscript is lost but which exists in two print editions. The first edition contains the line "the hedge rests in the sun," while the second edition prints the line "the hedge rusts in the sun." Both of these are possible lines of poetry. In one, the hedge is personified as resting. In the other, the way its leaves are turning brown in the sun is metaphorically described as rusting. Which version should the editor follow when preparing a new edition? Most editors would try to judge which text best reflects the author's intentions. To do so, editors rely on two kinds of evidence, which they call extrinsic and intrinsic. Extrinsic evidence is evidence from outside the text. Suppose that the diaries or letters of the author or publisher record that the author complained about several errors in the first edition and insisted on correcting the **proofs** of the second edition. This would provide extrinsic evidence that the second edition records the author's intentions more reliably than the first edition. In this scenario, the change from "rests" to "rusts" is likely to be the result of the author either correcting an error in the first edition or revising the poem. Intrinsic evidence is evidence from inside the text. Suppose a different scenario, in which the second edition contains many obvious misprints, such as impossible words, misplaced apostrophes, or misnumbered pages. This provides intrinsic evidence that the second edition is not reliable. In this scenario, the change from "rests" to "rusts" could have been another example of the printer's carelessness that just happened to create an intelligible reading. The distinguished literary critic F.O. Matthiessen once embarrassed himself over a textual variant of this kind. Matthiessen wrote that the image of the "soiled fish of the sea" in Melville's *White-Jacket* was a moment of genius; the "*discordia concors*, the unexpected linking of the medium of cleanliness with filth," he wrote, "could only have sprung from an imagination that had apprehended the terrors of the deep, of the immaterial deep as well as the physical." Unfortunately for Matthiessen, what Melville actually wrote was "coiled fish of the sea." He was talking about eels. "Soiled" was a printer's error in the edition Matthiessen had consulted.[8]

Having considered the evidence that a text is more or less reliable, the editor will then exercise his or her judgment about individual substantive variants in order to decide which variants are more likely to be mistakes or corruptions on the part of the typesetter or copyist, and which are likely to be corrections or revisions on the part of the author. To illustrate this process, Fredson Bowers helpfully works through three examples from Nathaniel Hawthorne's *Blithedale Romance*. The manuscript of this 1852 novel survives, but the first edition differs from it in several places. Hawthorne corrected a proof copy of the book, but the corrected proof has not survived. The editor, then, must figure out which differences between the manuscript and the first edition represent revisions that Hawthorne made on the lost proof, and which are printer's errors that crept into the first edition. For example, at one point the manuscript describes a "wintry day," while the first edition describes a "winter day." The scene is set in April, and Bowers says that one might call a day in April "wintry," but not a "winter day." So, on intrinsic evidence, we should prefer the manuscript reading. The first edition contains an error at this point that the editor can correct. At another point, the manuscript reads "to his credit," where the first edition says "creditable." Here, Bowers says that it's difficult to imagine that the typesetter misread the manuscript, so it is more likely that this is Hawthorne's revision. In this case, then, we should prefer the first edition's reading on intrinsic evidence. Finally, the manuscript says "inspirited" at a place where the first edition has "inspired." Here, Bowers argues that the typesetter is likely to have mistaken the more uncommon word "inspirited" for the more common one "inspired." The first edition's reading is therefore an error and the manuscript's reading should be retained, again on intrinsic evidence.[9]

Sometimes, deciding which variant to choose for a new edition gets very complicated or controversial, creating what is known as a textual crux. One textual crux that has given editors a lot of trouble is in Shakespeare's late play *The Tempest*.[10] In Act Four of that play, as it appears in the First Folio that collected Shakespeare's plays after his death, Ferdinand exclaims:

> Let me live here ever!
> So rare a wondered father and a wise
> Makes this place paradise. (IV.i.122–24)

In 1709 the editor Nicholas Rowe was the first to suggest that this should actually read "a wondered father and a wife." After all, Ferdinand is soon to marry Miranda: surely it's his wife-to-be, as well as his father-in-law, who makes the island seem like paradise to him. Rowe suggested that the Folio's **compositor** (or typesetter) had misread an f in the manuscript as an old long s, creating the error. Some subsequent editors followed Rowe's suggestion, which gained support in 1978, when Jeanne Addison Roberts examined multiple copies of the First Folio in detail and suggested that the word was actually "wife" but that the letter f had become damaged in the process of printing, making it look like a long s in most copies. More recently, Peter Blayney magnified by 200 times the relevant page of all the copies of the First Folio in the Folger Shakespeare Library in Washington, DC. This library has 82 copies of the First Folio, about a third of those still in existence and by far the largest collection in the world. He concluded that the letter had actually been a long s all along, and that ink blots, not a broken letter f, had misled earlier editors.

However, just because the compositor set a long s does not mean that the text he worked from contained an s. He might have misread the word, or a long s might have got mixed up with the f's by mistake in his typecase.

We know that there were five compositors working on the First Folio, and it is possible to compare their habits and level of skill.[11] All three compositors who worked on *The Tempest* were experienced, and therefore it is now generally acknowledged to be one of the most error-free of all Shakespeare's plays. Further, we know that as the first play included in the Folio, *The Tempest* was given pride of place and proofreading may have been careful as a result. Variants between surviving copies show stop-press corrections being made during printing.[12] So although we can't say with certainty, the generally high quality of **presswork** on this play reduces the likelihood that this word results from a printer's error.

It's also far from certain that the compositor was working from a manuscript in Shakespeare's handwriting. A legal scrivener named Ralph Crane is believed to have provided the manuscript, based on a copy in Shakespeare's hand. He might have inaccurately copied it. Faced with these uncertainties, editors have asked whether Shakespeare commonly put adjectives after the noun they referred to (as in "and a wise"), or whether the couplet rhyme produced by "wise" and "paradise" was characteristic of his verse, or whether his (or Ferdinand's) conception of paradise would have included wives, since the Bible taught that there were no marriages in heaven (Mark 12.25; Luke 20.35). Whether Ferdinand thinks of Miranda at this moment makes a significant difference to our understanding of his character, the play, and Shakespeare's attitudes toward women more generally, so when editors have to decide between "a wise" and "a wife," there is much at stake.

Given all the evidence from the Folio, then, substituting "wife" for "wise" remains a matter of conjecture. Sometimes editors introduce this kind of "conjectural emendation" to correct what seems to have been an error in the text, even when there's no positive evidence for the reading they suggest as a replacement. For obvious reasons, these kinds of emendation are the most disputed of all. The fourth version of the final lines from "Ode on a Grecian Urn" cited above from the Penguin edition edited by John Barnard represents a conjectural emendation, since Barnard's placement of the inverted commas does not follow any text of the work that Keats might have overseen. Another conjectural emendation occurs in *Romeo and Juliet*. There are three relevant texts of the play: a quarto book (Q1) published in 1597; another (Q2) in 1599; and the text in the First Folio of Shakespeare's collected plays, which appeared in 1623. In Q1, Mercutio says that a letter sent by Tybalt contains "Some Challenge on my life." In Q2 and the Folio, he says it contains "A challenge on my life" (II.iv.8). In all these texts, the line seems to mean that Tybalt is threatening to kill Mercutio. But this doesn't make sense in the context of the play. Tybalt is challenging Romeo to a duel, as the following scene makes clear. He is not threatening Mercutio's life. So modern editors conjecture that there should be a comma in this line, emending it to read "A challenge, on my life." With the comma, "on my life" becomes a mild oath, so Mercutio is saying—in his characteristically laddish way—"the letter contains a challenge, I'll bet."

The most famous conjectural emendation is probably from Shakespeare's *Henry V*. In the First Folio, when the Hostess is telling Bardolph and Pistol about the moment when she knew Falstaff was going to die, she recalls:

> [A]fter I saw him fumble with the Sheets, and play with Flowers, and smile vpon his fingers end, I knew there was but one way: for his Nose was as sharpe as a Pen, and a Table of greene fields. (II.iii.14–18)

"A Table of greene fields" doesn't seem to make much sense, so the editor Lewis Theobald conjectured in 1726 that the lines should read "and a babled of green fields." Here "a" is a short form for "he," which appears repeatedly in Shakespeare's plays, and Theobald conjectures that "Table" is a misreading of "babled" (for babbled). The Hostess, on Theobald's conjecture, is describing Falstaff falling into delirium as he approaches death, babbling suggestively but incoherently. Others since Theobald have challenged his conjecture, proposing other emendations to these lines or ingenious readings to make sense of the Folio's text.

Authorial Intentions

Most readers would say they want to read the words the author wrote. Most editors would agree that they aim to give readers the words the author wrote. To do this, they try to purge the text of errors introduced in the process of transmission by other people, such as scribes or compositors, in order to give us the work as the author intended it to be read. But what exactly are the author's intentions about the words he or she wrote, and how do editors discern them? That turns out to be a much more complicated question than it initially appears. Most authors' first drafts, when we have access to them, are messy affairs, scribbled over with crossings-out, alternative words, second thoughts, corrections, and ink blots. Some authors write fluently and with few corrections, but for most writers, most of the time, writing involves thinking again, and again, about how to express themselves. Depending on the author's working habits, this process may be extended through several drafts before the work is considered finished. And in many cases authors return to "finished" works at a later date and make further changes, sometimes after the work has appeared in print. W.H. Auden paraphrased the French poet Paul Valéry as saying "a poem is never finished; it is only abandoned," and "abandoned" works may be taken up again and revised (we'll see what this meant to Auden shortly).[13] A fundamental assumption of most textual editing has been that authors should be allowed their second thoughts. Editors often choose an early text of the work as a copy-text in order to exclude errors that have crept into later texts in the process of transmission. But they also emend their copy-text to reflect the author's second thoughts as expressed in later texts of the work. On the assumption that authors polish and improve their works as they revise them, many editors argue that a new edition should reflect the author's "final intentions."

To understand what this means, it is helpful to distinguish between three kinds of intention, as Michael Hancher does in a useful essay on this topic.[14] The first kind is the intention to write a certain sort of work: a novel, or a play, or a sermon, or an essay. An author has to formulate this kind of intention before beginning a work, although, as we'll see, he or she may modify it later. Hancher calls this the author's "programmatic intention." The second kind of intention is the intention to write this word rather than that one in a sentence or a line of poetry. This kind of intention is continually being worked out, questioned, and reconsidered as the author writes and revises. Hancher calls this "active intention." Third, the author will usually intend to accomplish something by writing the work, whether that is making money, producing social change, popularizing a set of ideas, consolidating a literary reputation, or several of those things at once. Hancher calls this the author's "final intention," but confusingly he does not use that phrase in the way that textual editors use it. Of these three kinds of intention, editors are mostly concerned with the second: the author's "active" intentions, or the intention to write one word rather than another on the page. When they use the term "final intention," scholarly editors mean the latest form of the active intention—the author's final choice of which words to use and what order to place them in.

The trouble with an author's active intentions is that they're radically unstable. Formed in the moment of composition, as the pen is moving across the page, they are liable to be revisited at later moments, reconsidered, and sometimes revised. The scholarly editor and theorist Thomas Tanselle borrows Hancher's threefold model of intention and uses it to distinguish between two kinds of revision (*BRBH* 139–55). He calls these "horizontal" revision and "vertical" revision. Horizontal revision occurs when an author aims to polish up the work, improve its clarity or intensify its effects, but without changing his conception of the work as a whole. In this kind of revision, the author changes his active intentions, but doesn't change his programmatic intention. The author is making changes of degree, not changes of kind. Vertical revision occurs when the author aims to alter the general character or purpose of the work. In other words, she stops trying to write one kind of work and starts trying to turn her material into a different kind of work. In this kind of revision, the author changes her programmatic intention, and the revisions she makes in her active intentions reflect that change. Horizontal revisions aim to improve the work as it's currently conceived. Vertical revisions reflect a new conception of the work and try to make it into something different. Horizontal revisions produce a new text of the work; vertical revisions effectively produce a new work.

Editors should treat these two kinds of revisions differently, in Tanselle's view. Where authors have changed their active intentions (producing horizontal revisions), the editor should include the revisions in a new edition of the work. Authors are allowed their second thoughts, and editors usually try to identify their final intentions (that is, the latest version of their active intentions). Editors include these revisions regardless of whether they think they're improvements—most editors would argue that it's their job to make judgments about what the author intended, not about the aesthetic value of those intentions. Where authors have changed their programmatic intentions (producing vertical revisions), editors may conclude that they're dealing with what are effectively two different works, or at least two distinct versions of a work. In this case, they may decide to edit the two works separately and present them both as part of a new edition.

An example is Wordsworth's long poem *The Prelude*. Wordsworth had written a version of the poem in two sections (or "books") by 1798, and he seems to have thought of it as finished at that time. But soon afterwards he returned to the poem and drastically expanded it, producing first a poem in five books and then, by 1805, a version in 13 books. At that point, Wordsworth again seems to have thought of the poem as finished. But, again, he returned to the poem and made further extensive revisions, recasting it into 14 books for the version that was published after his death in 1850. Accordingly, the Cornell edition of Wordsworth's poetry includes three different texts of *The Prelude*: the two-book version of 1798, the thirteen-book version of 1805, and the fourteen-book version of 1850. This decision could be justified on the grounds that, by 1805, Wordsworth was trying to write a very different kind of poem from the one he had written in 1798. The revisions he made between the three versions of the work were "vertical" revisions. In other words, his programmatic intentions had changed, and he was producing either a different work or a different version of the work.

In some cases, editors have argued that even where the author's final intentions are quite clear, they should not be followed. There are three distinct versions of this argument. First, editors may argue that the earlier texts are aesthetically superior. The editor of the Cornell University Press edition of Wordsworth's collected works, Stephen Parrish, argues that the earlier versions of *The Prelude* are often simply better poems (*BRBH* 157–63). He writes:

> [N]ot always, not even usually, but "often" we can confidently say that the early Wordsworth was a better poet than the late Wordsworth, for the plain reason that he was closer to the sources of his inspiration and less inhibited by the various orthodoxies—political, social, religious, and poetical—that he succumbed to in his later years. (160)

In order to recognize the value of the earlier versions of Wordsworth's poems, and to put them back into circulation for new generations of readers, Parrish suggests, editors need to question their commitment to respecting the author's final intentions. In accordance with this view, the Cornell Wordsworth usually reprints Wordsworth's poems in their earliest complete form, often from manuscript sources.

There's a second reason why editors might not want to follow the author's final intentions, even when they can figure out what they were. Where an author revised his or her works late in life, editors may resist reprinting the revised versions on the grounds that to do so obscures the author's development. Walter Scott and Henry James both revised most of their novels toward the ends of their lives for collected editions of their works (known as the "Magnum Opus" edition in Scott's case and the "New York Edition" in James's case). Scott and James had already sent their novels into the public domain in their original published versions. But late in their lives they not only corrected errors but also consciously changed many details of the texts. These late revisions often had the effect of smoothing out stylistic differences between earlier and later novels and in some respects made all the novels read as though they had been written at the end of the author's writing life. There's no doubt about the authors' final intentions in these cases, but editors—for example, those working on the recently completed Edinburgh edition of Scott's Waverley novels and the Cambridge Edition of the Complete Fiction of Henry James—have preferred to base new editions on the original published versions of the novels, so that readers turning from earlier novels to later ones can see the development of the author's style. The claim here is not that Scott's or James's early style is better than his late style, but that the two are different, and the difference is obscured when the later, revised versions of the works are the only ones reprinted in new editions.

Thirdly, and relatedly, editors may argue that the earlier versions of a work are worth reprinting because they allow us to read it in the same version as its first readers. In the final paragraph of the first edition of *On the Origin of Species* (1859), Charles Darwin concluded his theory of natural selection with this statement:

> There is grandeur in this view of life, with its several powers, having been originally breathed into a few forms or into one; and that, whilst this planet has gone cycling on according to the fixed law of gravity, from so simple a beginning endless forms most beautiful and most wonderful have been, and are being, evolved.[15]

Perturbed by the controversy his book produced, Darwin altered this sentence in the second edition (1860) so that it read "originally breathed *by the Creator* into a few forms or into one" (our italics). This was the most notable revision among many that Darwin made to his work over its first six editions, which appeared between 1859 and 1872. The changes amount to around 2,250 revised sentences (including sentences that were added or removed) and more than 15,000 changes in words or phrases. Darwin also added an extra chapter in 1872. The changes made the text less personal ("I think" was removed 29 times), as well as less colloquial and more authoritative, and incorporated new research to bring the volume up to date.[16] If we want an edition that reflects Darwin's final intentions, then, the sixth edition of 1872 is the best candidate for the copy-text. If, however, we want to understand why Darwin's book provoked such controversy and debate in 1859, an edition based on the first edition will allow us to read the text that so inflamed some of Darwin's earliest readers.

Other problems with discerning authorial intentionality persist. We have seen that most editors want to preserve or recover the text the author intended. Confusingly, however, authors do not always write what they intend to write. If, allowing his or her attention to wander for a moment, an author repeats a word in the manuscript, or writes "there" instead of "their," then an editor would quite reasonably conclude that the author had not written what he or she intended to write. Even a text in the author's handwriting is not a perfect guide to his or her intentions for the work. A new edition would, therefore, have to delete the repeated word or substitute "their" for "there" in order to present its readers with the text of the work that the author intended. It follows from this that someone other than the author can fulfil the author's intention. If the author sends a manuscript to his or her publisher and then telephones or writes to the publisher with a list of corrections, the publisher may write those corrections into the manuscript (and might throw the author's letter away). In this case, the manuscript in the author's handwriting will include changes in the publisher's handwriting. But the changes made by the publisher on the author's instructions will be no less "authorized" than the sections of the manuscript in the author's own handwriting. The same is true when, even without instructions from the author, an editor deletes a word repeated by mistake or corrects an obvious error. In these cases, **authorial intention** is not the same as authorial handwriting, and someone other than the author can fulfil the author's wishes.

If an author asks a publisher or **printer** for specific revisions to particular words, the situation is fairly straightforward. It's more complicated if the author gives a general instruction relating to the work as a whole, and still more complicated if an unspoken understanding exists between the author and the publisher about how the work will be edited in the process of publication. Lord Byron, returning a proof-copy to his long-suffering publisher John Murray, wrote, "If you have patience, look it over.

Do you know any body who can stop—I mean point-commas, and so forth? for I am, I hear, a sad hand at your punctuation."[17] Byron may have been unduly modest here. The punctuation in his manuscripts is irregular but expressive. Nonetheless, he seems to be giving Murray a free hand to alter the punctuation of his poem or to get someone else to do so. Where the punctuation in the printed version differs from the manuscript, then, editors have to decide which version to follow. John Clare's poetry provides another example of this problem. Clare was a self-taught poet from rural Northamptonshire who received no formal education. He often used dialect words in his poems, as well as non-standard spellings and punctuation. Some of his poetry was published by the London firm of Taylor and Hessey (who also published John Keats's work), and John Taylor "corrected" some of Clare's spelling and punctuation before printing his poems. Some of Clare's editors think Taylor patronized Clare and that his changes bleached out some of the distinctive local character of Clare's poetic voice. They prefer to base new editions of Clare's work on his manuscripts and retain their spellings, punctuation, and dialect words. Other editors disagree. They think that Clare viewed the manuscripts he sent to Taylor as unfinished and that he thought of the publisher's changes as polishing his work and making it ready for publication. These editors think that going back to the manuscript versions presents Clare's poems to the public in a state he would have been ashamed of, and they prefer editions based on the early printed texts.

What about cases where, instead of the author asking someone else to change the text, someone else suggests some changes to the author? Here, it's helpful to make another distinction. In some cases, authors may enthusiastically embrace changes suggested by friends, editors, and so on. In fact, Jack Stillinger, one of Keats's modern editors, has found that many of Keats's poems were not the product of his solitary labour, as he frequently invited his friends to make changes to them. Introducing the concept of multiple authorship, Stillinger contends that many literary works were in fact produced by a range of individuals, as opposed to a "solitary genius."[18] In other cases, authors may be prepared to accept suggested changes without really thinking that the changes are improvements. They may think the changes will make the work more saleable, better received by reviewers, or less likely to attract unwanted attention from censors. Editors, then, distinguish between changes the author endorsed and those the author only acquiesced in. Here, again, it's helpful to remember the difference between kinds of intention. An author who has the programmatic intention to publish a novel with a large **circulation** may accept that to achieve that goal he or she needs to delete a controversial scene or remove some swear words. For example, in 1928 D.H. Lawrence wanted to publish his novel *Lady Chatterley's Lover*, which contained both explicit sex scenes and swear words; however, he knew that it would be impossible to print the book as it was, without the controversial material being removed. As a result, an expurgated version of the novel was printed in 1928 (in the US) and 1932 (in the UK). No editor today (unless he or she was interested in the history of **censorship**) would print the expurgated version, given that it does not reflect Lawrence's active intentions. In this case, even if Lawrence acquiesced in the changes, an editor would be justified in restoring the original text as the author would have liked it to be published under ideal conditions.

Sometimes, authors censor their work not at the direct suggestion of others but as a result of their own anxieties. Worried about how their work will appear to readers and reviewers (as well as, in some cases, government censors), they tone down parts of the text that seem likely to attract criticism. Which parts of the work they worry about will depend on the author and the context of writing, but they might be those parts that are marked most strongly by the author's political views, religious beliefs (or lack thereof), sexual identity, gender, class, race, ethnicity, educational background, and so on. In these cases, revision is self-censorship. Seamus Heaney reflects on a line of poetry from his early poem "Follower" in these terms. In the first draft, Heaney wrote "My father wrought with a horse-plough." The word "wrought," Heaney explains, came naturally to him,

> because until relatively recently that verb was the common one in the speech of mid-Ulster [where he grew up]. Country people used the word "wrought" naturally and almost exclusively when they talked about a person labouring with certain tools and animals, and it always carried a sense of wholehearted commitment to the task. You wrought with horses or with a scythe or with a plough; and you might also have wrought at hay or at flax or at bricklaying.[19]

But Heaney reconsidered this word and changed it from the distinctive regional vocabulary of his childhood to a less localized, perhaps blander, standard English. The published text of the poem reads "my father worked with a horse-plough." In changing "wrought" to "worked," Heaney left behind a word that marked the poem as the product of a particular linguistic community—rural, agrarian, and Irish—and instead adopted one that, while more familiar to his readers, would have felt strange in his father's mouth. Heaney thought twice. "And once you think twice about a local usage you have been displaced from it," he wrote, "and your right to it has been contested by the official linguistic censor with whom another part of you is secretly in league."[20] Sometimes, writing is not only a struggle to convey meaning effectively but also a negotiation between what the writer wants to say and the various social, political, and linguistic constraints under which he or she works. When writing involves self-censorship, then recovering earlier texts of a work can be a way of belatedly liberating the writer from those constraints. This is controversial, because it goes against the usual editorial respect for final intentions.

Brenda Silver provides further examples of authorial self-censorship from early manuscript versions of works by Virginia Woolf (*BRBH* 181–98). Throughout 1932 and into 1933, Woolf worked on a text provisionally called "The Pargiters," which intertwined novelistic and essayistic sections. Eventually, she separated the two kinds of writing, turning the novelistic sections into her novel *The Years* (1937) and using material from the essayistic sections in her anti-war essay *Three Guineas* (1938). At a late stage of revision, she deleted or altered passages in *The Years* that included explicit sexual, feminist, and anti-war statements. She also seems to have toned down passages that might have seemed too obviously enraged. Woolf's modern critics debate whether these decisions were aesthetic choices or self-censorship reflecting the social oppression of women in Woolf's time. Recovering and editing "The Pargiters," with its angry, sexually frank passages intact, then, becomes a form of feminist intervention that reverses Woolf's act of self-censorship.[21]

A related complication arises when an author attempts to suppress a work he or she has already published. Marianne Moore continually revised her poems and chose not to reprint a number of her earlier ones in her 1967 *Collected Poems*. Her author's note to the volume read, in its entirety, "omissions are not accidents." In this case, Moore clearly intended not to recirculate some of her poems. But this has not stopped her recent editors from putting back into circulation poems that she omitted from her *Collected Poems*, or reprinting earlier versions of poems she included in

Collected Poems in altered forms. Moore's decision to omit some poems entirely from later publications raises a further question: if a poet is entitled to delete one word, one line, or one stanza of a poem, why not all the words? W.H. Auden first published his poem "Spain" in 1937, during the Spanish Civil War. Auden had travelled to Spain and hoped to participate in the war as an ambulance driver. Toward the end of the poem, Auden initially wrote, "To-day the deliberate increase in the chances of death, / The conscious acceptance of guilt in the necessary murder." When he republished the poem in 1940, he felt uncomfortable both with these lines and with the poem as a whole. He changed the title to "Spain, 1937" and the second line of the quotation above to "The conscious acceptance of guilt in the fact of murder." This still left the problem of the poem's final lines: "History to the defeated / May say Alas but cannot help nor pardon." Auden finally decided that these lines were indefensible. In the foreword to his *Collected Shorter Poems* in 1966, he wrote:

> To say this is to equate goodness with success. It would have been bad enough if I had ever held this wicked doctrine, but that I should have stated it simply because it sounded to me rhetorically effective is quite inexcusable.[22]

The lines, in Auden's view, could not be fixed. He omitted the poem from his *Collected Shorter Poems* and never again reprinted it in his lifetime. Auden's final intention regarding this poem is clear: he did not want it republished. But his editor and literary executor, Edward Mendelson, has reprinted the poem in his edition of Auden's *Selected Poems*, arguing that "the claims of history, and of readers who want the discarded poems are strong.... A historical edition of this kind, reflecting the author's work as it first appeared in public rather than his final version of it," he suggests, "should not be taken as implying that Auden's revisions or rejections were in any way misguided."[23] Rather, he suggests, readers need to know the early and the later versions, including the cases where Auden rejected whole poems, in order to get the measure of his poetic character and achievement.

Textual Pluralism

Faced with these complexities, some editors claim that we can never really find or construct the "best" text of a work. Brenda Silver, for example, advocates reading "backward as well as forward" through the process of revision (*BRBH* 194). The critic and editor Jack Stillinger has similarly argued that editors should stop privileging one text of a work over all the others and opt instead for what he calls "textual pluralism" (*BRBH* 165–80). Where an author put a work into the public domain in different forms at different times, Stillinger argues, editors should accept that the work has many "versions." Rather than privileging one version of the work in a new edition, editors should present multiple versions for readers to compare. This leads Stillinger to a distinctive understanding of what a work is and of how we should talk about an author's intentions. In his account, both the author's intention and the text of the work begin to seem radically unstable. "Textual pluralism," Stillinger writes, "is based on the idea that each version of a work embodies a separate authorial intention that is not necessarily the same as the authorial intention in any other version of the same work."[24] Rather than thinking of revision as a process of polishing and improving the text (as editors who seek the author's final intentions tend to), or thinking of it as a falling-off from the author's original inspiration (as editors who base their work on earlier texts of the work might), textual pluralists think of revision as producing a proliferation of different versions, none with more authority than any other. This approach begins to call into question the distinction between text and work on which so much editing traditionally relied.

In this view, a work isn't a single string of words but a field of discourse in which the work exists in multiple different states, none of which can be called definitive and all of which are provisional. This idea leads Stillinger to identify 18 different versions of Samuel Taylor Coleridge's poem "The Rime of the Ancient Mariner," some of which differ from the others very substantially and some of which differ in only one or two words. He sums up the changes like this:

> In his successive revisions from one text to another, Coleridge dropped some sixty lines and added (not necessarily as replacements) another twenty; removed most of the archaic spellings that were a distinctive feature of the first published text in *Lyrical Ballads*; made changes in the title and subtitle; altered the wording of the poem itself here and there all through the text; added a lengthy epigraph from a

seventeenth-century theological work in Latin by Thomas Burnet; and added fifty-eight explanatory and sometimes interpretative **glosses** in prose that were printed in the margins beside and underneath the verses.[25]

Given this degree of textual complexity, how can an editor choose a single text of "The Ancient Mariner" as a copy-text, or hope to emend it to produce a satisfactory edition of the work? Stillinger argues that, rather than making unsatisfactory choices, we should accept that "The Ancient Mariner" has no definitive text. "If *The Ancient Mariner* is one poem," he writes, "it *has* to be all its versions taken together. On the other hand, [. . .] *The Ancient Mariner* might theoretically be recognised as the title of eighteen different poems."[26]

But does anyone actually want to read 18 "Ancient Mariners," beyond a handful of Coleridge specialists? Although some recent editions of Coleridge's poem have printed two versions on facing pages, not even Stillinger attempted to reprint all of the 18 versions of the poem he identified.[27] The publisher that undertook such an edition would probably find themselves stuck with a lot of very thick and expensive books that no one wanted to buy. The teacher who attempted to put 18 "Ancient Mariners" on the syllabus would have to answer a lot of questions from students about which version of the poem they really needed to read. For most readers, most of the time, one text of a work is enough. Digital technologies may offer a different approach to this problem. Online archives of different versions can include interfaces that allow users to view and compare different versions side by side. As our written heritage from the past increasingly migrates into new media environments, some of the basic concepts that have structured scholarly editing—concepts such as text, work, intention, and edition—are being called into question. In a digital environment, some of the categories used by editors of printed editions may be reductive or redundant. We'll return to innovations in textual scholarship in the digital environment in Chapter 5.

The debates among textual scholars and editors that this chapter outlines can sometimes seem quite specialized, but they reflect underlying theoretical debates that should concern all readers. Thinking through editorial disagreements can help you to think about the nature of writing, reading, and the literary work. First, what is writing? If you think of writing as something inspired, or as something that pours forth from the mind of a genius in a moment of extraordinary creativity, then you're likely to want the text of the work that comes closest to that moment of inspiration. If you're looking for an edition of Jack Kerouac's novel *On the Road*, you may prefer an edition based on Kerouac's original draft.[28] Kerouac typed the draft over a period of three weeks in April 1951 in manic bursts on a continuous scroll of tracing paper sheets that he taped together, so that inserting new pages into the typewriter did not interrupt the flow of his creative outpouring. It's over 120 feet long. The scroll differs in several ways from the published novel: it uses the real names of Kerouac's friends, including Neal Cassady and Allen Ginsberg, and it includes several sexually explicit passages cut from later versions. If, on the other hand, you think of writing as a kind of craft, in which authors polish and refine their work, progressively improving it as a result of sustained attention and repeated revision, then you're likely to want the text of the work that reflects the latest, most polished version the author produced. You may prefer an edition of *On the Road* that reflects the many changes Kerouac made to the draft scroll between 1951 and the novel's publication in 1957, including cutting some passages and inserting others, dividing the novel into five parts, and changing the names of the characters.

Second, what is a literary work? If you think of a literary work as a linguistic construct, a string of words, then you will be quite happy with an edition that contains little or no information about the material forms in which the work has previously appeared. You may tend to view books as only the vehicles that convey texts of the work more or less imperfectly, and so think that nothing important is lost when a text of the work is conveyed in another format. For example, modern editions often renumber the chapters of three-volume novels into a continuous sequence, thus making it impossible to see where one volume ended and another began. If you think literary works are made only of words, this is unlikely to bother you too much, because the breaks between volumes may seem accidental and not substantive to you. If, however, you think of literary works as having a hybrid existence that is both linguistic and material, things will look rather different. You will probably want a new edition of the work to include at least some information about the physical format of the earliest editions. James Joyce's novel *Ulysses*, for example, played a complex game with the page numbers of its first edition in 1922. Joyce made a number of changes in the proof-copy to produce these effects, and they reflect his sometimes obsessive concern with numerology. The action of *Ulysses* takes place on one day in 1904; this was a leap year, a fact mentioned four times in the book. A leap year has 366 days and 366 nights, or 732 in total. The text of the 1922 edition of *Ulysses* covers 366 **leaves**, or 732 pages. Those pages divide exactly into two halves, with the first half taking place during the day and the second half at night: the sun sets on page 366, exactly halfway through the book. That page also contains the phrase "Done half by design."[29] Joyce makes the material form of the book an integral part of his artistry. New editions that do not contain information about the earlier physical forms in which the work appeared obscure the effects he laboured to produce.

Third, what is reading? If you think of reading as way of entering the mind of an author and understanding what he or she thinks, then you will probably want an edition that attempts to come as close as possible to what the author wrote and purges the changes introduced by collaborators, publishers, or others (even when the author acquiesced in those changes). You may prefer an edition of *Frankenstein* such as that edited by Charles Robinson in 2009.[30] This edition offers two texts of the novel: one based on Mary Shelley's earliest extant draft and another showing the additions and changes made by her husband Percy Shelley. By painstakingly analysing the manuscripts of the novel, Robinson worked out that Percy is responsible for about 5,000 of its 72,000 words. Percy also made many changes to the structure of Mary's sentences and to her choice of words; her direct and unadorned prose style is sometimes obscured by his edits. If you want to understand what Mary was thinking while she was writing, then this may be the edition for you. Better yet, you may want to view the Shelley-Godwin Archive (http://shelleygodwinarchive.org), an online remediation of the original manuscript notebooks with accompanying **diplomatic transcriptions** (a record of the original that attempts to reproduce its exact appearance, with minimal or no editorial intervention or interpretation). Viewing this digitized manuscript allows you to follow Shelley's process of creation, revision, and collaboration. On the other hand, if you think of reading as a way to understand literature in its historical context, then you will want an edition based on a text of the work that its first readers actually read, rather than one recovered from manuscript drafts that have lain unpublished for decades or even centuries. You will probably prefer an edition of *Frankenstein* based on the first published edition of 1818, or the revised edition of 1831, on the grounds that these are the editions that circulated historically and produced the novel's impact on its earliest readers. You might also be interested in the 1823 edition, which includes some revisions by Mary Shelley's father, William Godwin; these seem to have been made without Mary's knowledge or permission, although many of them were accepted by her in the 1831 edition. In any case, if you want to read the novel as its first readers saw it, you will have to read a version that includes contributions from someone other than Mary Shelley.

Very few readers of this book will become textual editors, but almost all of you will read editions of older literary works. All readers who use these editions should understand the work textual editors do and the debates they have about how best to do it. Before we can begin to understand any written work from the past, we should ask questions about the edition of that work we're reading. We should understand the basic textual history of the work, what versions of the work exist and how they differ from each other, and how the edition we're reading handles those different texts. We should think about which text of the work the editor has chosen as the basis for the new edition and, when the editor has changed that text, why he or she has done so. If the editor has reproduced multiple versions of the work or offered an image and/or transcription of one textual witness, then we should ask why that approach has been adopted. We can't start to talk about what a work means until we understand how its text has been handled by its editor, and the editorial process usually turns out to have been quite complicated. Most works from the past, whether they were initially circulated in manuscript or print, come down to us in several variant states. They frequently bear the traces of the author's second and third thoughts, and sometimes an author's intentions are impossible to pin down. These works may also bear the traces of the copyist's or typesetter's carelessness, inattention, or conscious censorship, or of the thoughtful contributions of editors and collaborators. And these kinds of traces can sometimes be difficult to tell apart. This complexity may be found in all kinds of writing, but literary works in particular possess a layered, unstable existence. Scholarly editors try to map these thickets to allow readers to find their way more easily, but they do not always agree on how best to approach their task. All of us who use modern editions—that is, all of us who read—need to know something about how they're made.

Notes

1. John Keats, *The Complete Poems*, ed. John Barnard, 2nd ed. (London: Penguin, 1988), 344–46, 672–77.
2. A helpful essay on this topic is Roger Chartier and Peter Stallybrass, "What Is a Book?," *The Cambridge Companion to Textual Scholarship*, ed. Neil Freistat and Julia Flanders (Cambridge: Cambridge UP, 2013), 188–204.
3. *Benjamin Franklin's Autobiography*, ed. J.A. Leo Lemay and P.M. Zall (New York: Norton, 1986), 36.
4. Fredson Bowers, "Textual Criticism," *The Aims and Methods of Scholarship in Modern Languages and Literatures*, ed. James Thorpe (New York: Modern Language Association of America, 1963), 23–42, 24.
5. Bowers agreed: he thought textual editing should be "an attempt to approximate an inferential authorial fair copy, or other ultimately authoritative document" ("Textual" 26).
6. Bowers coined this term in a discussion of Crane's works. See Fredson Bowers, "Multiple Authority: New Problems and Concepts of Copy-Text," *Library* 5.27 (1972): 81–115.
7. G. Thomas Tanselle, "Editing without a Copy-Text," *Studies in Bibliography* 47 (1994): 1–22.
8. F.O. Matthiessen, *American Renaissance: Art and Expression in the Age of Emerson and Whitman* (New York: Oxford UP, 1941), 329. The error was first pointed out in John W. Nichol, "Melville's 'Soiled' Fish of the Sea," *American Literature* 21 (1949): 338–39.
9. Bowers, "Textual" 32.
10. For a detailed discussion of this textual crux, which we have followed closely in this section, see William Shakespeare, *The Tempest*, ed. Virginia Mason Vaughan and Alden T. Vaughan, *The Arden Shakespeare* (London: Arden, 2011), 136–38.
11. Charlton Hinman, *The Printing and Proof-Reading of the First Folio of Shakespeare*, vol. 2 (Oxford: Clarendon P, 1963), 509–13.
12. Hinman, vol. 1, 265.
13. W.H. Auden, *Collected Poems*, ed. Edward Mendelson (London: Faber, 2007), xxx.
14. Michael Hancher, "Three Kinds of Intention," *MLN* 87.7 (1972): 827–51.
15. Charles Darwin, *On the Origin of Species by Means of Natural Selection, or the Preservation of Favoured Races in the Struggle for Life* (London: John Murray, 1859), 490. The word "On" was dropped from the title in the sixth edition. Different texts of Darwin's book can be compared using the "Online Variorum of Darwin's *Origin of Species*," ed. Barbara Bordalejo, *Darwin Online*, http://darwin-online.org.uk/Variorum/.

16 For an account of the revisions, see Barbara Bordalejo, "Introduction to the Online Variorum of Darwin's *Origin of Species*," *Darwin Online*, http://darwin-online.org.uk/Variorum/Introduction.html.
17 Byron to Murray, 26 August 1813, *Byron's Letters and Journals*, vol. 3, ed. Leslie A. Marchand (London: John Murray, 1973–94), 100.
18 Jack Stillinger, *Multiple Authorship and the Myth of Solitary Genius* (Oxford: Oxford UP, 1991).
19 Seamus Heaney, *The Redress of Poetry* (London: Faber, 2010), 86.
20 Heaney 87.
21 Virginia Woolf, *The Pargiters. The Novel-Essay Portion of* The Years, ed. Mitchell A. Leaska (New York: New York Public Library, 1977). See also Grace Radin, *Virginia Woolf's* The Years: *The Evolution of a Novel* (Knoxville: U of Tennessee P, 1981).
22 W.H. Auden, *Collected Shorter Poems, 1927–1957* (London: Faber and Faber, 1966), 15.
23 Edward Mendelson, "Preface," *Selected Poems*, by W.H. Auden, ed. Edward Mendelson (London: Faber and Faber, 1979), xvii–xviii.
24 Jack Stillinger, *Coleridge and Textual Instability: The Multiple Versions of the Major Poems* (Oxford: Oxford UP, 1994), 119.
25 Stillinger, *Coleridge* 60.
26 Stillinger, *Coleridge* 121.
27 The Everyman's Library edition of Coleridge's poems, edited by John Beer, prints the 1798 and 1828 versions of the poem on facing pages; the multi-volume Bollingen edition, edited by J.C.C. Mays, prints the 1798 and 1834 versions on facing pages. See S.T. Coleridge, *Poems*, ed. John Beer (London: J.M. Dent, 1999) and S.T. Coleridge, *Poetical Works*, ed. J.C.C. Mays. 4 vols. (Princeton, NJ: Princeton UP, 2001).
28 Such an edition was published in 2007 by Viking in the US and Penguin in the UK: Jack Kerouac, *On the Road: The Original Scroll*, ed. Howard Cunnell (London: Penguin, 2007).
29 These facts were first observed by John Kidd and reported by D.H. McKenzie, *Bibliography and the Sociology of Texts* (Cambridge: Cambridge UP, 1999), 58–60.
30 Mary Shelley (with Percy Shelley), *The Original Frankenstein*, ed. Charles E. Robinson (New York: Vintage, 2009).

CHAPTER 3

PRINTING AND READING

In this chapter, our longest, we focus on the histories of printing and reading in the four centuries of the **handpress** period, in Britain and, to a lesser extent, in Europe and America. During this period, nearly all books were created on presses operated by hand, using paper that was handmade, with **type** set by **compositors**, using methods that changed very little. (It was not until the widespread mechanization of the press, starting in the second third of the nineteenth century, that printing methods significantly changed and production capacity expanded.) But if the technology of print was relatively stable during this long period of time, the stories that historians, literary scholars, and bibliographers have told about it are anything but, and are fraught with many complexities and uncertainties. To begin, we might question why many scholars of printing and reading have tended to focus on the West, when the history of printing begins a millennium before the invention of the printing press in Europe in the mid-fifteenth century, in ancient China. We might also address the focus on the printed book, when books have been only a small proportion of the output of the press for much of its history. As well as books, presses produced **periodicals**, song-sheets, posters, visiting cards, and other printed matter. Further, the history of reading predates the arrival of printing by several millennia; the first known evidence of writing, and hence of reading, dates to 3600 BCE in ancient Mesopotamia. How does the history of the book relate to the quantitatively more significant history of print? How does the history of print relate to the much longer history of reading? In these entanglements we find the challenges involved in any attempt to narrate a straightforward account of the history of printing and reading.

Our chapter is necessarily limited in scope. We confine our attention to a period of roughly 400 years (rather than the five and a half millennia in which humans have been reading), and to a geographically limited area that neglects much of the global history of print. Nevertheless, by reviewing the major debates within our efforts to understand the "long period from the 1480s until around 1800 when the technology of printing was very stable,"[1] we believe the chapter establishes a solid foundation for further study.[2] For although the technology of book production was relatively unchanging during these four centuries, the history of this period is marked by great political, economic, and social upheavals in both Europe and North America. This history has shaped, and been shaped by, the output of the press.

As we have seen in the previous two chapters, many bibliographers and textual scholars invest themselves in the detailed study of physical aspects of printed books. Their work demonstrates how careful examination of a print book can expose the history of the print process used to create it, and how examination of various textual witnesses can be used to trace a textual history of a given piece of writing. In Chapter 1, we also introduced D.F. McKenzie's proposal for a "sociology of texts," one that "directs us to consider the human motives and interactions which texts involve at every stage of their production, transmission and consumption."[3] McKenzie's approach was important for expanding the range of bibliographical concerns beyond **descriptive bibliography**, which is chiefly concerned with the study of the physical book itself. His project initiated a shift in focus away from a narrowly conceived bibliography and toward the human interactions in making and circulating books, which became an important part of book history. Book historians attempt to understand both the material and the cultural history of print—of print as artefact and commodity—and its wider historical impact. Fundamentally, all historians of print culture ask how books have shaped knowledge; social, religious, economic, and political institutions; and local and national cultures. In this respect, the study of printing and reading is a deeply humanistic inquiry, as it allows for a close study of the printed book—one of the primary vehicles for disseminating knowledge, articulating religious and political views, expressing literary and cultural values, and embodying sociability. At the same time, as we have suggested above, difficulties inevitably arise when historians attempt to engage with these larger issues. The following sections explore some of these issues in an attempt to understand what is at stake in discussions about the history of the book. We begin with a section on "Print and the Book," in which we draw attention to the problematic nature of the term "book" in "book history."

Print and the Book

Traditionally, book historians have focused on the study of the printed **codex**: books that have been constructed from a number of folded **sheets** of paper which are then bound together (as discussed in Chapter 1). One of the primary reasons that the bound printed book has been book historians' chief object of study is that it has higher survival rates than unbound printed material, material that was often not meant to survive. As we do today, people in the past threw away most of the printed matter they came into contact with. We often throw away (or recycle) circulars we receive in the mail, or newspapers we find on the bus, but we are much less likely to treat a bound book in the same way. **Binding** also offers protection to the sheets within, and bound books arguably take a more concerted effort to discard or destroy than loose sheets. Even today, we are more likely to discard or recycle a newspaper or a circular than a book, which, if we no longer want it, we might try to sell or donate. Still, this focus on the *book* demands justification: What historical outcomes can we attribute to the codex form itself, as opposed to separates (single sheets or **broadsides**), folded sheets (like newspapers), sewn sheets in paper wrappers (like periodicals), or the earlier form of the **scroll**?

More **ephemeral** forms of print—tickets, letterheads, playbills, invoices, forms, notices, cards, labels, posters, receipts, and timetables, to name only a very few—are often described as "job printing," commercial printing undertaken by most printing houses to help them pay the bills. Job printing, though it is thought to account (quantitatively) for the largest output of the press, often vanishes without a trace.[4] Compare the materials we read on a daily basis now: Facebook pages and websites, printed advertisements and magazines. How much of it will remain in five years, to say nothing of fifty or five hundred? Likely very little of the material will survive, just as very little survives of the printed ephemera from the dawn of the printing press in the mid-fifteenth century. This material has largely been invisible to scholars, as it rarely survives, and if it does, it is in nothing like the quantity in which it once existed. But there are other, usually unstated reasons for the attention devoted to the book. The printed book has generally been assumed to be the most important material form for the conveyance of knowledge and culture. Therefore scholars have looked to books themselves as the most meaningful carriers of information about the past.

Recently, some scholars have suggested that we need to expand our attention beyond the book to the output of the press more widely conceived for what it can tell about print, social, and intellectual history. Peter Stallybrass, for example, has urged us to recall that "printers do not print books" but rather sheets.[5] He goes on to state that "[i]t is even more important to emphasize how frequently printers were not even trying to make books."[6] The first complete work that issued from **Gutenberg**'s press was a 39-line indulgence, an award by the Catholic Church for a remission of sin (see Figure 3.1). Printed indulgences were a form of "printed blanks,"

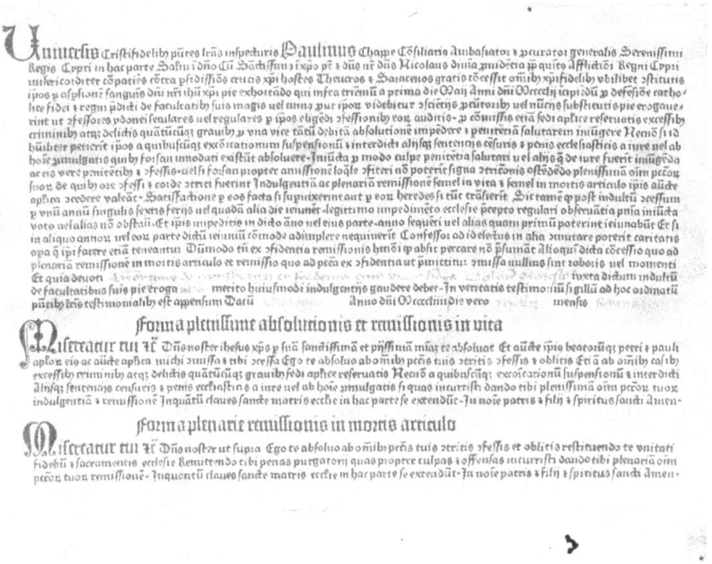

Figure 3.1: Copy of one of Gutenberg's 1454 indulgences (Rylands Library, University of Manchester).

ready-made receipts leaving an empty space to be filled in, in this case with the name of the individual who had paid to be pardoned. Gutenberg interrupted the printing of his Bible in 1454–55 to print these indulgences because they brought ready cash, which was needed to support the costly outlays involved in publishing more expensive works like the Bible. He was not alone. Millions of indulgences were printed in this period. It was profitable work that most **printers** needed to survive economically.[7] In addition to indulgences, most of the work of the press included the printing of periodicals, newspapers, and broadsides, and what we have described above as job printing. Studying material like indulgences sheds important light on daily religious practices and attitudes toward the Church, and other ephemera can be equally productive in attempts to reconstruct aspects of the past.

Stallybrass further demonstrates the prominence of job printing by giving an account of Benjamin Franklin's printing practices in colonial America. Before he became a founding father of the United States, Franklin was a commercial printer. As Stallybrass shows, his output was very similar to that of printers in fifteenth-century Britain: he was extensively involved in job printing, although little of his output survives. Of the 35,262 job-printed items that were printed in Franklin's shop in 1765, items such as tickets, notices, advertisements, and bills of sale, copies of only 20 items are extant, a survival rate of about 0.06%.[8] Examples like Franklin's publishing records tell us that sheets printed for books were only one part of the output of the press, and likely a small one. Furthermore, from the beginning, printers moved back and forth between grand projects (like printing the first Bible) and commercial activities (like printing indulgences). Beyond helping us to understand the day-to-day activities of printers, the great output of job printing (as well as **pamphlets**, newspapers, and periodicals, which enjoy higher survival rates) has encouraged many book historians to expand their objects of study beyond the printed codex. According to Stallybrass, "We only begin to understand the printing revolution when we start to look at the millions of sheets of printed paper that, beginning with Gutenberg's indulgences, transformed the texture of daily life."[9] The effects of print permeated far beyond the book, with the failure to account for its impact leading scholars like Stallybrass to critique "[t]he conceptual gluttony of 'the book' [which] consumes all printing as if all paper was destined for its voracious mouth."[10]

Scholars of periodicals have a similarly justifiable complaint against "the conceptual gluttony of 'the book.'" If we are interested in the history of the impact of print, the subject of our next section, then surely the newspapers, magazines, and journals that were printed and read in profusion in Britain, Europe, and America from at least the seventeenth century onwards demand attention alongside the book. Periodicals allowed the rapid **circulation** of information about current events, reviews of new books and plays, and reports on fashion and other topics of immediate interest that didn't necessarily appear in books. Periodicals were typically much cheaper and more portable, likely to be shared and passed around, meaning that they were accessible to far more readers than were books, which were costly and hence available largely to elites for much of the early print period. Reading periodicals brought readers together into communities with shared interests and concerns and connected people across geographical distances. Therefore we have reason to pay attention to what the history of the book excludes, and the consequences of these exclusions, as well as the assumptions, almost always implicit, about cultural value inherent in the focus on the book.

In the next section, we explore debates about the historical and cultural consequences of the coming of print, finding another strong conceptual knot that arises from the term "book history," this time focused on "history" rather than "book." Attempts to understand the effects of technological change brought about by the invention of the press in the West have been fraught. On the one hand, Gutenberg's printing press was a hugely important development that transformed the dissemination of knowledge and daily life for many; on the other hand, what is called **scribal culture** (the writing, copying, and circulation of handwritten texts) long predates the arrival of print and survives into the era of the handpress. Similarly, **oral cultures** of storytelling, conversation, lecturing, preaching, and performance both predate and survive the invention of print. The effects specifically resulting from the use of the press, then, are hard to isolate. Are the historical developments of the second half of the fifteenth century attributable to the invention of print, or is print merely a contributory cause? In a related question, did print replace and absorb the scribal and oral cultures that preceded it, or did it merely modify them, and how rapid or slow were these changes? These are some of the questions that scholars have debated for at least the last forty years, without the emergence of any consensus.

The Impact of Print

Elizabeth Eisenstein's groundbreaking study *The Printing Press as an Agent of Change* (1979) argues that print had an immediate and widespread effect on European culture (see *BRBH* 215–30). The shift from a culture in which all texts had to be produced by hand to one in which multiple copies could be reproduced quickly and efficiently by machine meant that knowledge could be more easily disseminated, accumulated, and preserved. According to Eisenstein, printing "revolutionized all forms of learning" and, with it, human society as we know it (*BRBH* 215). Indeed, her book makes the bold claim that print was a revolutionary "agent of change": the press's functions of dissemination, standardization, and preservation enabled scientific and artistic experimentation and religious debate, thereby ushering in the Scientific Revolution, the Renaissance, and the Protestant Reformation.

Eisenstein repeatedly identifies print as a trigger for significant intellectual and cultural change. She notes, for example, how the ability to print many copies of identical (or nearly identical) scientific manuals encouraged more research and resulted in more feedback for their authors, thus accelerating the pace of scientific discovery and knowledge: "new surveys led, in turn, to further interchanges, which set off new investigations and the accumulation of more data.... The sequence of ever-expanding reference works was a sequence without limits. . . ."[11] For Eisenstein, "systems of charting planets, mapping the earth, synchronizing chronologies, codifying laws, [and] compiling bibliographies were all revolutionized before the end of the sixteenth century," a direct result of the advent of print. She argues that the duplicative quality of print, combined with other features, such as typographical "fixity," constitutes the "basic requisite for the rapid advancement of learning."[12]

This "fixity" was achieved by print in a variety of ways. Printing was usually done on paper, as opposed to **parchment** or **vellum**, the basic materials for medieval **manuscripts**. Handwriting on vellum was often scraped away (for reuse), and manuscripts themselves, as rare and unique objects, did not circulate widely. They could be reproduced only by laborious handcopying, and the handling and moving involved in copying had the potential to degrade the original. The production of many print copies, Eisenstein claims, protected the original document from being lost or destroyed altogether and also preserved its text from the threat of miscopying, believed to be endemic to scribal culture. In essence, Eisenstein argues for the existence of a print culture that was markedly different from the scribal culture that preceded it. She claims that "the advent of printing" almost immediately and irrevocably "transformed the conditions under which texts were produced, distributed and consumed";[13] "[t]hus a knowledge explosion was set off," leading to revolutions in the arts and sciences.[14]

From her book's first publication, many of Eisenstein's claims have been met with scepticism. Her critics often object to her narrative of historical upheaval, pointing out that the adoption of the press, and its effects, were not instantaneous. Lucien Febvre and Henri-Jean Martin in *The Coming of the Book: The Impact of Printing, 1450–1800* (see *BRBH* 15–36) tackled the same question as Eisenstein, the transformational impact of print, but two decades prior. However, because Febvre and Martin adopt a more evolutionary approach to historical change (evident in one of Febvre and Martin's chapter titles, "The Book as a Force for Change"), their work has not attracted the same attention—both positive and negative—as Eisenstein's.[15] A related complaint directed against Eisenstein is that her work exhibits **technological determinism** (also called medium theory), a belief that changes in media technology inevitably produce profound cultural effects. These effects are said to take place both within individual consciousnesses and on the wider planes of social and political history. In contrast to Eisenstein, whom we might consider a technologist, Adrian Johns is a constructivist who tends to focus on the uses to which people put books and printing (see *BRBH* 267–88). When constructivists look at the arrival of printing in Europe, they tell a story about the people whose interests led them to promote print as a transformative technology, rather than one about the properties of the technology itself. The effects of print, they say, were culturally constructed rather than technologically determined. When they look at print culture, they tend to focus on the people who produce, disseminate, and use books, as much as on the books themselves.

The impact of print was not felt all at once, both because technology itself develops over time and because individuals adapt to new technology only gradually. For Johns, the qualities that Eisenstein argues are inherent to print—standardization, fixity, and ease of dissemination—are in fact not inherent to the technology at all but were developed by human actors over time through interaction and debate, trial and error. Johns studies the early use of print by astronomers to dispute the assertion that print itself revolutionized scientific discourse.[16] He and other scholars such as Febvre and Martin argue that the coming of print brought about evolutionary, rather than revolutionary, change; they also point to the ongoing use of old technologies such as handwritten script, rejecting a rise-and-fall model of media change. We explore these models of media change more fully in Chapter 4.

Another objection to Eisenstein's sweeping claims about the effects of print has been that if change was an inevitable consequence of print technology, why didn't these changes occur in China? Print had been invented in China as early as 200 BCE and was used continuously up until the early modern period, with various improvements and refinements.[17] That the Chinese (and later, the Koreans) had print for centuries before Western Europe, but without the political, religious, and scientific developments Eisenstein argues were the inevitable effects of printing, would seem to support her critics' rejection of her claim that such effects are inherent to print. Eisenstein seemed to offer a concession to this point in 2005, when she gave the second edition of her book the more geographically specific title *The Printing Revolution in Early Modern Europe*.

Notwithstanding these objections, some of the most influential theorists of the second half of the twentieth century made bold claims about the impact of technological change on human culture. Eisenstein was in large part attempting to historicize some of media theorist Marshall McLuhan's ideas, articulated in *The Gutenberg Galaxy: The Making of Typographic Man* (1962) and other books in the 1960s. For McLuhan, each new medium of communication alters "patterns of perception steadily and without any resistance."[18] Thus communication technologies (writing, printing, and electronic media) profoundly affect cognition and, as a result, social organization. McLuhan is also famous for his assertion that "the medium is the message," re-orienting study around the medium of communication itself as an independent source of meaning, just as worthy of study as the content of that medium.[19] Further, for McLuhan, one cannot understand the message as separate from the medium; the two are inseparable and mutually constitutive. Walter Ong, one of McLuhan's students and a scholar of oral culture, agreed. He argued that it was the invention of writing, rather than printing, that transformed human thought from a world of sound to a world of sight, leading to his conclusion that "more than any other single invention, writing has transformed human consciousness."[20] In Ong's view, the arrival of the press in Europe in the fifteenth century was merely one of a series of changes to affect human consciousness, the most important of which was writing, a technology that dated back millennia and was more diffuse and diverse than the coming of print.

 Another important theorist of the impact of technological change on human consciousness is Roger Chartier, a scholar of the history of reading. For Chartier, reading is a profoundly embodied experience: it "is not uniquely an abstract operation of the intellect: it brings the body into play, it is inscribed in a space and a relationship with oneself or with others" (*BRBH* 256). Studying the history of reading thus involves studying the history of our physical interactions with print, the spaces in which we read, and the social implications of reading. But while Chartier draws attention to how the material form of the book affects our reading practices, he claims, like Ong, that new material forms such as print do not produce changes in reading practices overnight, but rather do so over an extended period. He contends that "[b]etween 1500 and 1800"—that is, the first three centuries of print—"man's altered relation to the written word helped to create a new private sphere into which the individual could retreat, seeking refuge from the community."[21] Chartier attributes this shift neither to writing nor to print but to a set of cultural, economic, and social changes that enabled the practices of silent reading. Responding directly to Eisenstein, Chartier insists that "[a]lthough the invention of printing was indeed a 'revolution' in that it made it possible to produce a larger number of identical copies at a cost much lower than that of copying by hand . . ., it should not be credited with intellectual and psychological changes that were really the result of a new method of reading, regardless of whether the text was printed or manuscript."[22] Chartier's attempt to distinguish the history of printing from the history of reading reflects an important development in the field that we will return to at the end of this chapter. Chartier, like Johns, offers a nuanced understanding of the effect of technological change, suggesting that it evolves over centuries and that it may not stem from a single technological development, like the arrival of the press, but from a combination of forces that converge to stimulate cultural transformation.

For Ong, Chartier, Martin, Febvre, and Johns, the arrival of print transformed European history and culture, but not as instantaneously or comprehensively as Eisenstein claims. These theorists insist that what must be studied is how books were in fact read and used by consumers, leading us back yet again to D.F. McKenzie's call for a "sociology of texts" that "directs us to consider the human motives and interactions which texts involve at every stage of their production, transmission and consumption."[23] Several scholars have proposed models to help us conceptualize how books (and other forms of printed and written culture) shape the world, all of which implicitly adopt McKenzie's understanding that we must study books by studying how human beings interact with them.

Models for Book History

In 1982, Robert Darnton introduced his influential model of the **communications circuit** (see Figure 3.2) to emphasize the connections between disparate groups of actors (authors, **publishers**, printers, distributors, and readers) engaged in the production and dissemination of printed books.[24] Recently, Darnton has restated the key questions embedded in the model as follows:

How do books come into being?

How do they reach readers?

What do readers make of them?[25]

The last two questions move past book manufacture and address the dissemination and interpretation (or reception) of books (or other print or

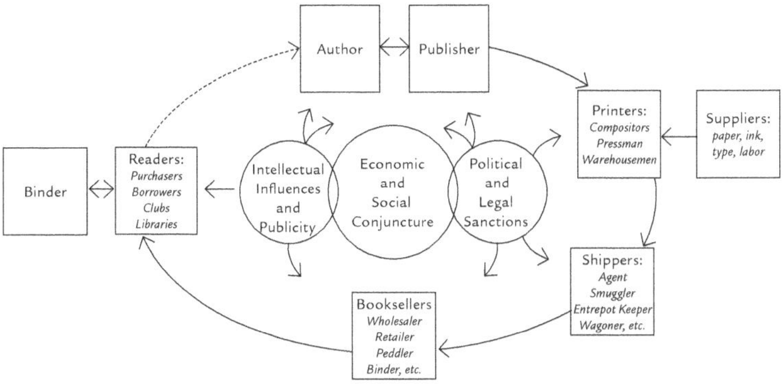

Figure 3.2: Darnton, "Communications Circuit."

manuscript material) by readers. In Darnton's model, the book becomes part of a much larger story of human interaction and activity that extends far beyond the printing shop.

Darnton's model presents a circuit through which the book is produced, disseminated, and interpreted—from author to publisher, printer, shipper, **bookseller**, reader, and back to the author—reflective of the book trades in England and some European countries in the handpress period. The circuit emphasizes that book production is a process that unfolds over time and involves multiple actors/groups. In essence, the circuit reminds us of the (potentially) lengthy prehistory of a book—that it comes into being, and reaches readers, only after a series of human and technological exchanges. Darnton's model has contributed to the decentring of the author from literary studies by reminding us that the author exists and operates within a much larger human network. His inclusion of the reader also expands this network beyond publication to consumption. Interestingly, the diagram first appeared with a dotted line between reader and author (in 1982) and was later replaced with a solid line (in 2007), suggestive of the potentially more direct power that readers can exert over authors. As an abstract model to describe the actors involved in book production and dissemination, Darnton's circuit has great explanatory force. One potential weakness is that, as an abstract model, it can fail to account for particular historical or local circumstances.[26] It is also largely geared toward commercial forms of printed book production as opposed to other forms of print and written culture.

In 1993, Thomas R. Adams and Nicolas Barker identified what they believe to be another shortcoming with Darnton's communications circuit, namely that "it deals with people, rather than the book." They continue:

> the principal emphasis is placed on the people who participate in the process through which the book went in providing a means of communication. For the purpose of the social historian it is a useful approach. For those who are concerned with the total significance of books (especially printed books) it has limitations.[27]

Adams and Barker advance a model for the life cycle of books (see Figure 3.3), tracking the movement of books rather than the people involved in making and moving them: "instead of the six groups of people who make the 'Communications Network' operation we have five events in the life of a book—publishing, manufacturing, distribution, reception, and survival."[28] Like Darnton, Adams and Barker follow McKenzie in thinking beyond production, recognizing both that the book continues its life cycle after it

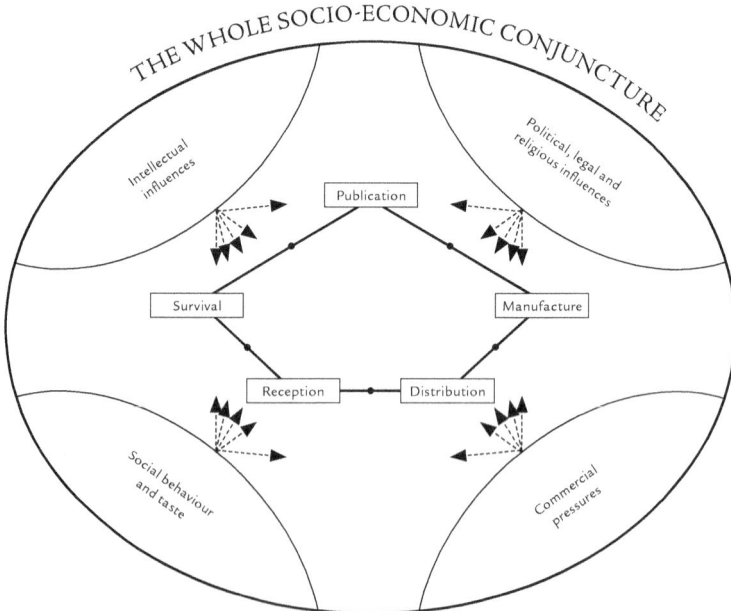

Figure 3.3: Adams and Barker, "A New Model for the Study of the Book."

is made and that there is both a physical and an intellectual history to the book's traversal of space and time.

Nevertheless, the separation between the study of people involved in the history of the book (or a sociology of the book, as embodied in Darnton's model) and the study of the material book itself (as reflected in Adams and Barker's, which is influenced by traditional **bibliography**) is of long standing, as we have seen in the divide between Greg and McKenzie. Yet there is no reason why a *détente* cannot be reached between these schools of thought: the models described above depict different aspects of print history, thus offering different and potentially complementary uses to scholars. Arguably, the disagreements between Eisenstein and her detractors can be framed in the same way: between scholars (like Eisenstein) who point to print technology as the driver of a cultural revolution and those (like Johns) who insist that "the very identity of print itself has had to be *made* . . . by virtue of hard work, exercised over generations and across nations" (*BRBH* 269). Both approaches have been enormously productive, even though they are in apparent opposition.

Print Economies

Both Darnton's and Adams and Barker's models situate the production, circulation, and reception of books in relation to a field of social, cultural, political, legal, and economic forces. These appear in the middle of Darnton's diagram and around the outside of Adams and Barker's. In this section, we will concentrate on the ways in which publishing, authoring, and reading take place within the economic realm, examining how printing has been a commercial endeavour throughout its history. Just as the technology of the printing press was relatively stable from the arrival of the press to the first third of the nineteenth century, so too were the economics of printing. To open a printing shop, certain fixed expenditures were required, namely a printing press and type fonts. Printing presses themselves could be relatively inexpensive, but the cost of type, made in foundries, was high.[29] In terms of book production, the variable costs (that is, costs that change depending upon the type and size of the book being produced) include paper, ink, and labour. As James Raven points out, the largest cost associated with printing, by far, was paper (*BRBH* 293). In the early modern period, the cost of paper could account for as much as two-thirds of the cost of publication. Its high price did not abate until the adoption of machine-made paper, made from wood pulp, became widespread from around 1825.[30]

Since economic conditions under which publishers operated were relatively consistent over time, fairly uniform business models were developed. For new titles (that is, books that had not been previously printed), the model was that of low volume and high prices. Once print became established, this marketing scheme was supplemented by a second business model, in which publishers produced a higher volume of older titles and sold them at lower prices. In the absence of surviving publishing **archives** it can be difficult to determine **edition** sizes, but it seems that most new books were printed in editions of between 500 and 1,000 copies until the second half of the nineteenth century. The practice of issuing small editions ensured that valuable paper was not wasted, as it would be if more books were printed than the demand warranted. This practice was also a consequence of the high cost of type. Most printers had to reuse the type used to set a book as soon as possible, and smaller presses had to reuse type from the first **pages** of the book they printed to print later pages. These practices meant that publishers needed to price a book high so as to recoup costs, since they couldn't make a profit by selling a high volume of books.

In the early days of print, of course, there were only newly printed books. The price of the Gutenberg Bible when it was first printed provides a sense of the high cost of books in 1452, at the birth of print in the West:

> Customers paid around 20 gulden for a paper copy of the Gutenberg Bible and 50 for a copy on vellum. By way of comparison, a stone-built house in Mainz would have cost between 80 and 100 gulden; a master craftsman would have earned between 20 and 30 gulden a year.[31]

Nearly 200 years later, Shakespeare's First Folio provides another example of the high cost of books in the early modern period. In 1623, the publishers printed 800 copies and sold them for £1, the price in large part determined by the large size of the **folio** format (a folio page is usually about 38 centimetres, or 15 inches, tall). Although it is notoriously difficult to translate historical prices into present-day ones, given significant changes in purchasing power, one measure involves finding the real price of a commodity by translating from 1623 into 2015 British pounds. Real price "measures the value of a commodity relative to the cost of a (fixed over time) bundle of goods and services such as food, shelter, clothing, etc., that an average household would buy." This would place the price of the First Folio at approximately £164.30 in 2015 currency. A more meaningful measure seeks to estimate the present-day value of the income that would be needed to buy the Folio—also known as income value—which calculates to an astonishing £6,746.[32] By either account, the cost of the First Folio was so high that only the elite would have been able to purchase it. Books remained expensive in Britain until the development of cheaper machine-made paper and the adoption of more efficient presses in the second half of the nineteenth century.

As mentioned above, for books that had been in print for some time and were being reprinted, a different model prevailed. With books that were known to be popular, publishers could produce more books but sell them more cheaply, because sales were assured. Publishers developed strategies for lowering the costs involved in print production. They worked together in what are known as "congers," spreading risk, pooling resources, and sharing costs. They produced books more cheaply, using smaller **formats** and lesser-quality paper, and printing text with smaller margins. Because most of these books were out of copyright (a topic we discuss shortly), there were also no fees to authors or other publishers to reproduce these works. Other forms of print—like broadsides, newspapers, **chapbooks**, and pamphlets—were also produced and sold cheaply, though they were not always produced in large numbers. For example, during the early seventeenth century, **playbooks** retailed for sixpence, a far more accessible price than the £1 cost (240 pence) of the First Folio. Using the same measures as above for calculating the present value of a playbook, the commodity value of a playbook would be £4.11 and the income value £168.60 in 2015 currency. Although they were far less expensive than the First Folio, most Britons would not have been able to afford playbooks either.

Because the cost of books remained high during most of the handpress period, publishers and booksellers developed additional strategies to reduce the price of books for individual readers. One innovative attempt to reduce the cost of books, and thus to make reading more accessible, was the development of **circulating libraries**. The first such library opened in Scotland in 1725. They soon spread throughout the United Kingdom and America. To join a circulating library, one would pay a membership fee entitling the member to rent a certain number of books at a time, comparable to present-day video-on-demand services like Netflix and Hulu. In effect, circulating libraries allowed eighteenth- and nineteenth-century readers to rent books, making reading accessible to a wider class of readers.

The fact that publishers and circulating libraries worked symbiotically to produce and distribute fiction provides a good example of how the histories of reading and publishing intertwine. For much of the nineteenth century, the three-volume (or triple-decker) format for novels dominated the market, as "the economics of the [circulating-library] system aligned with the specific properties of the three-volume format. Lending out triple-deckers by the volume meant that the libraries could circulate a single 'copy' of a novel among three subscribers at once."[33] Circulating libraries became so powerful by the mid-nineteenth century that many publishers would refuse to publish a book at all if they thought the major circulating libraries would decline to purchase it, and they often demanded that authors write in the three-volume format.[34] The circulating libraries represent the joining of forces between publishers and booksellers; this had the effect of making reading more accessible, albeit in a way that benefitted publishers and circulating libraries. Another strategy to share the cost of books was the formation of reading clubs by individuals who pooled their resources to collectively purchase and share books. Benjamin Franklin founded one of these clubs with some of his friends. He recalled, "by thus clubbing our books to a common library, we should, while we lik'd to keep them together, have each of us the advantage of using the books of all the other members, which would be nearly as beneficial as if each owned the whole."[35]

Another strategy that publishers used for lowering the cost of books and attracting less affluent readers was offering unsold books at a discount. The bookselling innovator who pioneered this approach was James Lackington (1746–1815). He opened his large and elegant Temple of the Muses in London in 1793 (see Figure 3.4) and is said to have sold around 100,000 books in the last decade of the eighteenth century alone. Lackington was able to lower the price of the books he sold by buying up unsold stock from other booksellers and refusing to sell books on credit. Because of his innovations, Lackington has often been referred to as an early incarnation of Jeff Bezos, the founder and CEO of Amazon. His enormous shop—it featured a 140-foot frontage and "was so capacious *that a mail-coach and four* was easily *driven round the counters*, at the time when it was *opened*"[36]—provides a potent visual symbol of the merging of commerce and culture during the period.

CHAPTER 3 • PRINTING AND READING

Figure 3.4: Messrs. Lackington, Allen & Co., Temple of the Muses, Finsbury Square (1809).

Throughout its history, the printed book was almost always a commodity, produced and sold for profit by those in the book trades, all of whom advertised themselves as such: from the mid-sixteenth century, as Raven notes, most **title pages** explicitly named the publisher, printer, and bookseller, often with full addresses to guide customers to the shop where the book could be purchased (*BRBH* 296). Book bindings, stamps, and other aspects of the book trade, such as publishers' **catalogues**, advertisements, and even bookshops themselves, also point to the commercial realm in which books were enmeshed. But books were also conveyors of information and ideas that could challenge religious beliefs and political systems. As is evident in the models we discuss above, legal and political sanctions influenced the ways in which books were made, sold, and read. Thus the history of books, and of all forms of print, is also the history of their state control and regulation.

Controlling Print / Controlling Reading

Prior to the arrival of print, all texts were copied by hand. Much of this copying was done within the church, particularly in **scriptoria**—rooms in medieval European monasteries devoted to the writing, copying, and illuminating of manuscripts by monastic **scribes**. Scribes not only performed intellectual and artistic labour; they also served as conservators of knowledge, safeguarding it through their curation and preservation of archives.

In a monastic scriptorium, decisions about what was copied, to whom copies were to be shown and given, and how changes (excisions/revisions) were made in the preparation of new copies were controlled by the same authority that sponsored the copying.[37] Therefore no external system of control was required.

The arrival of print posed new problems for religious and state control over the circulation of texts. Printers were often independent commercial agents, and they could produce multiple copies faster and more easily than scribes. As a result, measures were quickly introduced to control what could be printed, and by whom. For at least the first four centuries after the arrival of print, most states and religious authorities were eager to control access to printed matter deemed dangerous or undesirable, usually for reasons of religious or political content.[38] Consequently, licensing requirements were introduced almost at the origin of print, requiring government authorization to produce and trade printed books.

For much of the early modern period, print production in Britain was regulated by the **Stationers' Company**. Although it antedated print (it was formed in 1403), the Stationers' Company amassed greater powers after print's emergence. Raven notes some of the many powers vested in the Stationers' Company (*BRBH* 289–312):

1. it tightly regulated the number of printing presses, printers, and apprentices;
2. it enforced privileges granted to printers by state authorities (these licences were unique to print, and granted a printer an exclusive right to print particular works for a period of years);
3. it enforced copyright asserted by its members, after they had entered their ownership of books into the Stationers' Company register; once this right was asserted over a work, no other member was allowed to publish it;
4. it screened all books, starting in 1538, to ensure that they were acceptable for publication;
5. and, during the Tudor and Stuart reigns, it had power to seize books that were deemed offensive and bring those responsible for them before the church authorities.

The religious and political struggles of the period are thus intertwined with the history of print.

In 1695, the **Licensing of the Press Act 1662** lapsed and was replaced, in 1710, with the **Statute of Anne** (also known as "An Act for the Encouragement of Learning, by Vesting the Copies of Printed Books in the Authors or Purchasers of such Copies, during the Times therein mentioned"), which recognized **copyright** for a period of 14 years, with the possibility of extension for a further 14 years if the author were still alive at the expiration of the first period. This shift brought about several changes. First, the lapse of the Licensing Act brought an end to the *pre*-publication screening of printed works, replacing it with *post*-publication forms of control, including both civil and criminal **libel** (in which either a private individual or the state sued an individual for the words they had published). Second, the 1710 Act brought into effect a different means of controlling the right to copy books. Previously, authors and publishers acted as if copyright were perpetual—in other words, that they had a right to publish copies forever of works that belonged to them, without interference from others. After 1710, this copyright was limited to a fixed period of time, during which the copyright holder, whether an author or a publisher, had an exclusive right to copy. After the expiration of this period, however, the 1710 Act clarified that the right to copy would then be available to everyone.

Debates over copyright have usually tried to balance the interests of the public (as suggested by the title of the first copyright legislation) in a shorter period of copyright, and hence encouraging the free flow of ideas, and of authors/publishers, who favour a longer period of protection. Those who argue for longer copyright terms often claim that they encourage writers to write new works by allowing them to profit from their publications for longer periods. Throughout most of the nineteenth century—until the Berne Convention of 1886—no international copyright provisions were in place. As a result, the novels of Charles Dickens (and all other foreign authors) could be reprinted in America without any payment to the author or his English publisher. As Meredith McGill has shown (*BRBH* 439–56), the lack of international copyright kept prices for foreign books low and created a robust literary marketplace that helped to create a climate of open intellectual and literary exchange in the new American republic. Nevertheless, many authors were extremely vexed by this situation. Dickens, whose novels were extremely popular in America, somewhat ill-advisedly used the occasion of his 1842 tour of the country to bemoan his lack of remuneration. Dickens complained both that "scoundrel-booksellers should grow rich here from publishing books, the authors of which do not reap one farthing from their issue," and that excerpts from his novels could be published in "every vile, blackguard, and detestable newspaper" (444–45). It was not merely an economic objection that Dickens mounted, but one about his right to control the nature and extent of the reprinting of his fiction.

The authors'-right argument in favour of copyright (and longer copyright periods) has become complicated by the fact that a great deal of intellectual property is now held by large corporations, not individual creators. Indeed, the extension to American copyright law that passed in 1998 has become known as the "Mickey Mouse Protection Act," in part because Disney lobbied for the passage of the law to delay the entry of the earliest Mickey Mouse movies into the public domain. Those who advocate for short copyright terms claim that it is rarely original creators who benefit from long (or extended) copyright periods, and that once works come out of copyright and can be reprinted by anyone, they circulate more widely and therefore bring greater benefit to society. After the 1710 Statute of Anne, copyright provisions gradually expanded to include other forms of artistic production (such as songs, film, etc.), and the length of time these works were protected under copyright gradually extended: the current copyright period in the UK and the US is 70 years after the death of the author/creator. Given that many authors now have writing careers for decades, the current copyright period ensures that works can be protected for well over a century.

Copyright has always been one of the most important sources of economic power for publishers and authors, as it grants them the right to print material without competition. The state has traditionally recognized that copyright should be limited, as a perpetual copyright (which has been argued for at various times) would constrain the circulation of knowledge. To this end, the Statute of Anne was titled, "An Act for the Encouragement of Learning. . . ." Nevertheless, continual extensions of the copyright period demonstrate that commercial interests have generally prevailed over "the encouragement of learning." Among the forces acting on the circulation of books in the models discussed above, then, copyright produces both legal and economic impacts on authors and publishers. It is one example of the forces that make up what Adams and Barker call "the whole socio-economic conjuncture" in which books are situated (see Figure 3.3).

Another tactic that governments have employed to control access to books has been the strategic use of taxation. Like copyright regulation, taxation is too broad a topic to be covered in any detail here, but one snapshot from the late eighteenth and early nineteenth centuries suggests its huge impact in regulating access to books:

> The heavy taxes on paper and advertisements [in place during the late eighteenth century] were progressive, in the sense that the bigger the book, the bigger the tax, and those members of the aristocracy and gentry who bought the **quartos** and **octavos** helped to pay the interest on the national debt of which they themselves were the main holders. The stamp duties on pamphlets and newspapers, on the other hand, were flat rate and regressive, not so much a means of raising revenue as targeted attacks on the reading matter which the state most feared. All books below a certain size were taxed at the flat rate of 3 shillings per copy, equivalent to a third of the weekly wage of a working man. By taxing pamphlets, the government taxed political participation. . . . The stamp duty on newspapers at the flat rate of four pence a copy, equivalent in some cases to several hundred per cent, taxed the dissemination of information as such.[39]

In addition to these direct taxes on print, in Britain access to print was also indirectly affected by taxes on candles and on the number and sizes of windows (the former not repealed until 1831, the latter not until 1851), since light is necessary for reading. According to William St. Clair, these taxes significantly constrained the spread of knowledge via print. A comparison with the United States, which did not impose taxes on newspapers, demonstrates how such taxes impeded free speech. The US in the 1830s had almost double the number of newspapers for a similarly sized population. A comparison between Britain and the US also demonstrates the effect of copyright legislation on price: without any copyright protection for international authors in the US until 1891 (as discussed by McGill, *BRBH* 439–56), books by British authors were much less expensive in the US than in Britain for most of the nineteenth century. This culture of reprinting demonstrates the strong effect that regulatory schemes have on pricing and hence on access to books.

According to Elizabeth Ladenson, "the history of literary censorship is ... almost as long as that of literature itself."[40] We have seen that from the earliest days of print, licensing requirements were used to control the printing (and hence the dissemination) of ideas. Attempts to control reading can be found throughout recorded history. One example is recounted by Jonathan Rose:

> Henry VIII would try to suppress Scripture reading before the Reformation, and even after the Bible had been legally published in English. A 1539 proclamation limited discussion and reading of scripture to graduates of Oxford and Cambridge universities, and a 1543 Act for the Advancement of True Religion dictated that "No women nor artificers, 'prentices, journeymen, servingmen of the degrees of yeomen or under, husbandmen nor labourers" were permitted to read the English Bible.[41]

In the antebellum South, it was illegal to teach slaves to read or write, and for good reason: according to the great abolitionist, orator, writer, and former slave Frederick Douglass, it was learning to read that set him on the path of mental and physical emancipation.[42]

Ladenson has argued that the "development of religious censorship [in particular] was directly linked to the invention of **moveable type**," with the publication and circulation of certain works having resulted in the torture, dismemberment, and death of many people.[43] Raven (*BRBH* 289–312) refers to these individuals as "print martyrs"—the men who were tortured on the rack and/or burnt at the stake for reading proscribed religious writing during the tumultuous reigns of Mary I (1553–58) and Elizabeth I (1558–1603). Prosecutions for the common-law offence of public libel—whether seditious, blasphemous, or obscene—continued into the later nineteenth century. Although offenders were no longer punished with as much brutality as they had been in the past, the threat of prosecution had a so-called "chilling effect" on free speech, often a consequence of post-publication restrictions. Since it was difficult to anticipate whether a text would be found to be illegal, authors and publishers were forced to err on the side of caution. The common-law offences of public libel were no exception, as they were poorly defined and unevenly enforced.

One period of intense prosecution for public libel in Britain occurred between 1790 and 1832; for much of this period England was at war with France and the government was fearful of the influence of that nation's revolutionary politics and atheistic beliefs. During this 40-year period, there were more prosecutions for public libel than in the previous 90 years combined.[44] Radical booksellers complained that they were unfairly targeted because their printed works sold more cheaply and were thus available to the lower classes, whereas publishers who catered to elite clientele were rarely subject to prosecution. Robert Southey's comments on the **piracies** of Lord Byron's racy, satirical *Don Juan* perfectly capture this reality: "'Don Juan' in quarto and on hot-pressed paper would have been almost innocent—in a whity-brown **duodecimo**, it was one of the worst of the mischievous publications that have made the press a snare."[45] Southey expresses a commonly held view that it is not the content of the book *per se* but rather access to it that demands strict control.

State-sponsored **censorship** continued in Europe and America until the 1960s, when publishers sought to print books that had been suppressed for decades because of their explicit sexual content. D.H. Lawrence's *Lady Chatterley's Lover* was first printed privately (meaning that Lawrence paid for the cost of printing and the book was not widely distributed) in 1928. The class politics of the novel—it depicts a sexual relation between a working-class man and an upper-class woman—made it especially shocking. Because of this, Lawrence did not attempt to have his original version of the novel published in England and the US; instead, he consented to heavily censored editions being published in the US in 1928 and in England in 1932. In 1960, Penguin finally published the novel in Britain as Lawrence had originally intended, bringing to an end "[t]he era of routine literary censorship in the West."[46] The publisher was promptly brought to trial under the new Obscene Publications Act of 1959. Under this law, it was possible for a publisher to defend a work if it could be said to possess literary merit. Dozens of expert witnesses testified in favour of Penguin and the novel, defending Lawrence's use of offensive language (particularly the repeated use of the word "fuck") and the book's sexual content as an essential part of its artistic integrity. The prosecution had difficulty finding any witnesses to support its claim that the book lacked literary merit, and the jury acquitted

Penguin. Many regard the ruling as a watershed in the long march toward a free press in Britain.

Other books that had long been suppressed, such as John Cleland's *Fanny Hill; or Memoirs of a Woman of Pleasure*, first published in England in 1748–49 and popularly known as *Fanny Hill*, were also published in their original form for the first time in the 1960s. Soon after the first publication of Cleland's novel, the publisher was prosecuted for public libel; Cleland disavowed the novel and withdrew it, though pirated versions remained in print. He then published a heavily edited version. More than two hundred years later, in 1966, *Fanny Hill* became the subject of a famous US Supreme Court judgment, *A Book Named "John Cleland's Memoirs of a Woman of Pleasure" v. Attorney General of Massachusetts* (383 U.S. 413). The Court held that under the US Constitution, a modicum of merit precluded its condemnation as obscene. The uncensored version was finally legally published in the UK in 1970, 222 years after its first publication.

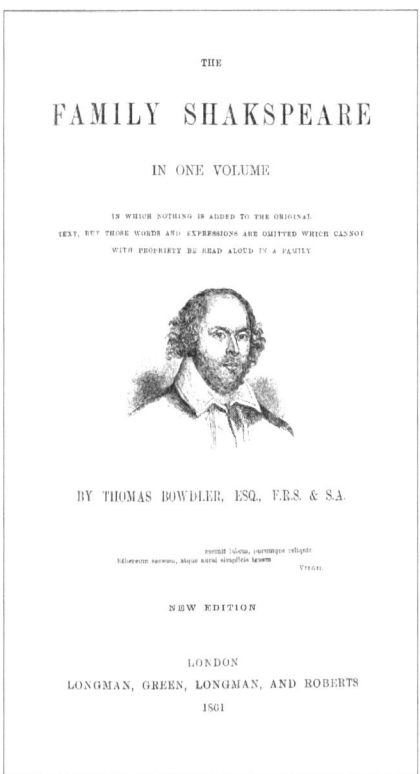

Figure 3.5: Thomas Bowdler, *The Family Shakspeare* (1861).

When the chief prosecutor in the 1960 trial of *Lady Chatterley's Lover* asked the jury whether it was the kind of book "you would wish your wife or servants to read," he was invoking scare tactics that had been used for centuries to control what could be printed and read. The eighteenth and nineteenth centuries proliferate with examples of books that were either banned outright (though this could result in the book being printed and distributed surreptitiously) or edited in such a way so as not to offend (or inflame, or radicalize) wives and servants. Thomas Bowdler first published an expurgated version of Shakespeare's plays in 1807, omitting those passages "which with propriety cannot be read aloud in a family" (see Figure 3.5 for a title page from a subsequent edition). The text of the plays was edited to conform to standards of propriety deemed acceptable for family reading. Thus, in the *Family Shakspeare*, Ophelia's death becomes an accident, not a suicide, and Lady Macbeth's "Out, damned spot" becomes "Out, crimson spot!" This process of sanitizing rapidly became known as "bowdlerization." A great irony exists in this censored edition of Shakespeare's plays: it was Bowdler's sister and wife who did much of the work on these editions. They could not be named as co-editors, however, because that would demonstrate their familiarity with the objectionable, unexpurgated Shakespeare.

Of course, the punishment of authors and publishers by the state, and the banning and burning of manuscripts and books, is not a thing of the past. The American Library Association maintains records on banned and challenged books and publishes a yearly list of the most frequently challenged books, many of which have been printed in the last decade.[47] Recently, print has provoked extreme acts of violence. On 7 January 2015, two gunmen charged the offices of the satirical magazine *Charlie Hebdo* in Paris, France, killing twelve people and wounding eleven, including cartoonists, editors, and other staff who worked at the magazine. The attack was motivated by a series of satirical cartoons of the prophet Muhammad. The phrase "Je suis Charlie," French for "I am Charlie," was adopted by supporters of freedom of expression after the shootings, reflecting the enormous outpouring of support in solidarity with the victims of the attack.

Methods for a History of Reading

The controls that have been placed on books—from window taxes and stamp duties to state-imposed censorship—form part of a larger history of reading. As with the history of printing, the history of reading has demanded scholarly ingenuity, as the practice, according to Roger Chartier, "only rarely leaves traces, [its history] is scattered in an infinity of singular acts" (*BRBH* 252). The box labelled "readers" in Darnton's diagram (Figure 3.2) contains a wide variety of activities and practices (Adams and Barker use the terms distribution, survival, and reception to indicate some of the activities which readers are often involved in; see Figure 3.3). However, these activities are difficult for historians to reconstruct. Just as printers rarely left behind detailed accounts of their working process, requiring scholars to draw inferences from printed works themselves, historians of reading have turned to printed works for evidence of ownership and use. As discussed in Chapter 1, copy-specific evidence, such as bindings, bookplates, library stamps, and inscriptions can tell us about how books have changed hands and been used. **Marginalia**, comments written in the margins and elsewhere through a book, can provide direct evidence about a reader's response to the work, as can corrections, underlining, dog-earing, and other marks left on the page. The traditional practice of **commonplacing**, whereby readers copied passages from other sources (both manuscript and print), sometimes arranged according to particular topics, also informs scholars about what was being read and how readers repurposed that material. Surviving **libraries** and collections, and catalogues of libraries that have now been dispersed, have also been used to reconstruct reading patterns.

Jonathan Rose's *The Intellectual Life of the British Working Classes* (2001) has proven to be one of the most impressive reconstructions of reading history. In his chapter "The Welsh Miners' Libraries," Rose examines lending-library records and working-class autobiographies to offer a rich portrait of the reading lives of Welsh miners in the early twentieth century (*BRBH* 313–31). He finds a flourishing cultural and intellectual life within these mining communities. The miners did not read the **canon** of what we now consider to be high literary modernism, such as the novels of James Joyce and Virginia Woolf (321). Nor did they all read Karl Marx's writings, as had been believed. According to Rose, "[a]ny historian of working-class culture in early twentieth-century Britain must deal with this inescapable fact: the readers of Marx and Lenin were infinitesimal compared with the fans of Mrs. Henry Wood," a Victorian sensation novelist (323).

Publishing archives have also been used to reconstruct reading history. In *The Reading Nation in the Romantic Period* (2014), William St. Clair provides a meticulous account of the edition sizes and retail prices of books by a wide range of authors, in order to gain a better understanding of what books were popular and widely read, and by which classes of society, during the period. He finds a startling disparity between what has long been deemed the canon of Romantic British literature (essentially the major male poets: Coleridge, Wordsworth, Blake, Byron, Shelley, and Keats), and what was in fact read during the period. St. Clair demonstrates that, with the exception of Lord Byron, these poets garnered very little of the reading nation's attention. Lord Byron and Sir Walter Scott were extremely popular authors, with over 100,000 copies of *Don Juan* selling before Byron's death in 1824 and over 50,000 copies of Scott's novel *Guy Mannering* selling by 1836. When these figures are placed alongside what are now some of the most revered volumes of poetry in the Romantic canon, a significant disparity emerges: Wordsworth and Coleridge's *Lyrical Ballads* (1798) sold 2,000 copies at most over a seven-year period, and Keats's *Lamia, Isabella, The Eve of St. Agnes, and Other Poems* (1820) had sold fewer than 500 copies by the time of his death the following year. St. Clair contends that the largest portion of most people's reading material was not contemporary (or recently written books—such as those written by Wordsworth or Keats) but rather what he terms "the old canon," seventeenth- and eighteenth-century literature that could be reproduced cheaply, in part because it was no longer in copyright. The history of what was read during a particular period may depart significantly from what was written in that period.

Both Rose and St. Clair deploy archival methods to present a more complete history of what was actually read during various historical moments and within particular communities. Evidence of reading exists in other sources, such as diaries, letters, and novels, as well. Yet, to repeat Chartier's words, this history exists "scattered in an infinity of singular acts." The *Reading Experience Database* (RED), *1450–1945* attempts to gather together these "singular acts" in an online database that crowd-sources the history of reading by asking users to enter accounts of "reading experiences" found in journals and letters, in the United Kingdom, written between 1450 and 1945. This database defines a reading experience as "a recorded engagement with a written or printed text—beyond the mere fact of possession" and has amassed over 30,000 records of reading experiences of British subjects.[48] Affiliated sites track reading experiences in Canada, Australia, New Zealand, and the Netherlands. Such projects are beginning to collect the necessary evidence to construct broader national and comparative accounts of the history of reading.

Another approach to the history of reading is to understand it as an embodied experience. According to Chartier, "we need to remember that there is no text apart from the physical support that offers it for reading (or hearing), hence there is no comprehension of any written piece that does not at least in part depend upon the forms in which it reaches its reader."[49] The physical surfaces that humans have read from are various: parchment, vellum, paper, stone, and now screens made of several different materials. All affect our experience of reading. As we have seen, scholars as varied as McLuhan, Chartier, Ong, and McGann have claimed that how we access texts produces significant differences in how we understand their content.

We might also consider the differences between reading handwriting and print. Although handwriting can be more difficult to decipher, it can be a carrier of personality and feeling. Handwriting necessarily varies from individual to individual and can also change for a single individual over time. The uniqueness of handwriting has been used to distinguish it from print. For Ong, printed texts "look machine-made, as they are.... This is an insistent world of cold, non-human, facts."[50] Anna Chen describes the "chilly impersonality of print," in contrast to the warmth of handwritten documents.[51] For Marta Werner, manuscript is "suggestive of intimacy. Again and again," she contends, "we find references to the 'face' or 'physiognomy' of the manuscript, or to the manuscript as a 'mirror' of the writer's thoughts."[52] It is important to note that these associations with reading in one medium rather than another are culturally and historically specific. In periods and places where handwriting styles were highly regulated, script might be felt to be less revealing of character and more reflective of other norms, such as conformity. To complicate matters further, currently most of us read text in a variety of forms—handwriting on paper, print on paper, and e-ink and pixels on screens. We move back and forth between these different reading environments, making it difficult to know precisely how one medium differs from another in terms of its effect on us as readers.

We know, however, that even within a specific medium like print, physical differences can be significant: the physical presence of the printed sheet or book, its paper, **typography**, margins, binding, format, colour, and illustrations all affect the reading experience. Consider, for example, the format of newspapers. Typically, the largest size of newspaper is what is known as a broadsheet, which is folded once and sometimes folded again

Figure 3.6: Men Reading newspapers in Chicago, outside the *Chicago Daily News* offices.[53]

for reading purposes. Many major papers in the US, Canada, and the UK are published in this format.[54] Figure 3.6 depicts the large size of the broadsheet format and the variety of ways in which newspapers of this size are held, manipulated, and read. Some newspapers use smaller formats, such as tabloid. This size difference conveys to some people a change in content and quality, hence the term "tabloid journalism" to characterize newspapers whose stories focus on celebrity gossip and sensational crime. Nevertheless, some newspapers published in smaller formats do not fit this characterization. The Berliner format, for example, which in size falls between the broadsheet and the tabloid, is commonly used in many parts of Europe and is associated with serious journalism.

One final insight into the history and theory of reading has been the understanding of it as a powerfully creative act. In his famous 1967 essay "The Death of the Author," Roland Barthes contends that the modern author is merely a "scriptor" and that "every text is eternally written here and now" by its readers.[55] Barthes objects to the sacralization of the author, contending that the meaning of texts has been "tyrannically centered on the author, his person, his history, his tastes, his passions."[56] For Barthes, "the birth of the reader" must come at the expense (or death) of the author.[57] Literary historians have often witnessed the power of readers—to resurrect favourite characters, for example, both by direct appeals (the fans of Sherlock Holmes successfully prevailed on Arthur Conan Doyle to bring him back to life) and by parody and imitation. What we now call fan fiction, in which characters or settings from an original work of fiction are used as inspiration for new writing by fans, has existed for centuries. Michel de Certeau has analogized reading to poaching, insisting that reading is a productive (and not merely a consumptive) act.[58] This understanding of the power of reading and readers brings us back to the later incarnation of Darnton's model of the communications circuit, in which he depicts a solid line running from readers to author. Through this line, Darnton suggests the influence readers can exert on writers, and perhaps how readers can transform themselves into writers as well. The evolving relationship between author and reader today is apparent in fan fiction disseminated online, through self-publication platforms like Kindle Worlds.

    Throughout this chapter, we have attempted to show how book historians situate their study of the material book within its wider context, attentive to the human interactions that shape the production, circulation, and reception of books at every stage: the economic realities that drove Gutenberg to publish indulgences and bibles; the religious and political controversies that ended in print martyrdom; the copyright laws that enriched some authors and corporations, and excluded others; the moral battlefield over the publication of books like *Lady Chatterley's Lover*; the power that readers have to rewrite the stories of others. The following chapters extend this focus on how print shapes and is shaped by "the whole socio-economic conjuncture," to consider how printed matter is embedded in complex relations with other media and has always been part of a multimodal world. To return to Doyle's detective, we find that Holmes appeared not only in multiple print forms during Doyle's lifetime, in the *Strand* magazine and in book collections of various stories, but also in multimedia forms, such as illustrations that helped shape the image of Sherlock Holmes for the public. Doyle's illustrators significantly shaped the image of the famous detective: Holmes's characteristic deerstalker hat was never mentioned by his original creator. Instead, Doyle refers to "a close-fitting cloth cap" in the early story "The Boscombe Valley Mystery" (1891); his illustrator Sidney Paget included an image of Holmes wearing the deerstalker in his illustration of the story for the *Strand Magazine*, and so the iconic image was born.[59] Today, Holmes and Watson occupy the entire media spectrum, from every form of print and e-book publication, to online fan fiction, stage plays, Hollywood films, television series, and licensed merchandise. This intermingling and intertwining of media forms is where we begin in Chapter 4.

Notes

1 James Mosley, "The Technologies of Print," *The Book: A Global History*, ed. Michael F. Suarez, S.J., and H.R. Woudhuysen (Oxford: Oxford UP, 2013), 135.
2 We urge students interested in this broader field to consult Simon Eliot and Jonathan Rose's *A Companion to the History of the Book* (Oxford: Wiley-Blackwell, 2007); Michael F. Suarez, S.J., and H.R. Woudhuysen's *Oxford Companion to the Book* (Oxford: Oxford UP, 2010) and *The Book: A Global History* (Oxford: Oxford UP, 2013); and Leslie Howsam's *The Cambridge Companion to the History of the Book* (Cambridge: Cambridge UP, 2015).
3 D.F. McKenzie, *Bibliography and the Sociology of Texts* (Cambridge: Cambridge UP, 1999), 13, 15.
4 Peter Stallybrass, "'Little Jobs': Broadsides and the Printing Revolution," *Agents of Change: Print Culture Studies after Elizabeth L. Eisenstein*, ed. Sabrina A. Baron, Eric N. Lindquist, and Eleanor F. Shevlin (Amherst: U of Massachusetts P, 2007), 318.
5 Stallybrass 315.
6 Stallybrass 340.
7 Stallybrass 320.
8 For further discussion of the little that survives of job printing from the early modern period, see James Raven, "Markets and Martyrs: Early Modern Commerce," *BRBH* 290, 292–93.
9 Stallybrass 340.
10 Stallybrass 340.
11 Elizabeth L. Eisenstein, *The Printing Press as an Agent of Change: Communications and Cultural Transformations in Early-Modern Europe* (Cambridge: Cambridge UP, 1979), 84.
12 Eisenstein 87.
13 Eisenstein 168.
14 Eisenstein 110.
15 Lucien Febvre and Henri-Jean Martin, "The Book as a Force for Change," *The Coming of the Book: The Impact of Printing 1450–1800*, ed. Geoffrey Nowell-Smith and David Wooton, trans. David Gerard (London: Verso, 1976), 248–332.
16 See Adrian Johns, *The Nature of the Book: Print and Knowledge in the Making* (Chicago: U of Chicago P, 1998).

17 Mosley 131.
18 Marshall McLuhan, *Understanding Media: The Extensions of Man* (1964; New York: McGraw-Hill, 1974), 27.
19 McLuhan 27.
20 Walter J. Ong, *Orality and Literacy: The Technologizing of the Word* (London: Methuen, 1982), 78.
21 Roger Chartier, *The Practical Impact of Writing* (Cambridge, MA: Belknap, 1989), 157.
22 Chartier, *Practical Impact* 165.
23 McKenzie 13, 15.
24 Robert Darnton, "What Is the History of Books?" *Daedalus* 111.3 (1982): 65–83.
25 Robert Darnton, "What Is the History of Books? Revisited," *Modern Intellectual History* 4.3 (2007): 495.
26 For a discussion of some of the weaknesses of the model, consider its inability to take into account issues of gender. See Michelle Levy, "Do Women Have a Book History?," *Studies in Romanticism* 53.3 (2014): 297–317.
27 Thomas R. Adams and Nicolas Barker, "A New Model for the Study of the Book," *A Potencie of Life: Books in Society: The Clark Lectures 1986–1987*, ed. Nicolas Barker (London: British Library, 1993), 5–44.
28 Adams and Barker 15.
29 In the first decades of the nineteenth century in Britain, a press could be bought for anywhere from £3 to £70. See William St. Clair, *The Reading Nation in the Romantic Period* (Cambridge: Cambridge UP, 2004), 312.
30 Alexis Weedon, "The Economics of Print," Suarez and Woudhuysen 159–60.
31 Andrew Pettegree, *The Book in the Renaissance* (New Haven, CT: Yale UP, 2010), 29.
32 All figures were calculated using the calculator at https://measuringworth.com. The definition of real price is from the glossary on this same site.
33 At the same time, as Richard Menke discusses, authors and their publishers formatted their books for sale to circulating libraries, and this could result in an increased price for novels: "Archibald Constable raised the price of the three-volume *Kenilworth* (1821) to a guinea and a half (thirty-one shillings and sixpence), where it would long remain." Richard Menke, "The End of the Three-Volume Novel System, 27 June 1894," *BRANCH: Britain, Representation and Nineteenth-Century History*, ed. Dino Franco Felluga, extension of *Romanticism and Victorianism on the Net*, http://www.branchcollective.org/?ps_articles=richard-menke-the-end-of-the-three-volume-novel-system-27-june-1894.
34 St. Clair 244.
35 Benjamin Franklin, *Autobiography of Benjamin Franklin*, Penn Reading Project Edition (Philadelphia: U of Pennsylvania P, 2005), ProQuest ebrary, 56.

36 R.A. Davenport, *Lives of Individuals Who Raised Themselves from Poverty to Eminence or Fortune* (London: Thomas Tegg, 1841), 240.
37 Roger Chartier, "*The Order of Books* Revisited," *Modern Intellectual History* 4.3 (2007): 511.
38 Elisabeth Ladenson, "Censorship," Suarez and Woudhuysen 169.
39 St. Clair 309–10.
40 Ladenson 169.
41 Jonathan Rose, *The Intellectual Life of the British Working Classes* (New Haven, CT: Yale UP, 2001), 13.
42 Frederick Douglass, *Narrative of the Life of Frederick Douglass, an American Slave. Written by Himself* (Boston: Anti-Slavery Office, 1845), 33–36, 38–40.
43 Ladenson 173.
44 Philip Harling, "The Law of Libel and the Limits of Repression, 1790–1832," *The Historical Journal* 44.1 (2001): 108–11; Hannah Barker, "England, 1760–1815," *Press, Politics and the Public Sphere in Europe and North America 1760–1820*, ed. Hannah Barker and Simon Burrows (Cambridge: Cambridge UP, 2002), 98.
45 [Nassau William Senior,] "Cases of *Walcot v. Walker; Southey v. Sherwood; Murray v. Benbow*, and *Lawrence v. Smith*," *Quarterly Review* 27.53 (1822): 128.
46 Ladenson 181.
47 "Frequently Challenged Books," *Banned and Challenged Books*, Office for Intellectual Freedom of the American Library Association, http://www.ala.org/bbooks/frequentlychallengedbooks.
48 *The Reading Experience Database* (RED), *1450–1945*, The Open University, http://www.open.ac.uk/Arts/RED/.
49 Roger Chartier, *The Order of Books: Readers, Authors and Libraries in Europe between the Fourteenth and Eighteenth Century*, trans. Lydia G. Cochrane (Stanford, CA: Stanford UP, 1992), 9.
50 Ong 120.
51 Anna Chen, "In One's Own Hand: Seeing Manuscripts in a Digital Age," *DHQ* 6.2 (2012): n. pag., para. 4.
52 Marta L. Werner, "'Reportless Places': Facing the Modern Manuscript," *Textual Cultures: Texts, Contexts, Interpretation* 6.2 (2011): 63.
53 "Old Photographs from the Chicago Daily News: 1902–1933," *Vintage Everyday: Bring Back Nostalgia and Memories*, http://www.vintag.es/2012/11/old-photographs-from-chicago-daily.html.
54 In recent years, three British newspapers, *The Independent*, *The Times*, and *The Scotsman*, have changed to tabloid format.
55 Roland Barthes, "Death of the Author," *The Norton Anthology of Theory and Criticism*, 2nd ed., ed. Vincent B. Leitch (New York: Norton, 2010), 1324.
56 Barthes 1322.
57 Barthes 1326.

58 Michel de Certeau, "Reading as Poaching," *The Practice of Everyday Life*, trans. Steven F. Rendall (Berkeley: U of California P, 1984), 165–76.
59 *The New Annotated Sherlock Holmes*, ed. Leslie L. Klinger, 3 vols. (New York: Norton, 2005), I, 103–04.

CHAPTER 4

INTERMEDIALITY

In the first decade of the twenty-first century, a spate of books and articles, with titles like *The Gutenberg Elegies: The Fate of Reading in an Electronic Age*,[1] appeared prognosticating the death of the book. Alexandra Alter, in 2015, sums up the thinking that characterized these writings as follows:

> Five years ago, the book world was seized by collective panic over the uncertain future of print.
>
> As readers migrated to new digital devices, e-book sales soared, up 1,260 per cent between 2008 and 2010, alarming booksellers that watched consumers use their stores to find titles they would later buy online. Print sales dwindled, bookstores struggled to stay open, and publishers and authors feared that cheaper e-books would cannibalize their business.
>
> Then in 2011, the industry's fears were realized when Borders declared bankruptcy.[2]

However, in what Alter describes as a "plot twist," the book seems to be making a recovery, rendering reports of its demise premature. In fact, the

> digital apocalypse never arrived, or at least not on schedule. While analysts once predicted that e-books would overtake print by 2015, digital sales have instead slowed sharply.
>
> Now, there are signs that some e-book adopters are returning to print, or becoming hybrid readers, who juggle devices and paper. E-book sales fell by 10 per cent in the first five months of this year [2015], according to the Association of American Publishers, which collects data from nearly 1,200 publishers. Digital books accounted last year for around 20 per cent of the market, roughly the same as they did a few years ago.

When we look deeper into the past, we find the same phenomenon. A new technology is touted as revolutionary and expected to supersede what came before. Instead, the earlier technology persists, even flourishes, alongside the new one. The "hybrid readers, who juggle devices and paper," and their predecessors, who juggled **manuscript** and print, and oral and written culture, are in large part of the subject of this chapter.

We explore in this chapter the concept of **intermediality**, which we define as the interactions between various media. Its fundamental premise is that no single medium exists independently of others. Rather, a medium's existence and identity is necessarily conditioned by its co-existence with a range of other media. Further, media history cannot simply be regarded as a series of new technologies whose emergence made older ones outmoded. Until very recently, the prevailing narrative of media change was, according to Paul Duguid, that of the "rhetoric of supersession," whereby it was assumed that "each new technological type vanquishes or subsumes its predecessors."[3] Put most crudely, it was believed that oral culture transitioned to written culture after the invention of writing; that written culture was abruptly transformed by the invention of print; and that, with the emergence of digital culture, print itself will quickly pass away. There are many problems with this model, not least of which is that it fails to conform to the evidence we have about media change, evidence that will be presented throughout this chapter.

If we turn back to the Early Modern period, we find that scholars have accepted "that 'this'—the printing press—did not kill 'that'—the manuscript."[4] The "reverse migration to print" that many **booksellers** interviewed by Alter identify also seems prevalent in earlier periods. According to Peter Stallybrass, "the attempt by recent scholars to argue for the *persistence* or even the *coexistence* of manuscript and print is misconceived, depending upon an elision of printing with the printing of *books*."[5] In other words, the notion of manuscript persisting in the print era makes sense only if we are equating books with print; but if we are thinking about the entire output of the press, which (as we saw in the previous chapter) is Stallybrass's aim, then print did not simply co-exist with manuscript. Rather, Stallybrass argues, the "most radical effect" of the invention of the press was "its incitement to writing by hand."[6] He identifies the printed blank form—one "that only fulfills its function *as* a form when it has been completed by hand"[7]—as one of the major outcomes of the print revolution. "Printing-for-manuscript," as he terms it, describes a hybridized form of practice, not dissimilar from Alter's description of us all now as "hybrid readers."

There is an even more profound problem with the rise and fall model of media history, which is that it has often been teleological, regarding each new technological development as an improvement on what came before.

For example, Thomas Astle, who in 1784 wrote one of the first comprehensive histories of writing, presents the following developmental account of media history: "The noblest acquisition of mankind is SPEECH, and the most useful art is WRITING. The first, eminently distinguishes MAN from the brute creation; the second, from uncivilized savages."[8] For Astle and many other enlightenment thinkers, the emergence of print reflects the high-water mark of technological sophistication and hence intellectual improvement: it allows "knowledge [to be] diffused through most nations, and . . . attainable by the generality of the people in every free country."[9] But such a progressive narrative necessarily implies that those without the most advanced technology are backward, as in Astle's characterization of the members of cultures without writing as "uncivilized savages."

Astle's views reflect a prejudice against cultures without written history that is still very much with us. In a 1991 judgment of the Supreme Court of British Columbia, *Delgamuukw v. British Columbia,* Justice Allan McEachern concluded that oral history could be given no weight because the Gitksan and Wet'suwet'en people's ancestors were a "people without culture" who had "no written language, no horses or wheeled vehicles."[10] On appeal to the Supreme Court of Canada, the decision was overturned, with the high Court recognizing for the first time that oral evidence had to be placed on an equal footing with historical documents.[11] Nevertheless, the case demonstrates long-standing and deeply problematic understandings of oral culture and media history, understandings that have serious moral and political implications.

Models of Intermediality

In Chapter 3, we described several models of print culture, including Robert Darnton's **communications circuit**. One potential critique of his model is that it focuses on print to the exclusion of other forms of communication. Three models have emerged that provide a more robust account of media interactivity. One is that of media ecology, which has been defined as "the study of complex communication systems as environments."[12] Borrowing from the biological theory of ecology, which addresses the interrelations of living organisms and their environments, media ecologists assume a complex set of human engagements with and between media. This idea has often been associated with **technological determinism**, since some of its most influential theorists, such as Marshall McLuhan, assert that technology has a pervasive power in our lives from which we cannot escape. According to McLuhan,

> All media work us over completely. They are so persuasive in their personal, political, economic, aesthetic, psychological, moral, ethical, and social consequences that they leave no part of us untouched, unaffected, unaltered. The medium is the massage. Any understanding of social and cultural change is impossible without a knowledge of the way media work as environments.[13]

You don't have to agree entirely with McLuhan, however, that the effects of media are inescapable, to see how thinking of media as environments helps us to understand their relational and interactive nature.

A second model of media interactivity may be found in Pierre Bourdieu's concept of the "the field of cultural production." One of his most famous essays (*BRBH* 335–52) provides a description of the French literary field in the second half of the nineteenth century. In this essay Bourdieu describes a field as an arena in which social actors take positions. He describes the literary or artistic field as *"a field of forces"* and *"a field of struggles"* (337; italics in original) because every position taken within the field is relative to every other position, where the success of one comes at the expense of others. Each actor's position and hence success in the field is determined by the distribution of capital—economic, social, and cultural. Bourdieu argues, therefore, that it is impossible to examine one form of cultural production—such as poetry, or the novel—apart from others, such as vaudeville, or cinema, as they all exist within an interrelated system. As with the ecological system model, Bourdieu's "field" is complex and interactive. Bourdieu diagrams the differing amounts of audience appreciation (or commercial success) and "consecration" (or cultural respect) afforded to different types of cultural productions across a range of media, demonstrating that they have an inverse relationship to one another (348). He claims that no one form of cultural production can be understood apart from others, and that cultural production itself is constrained by economic and political power.

Theories of new media provide a final conceptual model for intermediality. One of the most valuable insights of new media studies is its awareness that "mediation forms the very basis of human existence." According to Mark B.N. Hansen,

> from the outset, human beings have evolved not simply genetically but culturally, which is to say, by exteriorizing their know-how and collective memory in the form of cultural artifacts and object memory supports. This means, of course, that the evolution of the human can be characterized in terms of a long series of "new media" revolutions. . . .[14]

Drawing upon the theories of Bernard Stiegler, Hansen contends that human beings "are 'essentially' correlated with technical media."[15] If we understand our dependence on technology as inevitable, human history itself can be rewritten as a series of new media events. And furthermore, because it "introduce[s] modes of experience that challenge the familiar," the introduction of new media is "bound to occasion anxiety, resistance, even hostility."[16] Like the concepts of media ecology and the field of cultural production, new media theory insists upon a constantly evolving suite of media, and the inevitability of these developments' evoking both excitement and trepidation.

To further explore the concept of intermediality, the following sections focus on three media contact zones: between orality and writing, between print and manuscript, and between text and image. These contact zones are often represented as transitional aspects of media change, and the media involved are often framed as qualitatively different or somehow intractable to combination. Our approach instead emphasizes historical overlap and relationality between these media.

Orality and Writing

In our current media environment, it may be "easy to overlook the fundamental importance of speech, the oldest form of intelligent communication, and of its reception and counterpart, hearing."[17] Most of us learned to talk in a media-rich environment, with access to printed and handwritten texts, television and recorded sound. In the same way that we could not isolate our earliest experiences of hearing and speech from exposure to other media, historians of orality find it difficult to separate orality from other forms of mediation. Oral tradition, which is the store of cultural material transmitted orally from person to person, over time, in the form of stories, song, folk tales, and so on, can be almost impossible to disentangle from the representation of the same or similar cultural material in other media forms.

One of the earliest accounts of orality appears in Plato's Socratic dialogues. In the *Phaedrus*, Socrates addresses written culture's impact on orality, delivering a profoundly negative assessment of its outcomes. He presents the myth of Theuth,

> ... the inventor of many arts, such as arithmetic and calculation and geometry and astronomy and draughts and dice, but his great discovery was the use of letters. Now in those days the god Thamus was the king of the whole country of Egypt;.... To him came Theuth and showed his inventions, desiring that the other Egyptians might be allowed to have the benefit of them;.... But when they came to letters, This, said Theuth, will make the Egyptians wiser and give them better memories; it is a specific both for the memory and for the wit. Thamus replied: O most ingenious Theuth, the parent or inventor of an art is not always the best judge of the utility or inutility of his own inventions to the users of them. And in this instance, you who are the father of letters, from a paternal love of your own children have been led to attribute to them a quality which they cannot have; for this discovery of yours will create forgetfulness in the learners' souls, because they will not use their memories; they will trust to the external written characters and not remember of themselves. The specific which you have discovered is an aid not to memory, but to reminiscence, and you give your disciples not truth, but only the semblance of truth; they will be hearers of many things and will have learned nothing; they will appear to be omniscient and will generally know nothing; they will be tiresome company, having the show of wisdom without the reality.[18]

Here Plato speaks as Socrates speaking as Thamus, lamenting the loss of mental capacity, in the form of memory, that writing introduces. Writing, he argues, induces mental laziness, "forgetfulness." In this dialogue, writing is also condemned as introducing a false kind of knowledge. Learning acquired from the written word bears "only the semblance of truth," only "the show of wisdom without the reality."

The *Phaedrus*'s critique of writing as mediated communication persists. John Durham Peters has remarked that

> Socrates complains about writing in terms that are strikingly relevant for later mass media: it is unresponsive, saying the same thing over and over; it stimulates intelligence and personal care but cannot interact with a reader; it is indiscriminate in its audiences, speaking to anyone who happens upon it; it disrupts memory and the interactive intensity of dialogue.[19]

Plato's argument against writing is that it is impersonal and exteriorizes memory. Similarly, some people have objected that calculators (and their use in educational contexts) impair the development of computational skills,[20] or that GPS systems erode our navigational capacities.[21] Dependence on social media has also been correlated to feelings of depression and isolation. All of these contentions share, with Plato, a fundamental anxiety that technology, by exteriorizing memory and mediating communication, compromises our cognitive abilities and impedes social interactivity.

Walter Ong (1912–2003), one of the most important theorists of oral culture, developed a more complex and nuanced understanding of orality. His best-known work, *Orality and Literacy: The Technologizing of the Word* (1982), attempts to identify the distinguishing characteristics of orality by studying those cultures without **literacy**, what he terms "primary orality." According to Ong,

> A deeper understanding of pristine or primary orality enables us better to understand the new world of writing, what it truly is, and what functionally literate human beings really are: beings whose thought processes do not grow out of simply natural powers but

out of these powers as structured, directly or indirectly, by the technology of writing. Without writing, the literate mind would not and could not think as it does, not only when engaged in writing but normally even when it is composing its thoughts in oral form. More than any other single invention, writing has transformed human consciousness.[22]

For Ong, writing involves "the technologizing of the word" and "heightens consciousness," in part by alienating us from ourselves, since we not only put our thoughts into words, but also put our utterances into an external form.[23]

Nevertheless, Ong understood that orality necessarily survives in any culture with writing technology: in his words, "[w]riting can never dispense with orality."[24] Most modern societies are simultaneously oral and written cultures, though some may lean more to one end of the spectrum than the other. According to Harold Innes, a balance between the spoken word and writing contributed to the cultural and intellectual vitality of ancient Greece in Plato's time. Plato conveyed his ideas by writing down Socrates' conversations, thus "preserving the power of the spoken word on the written page."[25] Innes's observation underscores the challenge in studying what Ong calls primary orality. It is not only the case that "[t]oday primary oral culture in the strict sense hardly exists, since every culture knows of writing and has some experience of its effects," but also that most of our knowledge about oral culture is transmitted via writing.[26] As Ong explains,

> One weakness in Plato's position was that, to make his objections effective, he put them into writing, just as one weakness in anti-print positions is that their proponents, to make their objections more effective, put the objections into print. Writing and print and the computer are all ways of technologizing the word. Once the world is technologized, there is no effective way to criticize what technology has done without the aid of the highest technology possible.[27]

In other words, most of our access to oral tradition has been mediated. Thus, we study the dialogues of Socrates not in their original form, but as they have been written down. The same is true for many other forms of oral culture that historians may wish to recover, such as debates, songs, sermons, lectures, nursery rhymes, fairy tales, political speeches, and dramatic performances. Before the age of sound recording, no access to these forms of oral culture existed except via another media, like handwriting or print—and of course, even sound recordings technologically mediate speech. Some oral culture does survive without technological mediation, a point to which we return at the end of this section. But, by and large, our understandings of oral culture have been shaped by their remediations.

It is, therefore, important to bear in mind that representations of orality are historically constructed. To Plato, writing in the fourth century BCE during a transitional period with overlapping oral and written cultures, written culture was conceived as a threat to the longer-standing traditions of orality. Consequently, Plato valorized the oral as more cognitively demanding and "as more immediate and personal than the written."[28] In the later eighteenth century, an expanding print culture initiated a new wave of concerns about the loss of orality, which was praised for its warmth, naturalness, and authenticity. As with Plato, however, Ong's "highest technology possible," now print, was used to collect and memorialize oral tradition. As ballads (such as those collected in Sir Walter Scott's *The Minstrelsy of the Scottish Border*, published in 1802–03) and folklore (such as the tales collected by the Grimm brothers in *Children's and Household Tales [Kinder- und Hausmärchen]*, published in 1812) were committed to the press, oral tradition was reshaped by **editors, publishers**, and readers, changed by the process of fixing it in print.

Just as Plato privileged orality over writing, eighteenth-century thinkers like Jean-Jacques Rousseau, experiencing a later moment of media shift, could idealize oral culture in relation to print:

> Building on two centuries of European encounters with largely non-literate New World peoples, [Rousseau] romanticized oral culture in his *Essay on the Origin of Language* [1781], becoming perhaps the first to conceive of the oral-literate transition as an intellectual and cultural problem. This so-called "privileging" of orality as a more natural and primary human form of communication has been a recurrent theme in Western thought.[29]

Of course, Rousseau's idealized depiction of oral culture reverses the usual narrative of media change: instead of perceiving a movement from a less to a more enlightened form of communication, he sees print literacy as a falling away from an earlier ideal.

Rousseau's attraction to orality must be understood within a larger historical context, in which there was widespread concern about the moral corruption of "civilized" society in central Europe, and a fascination with the "primitive." Poets and novelists responded to this fascination by representing different regional vocabularies and speech patterns; or, as William Wordsworth proposed in the preface to *Lyrical Ballads* in 1800, employing "a selection of the real language of men."[30] Such attempts to reproduce orality have always been disputed; when the *Lyrical Ballads* was first published, many readers denounced Wordsworth's use of natural language as infantile and an improper basis for poetry. More recently, it has been condemned as cultural appropriation: Wordsworth was, after all, not of the class of many of his poetic characters. The use of dialect to represent the Irish, or African-American slaves, has also been a long-standing source of controversy.[31]

Paula McDowell, a literary historian of the eighteenth century, argues that the very concept of orality is itself a creation of that period, a product of and response to print culture (*BRBH* 395–415). McDowell proposes that the rising dominance of a commercialized print marketplace prompted the formulation of "**oral culture**" as non-commercial, natural, and sociable precisely because these are things that print is not perceived to be. In other words, orality emerges as a back-formation, first of writing and then print. The phrase "oral culture," then, works a bit like the phrase "acoustic guitar." Before electric guitars were invented, an acoustic guitar was just a guitar. Just as the concept of acoustic guitars relies on the existence of electric guitars, so oral culture relies on written culture or print culture.

For McDowell and many other scholars of orality, written works purporting to reflect oral tradition do not do so in a transparent way, as all such written works actually reflect a history of continuous remediation. In the early modern period in Europe, for example, "much of the repertoire of story and song, phrase and fable, which was passed on one to another by word of mouth was by no means the pure water of unmediated oral tradition," for it originated in "the highly learned and literate traditions of bardic and monastic culture."[32] Thus "many of the inherited forms of oral culture in the various parts of Britain were already the distillation of a long series of interactions between the spoken and the written word."³³ The same holds true for many other cultures and at other times, where stories inevitably flowed back and forth between spoken, written, and print culture.

The remediation of the Arthurian legends provides a strong example of the overlapping nature of oral, written, and print cultures. The legends derived from both local folklore and the learned tradition of great monastic chronicles, though it was "[w]ith Malory's *Le Morte D'Arthur* (printed in 1485) [that] the legend came to receive even more elaborate literary treatment and, recycled thereafter in poetry, prose and song, no less than in ritual, pageantry and drama, it became in its many forms a staple of the developing mass media."³⁴ Such an example confounds any narrative of history in which one medium supersedes another, instead showing how a new medium (like print) could revitalize and mingle with older ones (like oral and written culture). As Adam Fox and Daniel Woolf argue,

> the circulation of the printed word was not something that necessarily served to undermine the vitality of oral traditions or the independence of the spoken word, but could, instead, help to augment and invigorate it. It is less instructive to think in terms of inversely correspondent relationships between oral, scribal and print cultures, in which an advance in one must entail a consequent retreat in another, than to regard these three media as complementary and mutually sustaining.³⁵

Another example helps illustrate the flourishing of orality alongside print. William Shakespeare is today an author of unrivalled cultural status. Yet, as David Scott Kastan has shown, in his own lifetime he was not thought of as a print author but as a commercial playwright, and his primary interest was in the production of his plays on stage, not in the printing of them (*BRBH* 354–55). When others printed his dramatic works during his lifetime, they rarely invoked his authorship of them. Though he lived in a print era, the realm in which Shakespeare operated, and understood his writing to operate, was that of oral performance, with the print record being, for him, largely insignificant.

A final example of a sophisticated model for understanding orality intermedially may be found in Matt Cohen's 2009 book *The Networked Wilderness* (*BRBH* 417–37). Cohen argues that relations between settlers and Native Americans cannot simply be viewed, as has often been the case, as a clash between written and oral cultures, because both groups simultaneously used oral and written forms of communication. To comprehend their interactions, he argues, we must expand our notions of what counts as communication. For Cohen, "traps, paths, wampum [shell beads], monuments, medical rituals, and other messaging systems" uncover a broad set of communication practices that allowed for meaningful exchanges between different cultural groups who had little common ground linguistically.

Cohen's attention to this broader set of cultural practices echoes recent movements to recognize and preserve Intangible Cultural Heritage (ICH). According to UNESCO, ICH includes "oral traditions, performing arts, social practices, rituals, festive events, knowledge and practices concerning nature and the universe or the knowledge and skills to produce traditional crafts." UNESCO defines ICH as

> the practices, representations, expressions, knowledge, skills—as well as the instruments, objects, artifacts and cultural spaces associated therewith—that communities, groups and, in some cases, individuals recognize as part of their cultural heritage. This intangible cultural heritage, transmitted from generation to generation, is constantly recreated by communities and groups in response to their environment, their interaction with nature and their history, and provides them with a sense of identity and continuity, thus promoting respect for cultural diversity and human creativity.[36]

One important aspect of this movement to recognize ICH is the understanding that oral tradition may be different from recorded accounts (whether in handwritten, print, or digital forms) of that culture. Acknowledging the importance of what UNESCO calls the "oral heritage of humanity" has instigated important efforts to respect and safeguard oral tradition.[37]

Manuscript and Print

Until the invention of the typewriter in the late nineteenth century, nearly all printed texts began as handwritten manuscripts. Thus, the imbricated nature of manuscript and print exists from the invention of print, much in the same way that oral and written culture were conjoined from the invention of writing. Nevertheless, it is often asserted—following the same rise-and-fall model of media change previously discussed—that at some point, usually in the eighteenth century in Britain, manuscript culture gave way to print as a means of circulating texts and information. But this assertion is also false. Individuals continued to produce and use handwritten documents for the **circulation** of literary texts, for record keeping in business and the law, and for correspondence. Indeed, as we indicated earlier in this chapter, scholars now contend that the introduction of print provided more opportunities for people to create and use script, in printed blank forms, in annotations to printed texts, and in the culture of letters that accompanied rising literacy.

The persistence of handwritten culture derives from its distinct affordances as a technology. Much in the same way that writing could not take the place of speech, print did not replace the need for handwriting. Printing required equipment such as the printing press, and the expertise to use it. A typical press required a **compositor** and a pressman, and, as we know, the press produced only **sheets**, not books. To prepare books, the sheets had to be folded, sewn, and bound, usually the province of another workshop altogether. Printing also required capital investment—chiefly for the cost of the paper but also for **type** and the press itself and the labour costs of **composition**. By contrast, handwriting required less of an economic investment and less expertise. Although an individual had to learn how to make a quill, load it with ink, prepare the paper, and write with a quill, this was a skill that could be easily mastered by most children. Writing is also a portable technology, well suited to domestic life and travel, and equally accessible to men and women, provided they had fundamental literacy. Although access to the printing press grew during the eighteenth and nineteenth centuries, the instruments of writing were always more available than those of the printing house, a situation that would not change until the typewriter (and later the home computer and printer) enabled easy and inexpensive self-printing.

In addition to being more accessible, handwriting was a more intimate form of communication, as it was produced directly from the hand of the writer, not mechanically reproduced in identical (or nearly identical) copies. Handwritten documents could be revised more easily than print: individual copies could be tailored for different recipients, and they could be easily amended, or added to, by others. In other words, handwriting enabled a textual fluidity less possible in print. Many authors preferred to circulate their writings in handwritten form. Margaret Ezell (*BRBH* 375–94) has shown how a great deal of literary writing during the seventeenth and eighteenth centuries was disseminated in handwritten form and "existed independently from the conventions and the restrictions of print and commercial texts" (378). She also describes how the scholarly focus on print—deemed the primary medium for the communication of literary texts with value—has resulted in large quantities of writing by women being ignored. Ezell demonstrates that both women and men had good reasons for choosing manuscript circulation, and that the fact that a text was circulated via a handwritten document and not print cannot be taken as a signal that it lacked quality. Further, she warns that we neglect a large sociable realm of literary production and circulation—one that flourished for centuries—by confining our attention to print.

One of these reasons for choosing handwriting is still relevant today. Handwriting was simply the more efficient medium for producing texts that did not need to be circulated in multiple copies. As a result, many forms of documents, including letters, wills and contracts, and family recipes, were handwritten. Today, most of us continue to handwrite lists, such as shopping and "to do" lists, though we could type them up and print them or make a digital list on a portable device. Again, many factors dictate our choice of what medium to use, including convenience, what materials are at hand, the need (or lack thereof) for sharing or preserving our writing, and so on.

Handwriting has also been a first resort for copying. For most of the print era, copying by hand was an important means through which a whole range of texts were multiplied and disseminated. Although print technology, when available, was superior for reproducing multiple copies of longer texts, many texts lent themselves to hand-copying. Copying could be done for record-keeping purposes, as when a copy of a letter was made before it was sent to a recipient, or as an aid to reading or studying, as from lecture notes. Hand-copying was necessary to reproduce material that could not be safely printed, lest it be censored or fall into the wrong hands, and it could be used to preserve rare texts. One reason that hand-copying was so prevalent during the **handpress** period is the high price of books. Passages from printed texts were regularly copied into **commonplace books** partly because doing so was cheaper than buying a copy of the book. Copying from printed music was also widespread. During this period, then, texts moved back and forth between manuscript and print forms: manuscripts could become print, and print was transformed back into handwritten copies.

In our own time, when many of us compose by typing on computers, handwriting can feel like an individualized and immediate form of technology. When studying for exams, or reading material we want to retain or re-use in some way, we often use marginal notation or underlining or dog-earing of pages, and reading with pen or pencil in hand has helped us to work with and understand print from its origins. Before the age of the stenotype and the audio-recorder, special forms of handwriting like shorthand were developed to capture human speech. Evidence is emerging that putting pen to paper as a means of note-taking is cognitively superior to its digital counterpart (such as typing on a laptop keyboard).[38] Perhaps these studies explain the endurance of handwriting, which, like print, was declared dead only a few years ago. Recent reports show that even in Silicon Valley, ground zero for handheld and laptop devices, tech entrepreneurs have returned to taking notes in physical notebooks.[39]

Even as printed texts proliferated throughout the eighteenth and nineteenth centuries, manuscripts continued to be produced not exclusively for print but for circulation as manuscripts. Although many texts began as manuscripts destined for print, many others were written to be shared with friends and family, students and colleagues. The novel is often considered a commercial genre, at least from the eighteenth century onward, and so we might expect that most manuscripts of novels were printed. But even this assumption would be false. Novels often languished en route to a publisher, and some authors did not want their novels printed at all. In less commercial genres, like poetry, memoir, and travel narratives, we find that many texts were composed with a domestic or social audience in mind, with no view toward print publication, though these works were often eventually printed, with or without the consent of the author.

We tend to think that authors wrote either for print or for manuscript, but in fact many wrote for both. Into the nineteenth century, and likely beyond that too, even the most commercially and/or critically successful of authors might decide to circulate some of their writing in handwritten rather than print form. Lord Byron, the most successful poet of the early nineteenth century, is a case in point: of his 378 shorter poems, he elected to disseminate 207 of them via scribal means. His reasons for doing so are comparable to those of authors from previous generations: because the poems were intended for an intimate or knowing set of readers; because they were risky, politically or socially; and/or because they were otherwise deemed unsuitable for print. Thus, although some authors relied exclusively on the technology of script to circulate their writings, many authors used both script and print for various reasons over the course of their careers.

Two other authors, Dorothy Wordsworth and Emily Dickinson, provide further examples of the co-existence of print and **scribal publication** practices during the nineteenth century. Both authors disseminated their work primarily through manuscript, and they have often been deemed outliers, even oddities, of literary history as a result. According to her best-known editor, Ernest De Selincourt, Wordsworth is "the most distinguished of English prose writers who never wrote a line for the general public."[40] According to Wendy Martin, "Often, Dickinson is painted as a young woman in white, closeted in the upper rooms of her home, isolated not only from her neighbors and friends, but also from the historical and cultural events taking place outside her door."[41] These views of Wordsworth and Dickinson derive from misunderstandings about the history of manuscript and print. These authors are perceived as anomalous because they did not print their writing during a period when it is assumed that "[w]hat was kept in manuscript was increasingly what lacked the quality required for print publication."[42] As a result, critics have struggled to understand why neither Wordsworth nor Dickinson printed her work when it does not lack "the quality required for print."

Wordsworth and Dickinson challenge myths of authorship and media history in two ways. First, they exemplify a media ecology in which manuscript circulation is not diminished by a highly developed print culture. Wordsworth kept notebooks of her poetry, travels, and local history, which were shown to and often copied for others within her domestic circle, and some of her writing was well known by a larger social circle. Similarly, Dickinson circulated her poems in manuscript, chiefly through her letters. She often "drafted multiple versions of letters and changed them slightly to suit the different people they were being sent to."[43] Dickinson's practices were not anomalous but rather were part of a long tradition of circulating poems in letters and writing letter poems.[44] Margaret Ezell has challenged the assumption that early modern "manuscript culture was ... the province of women, in opposition to print culture as being the domain of men," rather showing that men used manuscript circulation, women used print, and both men and women could resort to either method of dissemination, as suited their needs (*BRBH* 389).

A study of Wordsworth and Dickinson challenges received views of authorship and media history in a second way, by undermining the belief that authors wrote for either manuscript or print dissemination. Although Wordsworth and Dickinson are thought of as "manuscript writers," both saw some of their writing appear in print in their lifetimes. Several of Wordsworth's poems, two of her travel narratives, and lengthy excerpts from her journals appeared in print, with her authorization, while she was alive.[45] Although scholars debate whether Dickinson chose to publish her poems, we do know that eleven of them appeared in six different **periodicals** printed in Massachusetts and New York State during her lifetime, although not one was published under her own name.[46] It was common, during this period, for writing to be published without the consent of the author, particularly shorter pieces appearing in magazines and newspapers. But even if they were published without her permission, there is no evidence she objected, and they must have travelled some distance beyond her home to have been printed, whether with her consent or not. Dickinson's career suggests that even a poet highly resistant to publication could not prevent her writing from appearing in print. In the absence of evidence, however, we simply don't know whether Dickinson's poems were published with or without her consent—whether she acquiesced in or resisted or approved their publication.

Dickinson's production of her manuscripts provides another avenue for exploring the complex, ongoing interactions between script and print. In her thirties, Dickinson began to write poems in folded pages hand-bound with string, small booklets called fascicles by her first editors.[47] Thus "she collected and organized, and some say self-published, her poetry."[48] On the one hand, these fascicles demonstrate how Dickinson fully inhabited a print world. By selecting, copying, arranging, and binding her poems into small booklets, Dickinson reproduced aspects of the printed book, essentially taking upon herself the roles distributed along the communications circuit diagrammed by Darnton in the previous chapter. According to Martha Nell Smith, when Dickinson began compiling her first eight fascicles, she "was obviously writing bibliographically, or with the book and the printed page in mind—her poetic forms in these [fascicles] are regularized variations on the tercet and quatrain, predictably lineated."[49] Dickinson's fascicles thus share the bibliographical conventions, presentational quality, and production methods of print.

At the same time, many of her practices depart significantly from what we would expect in the print sphere. There is no evidence that Dickinson shared the fascicles with others during her lifetime, thus separating her from both the commercial world of print and even from the realm of manuscript circulation. Moreover, as she continued to compile and collect her fascicles, she seems to have become more attuned to the distinct affordances of manuscript. As Smith observes,

> By the ninth and in all subsequent fascicles, Dickinson writes as if "the joint work of eye and inner ear" is being shaped by her persistent encounters with the manuscript page, a striking visual contrast to print, and with patterns guided entirely by her hand. The material record suggests that she began to focus more and more on the possibilities afforded by the manuscript page, and experimented with lineation, calligraphic orthography, angled marks of punctuation, and with leaving alternative word choices from which readers can choose. In other words, she began to render her poetic embodiments in terms of her holograph and cottage industry rather than in terms of typography and the publishing industry.[50]

Thus Dickinson's poetry, though handwritten ("**holograph**"), was necessarily shaped by her interactions with the realm of print, whether she imitated the conventions of the printed page or rejected them.

Dickinson's disruption of print conventions has posed significant difficulties for her editors, who have had to decide how to reproduce her poetry (particularly the fascicles) in print. As we have seen, Dickinson did not write for print and her poetry challenged many of the **bibliographical** and **typographical** codes of the time. Further, her poetry inhabits its physical embodiment (on the page, in the facsicle) in ways that make it resistant to remediation in print. Dickinson's chosen writing implement was a pencil, and her written words "were light, small, and difficult to decipher"; she wrote on "scraps of stationery, notepaper, or wrapping paper, on discarded letters, envelopes, Commencement programs for Massachusetts

Agricultural College, advertising circulars, and the like"; and, after her death, her "[p]apers were [found] bundled, loose, boxed, pinned, stitched, collected, and folded."[51] She wrote at night and suffered from failing eyesight, compounding the problems of legibility that these manuscripts already pose. Thus, the task facing both early and modern editors of her poetry has been one of many challenges.

The print **editions** of Dickinson's poetry that have appeared since her death in 1890 are fruitful sites of intermediality. According to Martin, "[t]urning Dickinson's handwritten words into typewritten script was much more difficult than it might seem. Her writing and symbols had to be interpreted, translated, and adapted to type." Dickinson's first editors, Mabel Loomis Todd and Thomas Wentworth Higginson, "edited the poems to regularize their capitalization, punctuation, lineation, and rhyme in order to align them with nineteenth-century poetic standards."[52] They also added titles, and in an attempt to impose order, rejected the fascicles' arrangement of the poems. For these first editors, many of Dickinson's poetic choices, which were specific to her manuscript practices, had to be stripped from the poems to render them suitable for print.

In his 1955 edition of Dickinson's poetry, Thomas Johnson restored her irregular capitals and dashes and presented her poems in chronological order, restoring some of their original features. However, Johnson did not replicate the visual arrangement of words in the manuscripts, instead transcribing the poems as metrical stanzas. Furthermore, he did not present Dickinson's variant word choices: within many of her individual manuscripts, Dickinson would allow alternative words to exist without deciding upon one or the other, what Sharon Cameron has described as the poet's "choosing not choosing."[53] Both the lack of stanza breaks in Dickinson's manuscript poems and her inclusion of variant words are distinctive to handwritten literary documents. Even though Johnson was far more committed to reproducing certain aspects of the original manuscripts than previous editors had been, his edition nevertheless reflects the expectation of textual stability within print.

The question that Johnson's edition continues to raise is whether transforming Dickinson's handwritten poems into printed text at all risks sacrificing too much of them. The editors of the *Emily Dickinson Archive*, an online collection of images of her manuscripts and various transcriptions, summarize the debate as follows:

Some critics argue that Dickinson's manuscript pages are mediated primarily by metrical and stanzaic conventions. Other critics assert that her manuscript page, with its spaces between words, lines, and stanzas, its ambiguous capitalization and idiosyncratic punctuation, represents Dickinson's radical revision of these conventions. Some critics believe that Dickinson, over the course of her writing life, came to conceive of her poems as fully realized in their manuscript condition rather than as drafts designed with the printed page in mind.[54]

Once again, we return to the difference between what McGann theorized as linguistic and bibliographical codes, though here in relation to manuscript writing. Some claim that the linguistic and literary features of the poetry are separable from their material incarnation and therefore can be remediated in print. Others see the poetry as inseparable from the paper, pencil marks, string, and other material elements that Dickinson

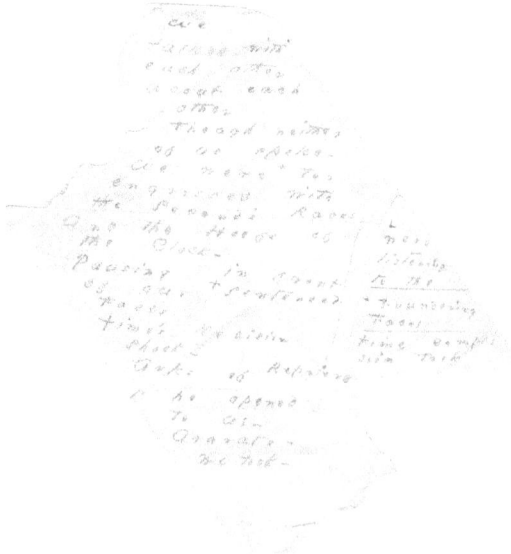

Figure 4.1: Emily Dickinson, "We talked with each other about each other," c. 1879, Amherst Manuscript #514. Pencil on Envelope, 1 sheet, 5 $^{1}/_{10}$ x 7 $^{9}/_{10}$ inches (13 x 20 cm). Courtesy The Emily Dickinson Collection, Amherst College Archives and Special Collections.

used to create them, and that to print them is to contravene their very essence. The comparison between a photo facsimile of the manuscript of Dickinson's "We talked to each other about each other," written in pencil on an envelope around 1879 (see Figure 4.1), and its first publication in 1945 (Figure 4.2), offers a study in contrasts, with variants, lineations, and other physical elements of the manuscript poem lost in their translation into print.

One apparent solution to this issue emerged in the 1980s, with several editions of Dickinson's poems that sought to capture more fully the scriptural nature of her poetry. A **facsimile** edition by R.W. Franklin, with photographic reproductions of the manuscripts, appeared in 1981.[55] In 1986, *The Master Letters of Emily Dickinson* was published, also edited by Franklin, complete "with an envelope that included a few photographic reproductions of letters, printed onto folded sheets just like the original documents."[56] Franklin argued that a facsimile edition, which seeks to represent not only the page but the physical form of the original itself, was "[t]he best way for readers to experience what Dickinson's letters looked like."[57] Digital remediations, which provide high-quality photo-facsimiles of manuscript images, offer another evolution of this approach, as we will discuss in the next chapter.

Though inviting less controversy, the regularization and print publication of Dorothy Wordsworth's *Grasmere Journals*—her most famous writing—present similar issues. Written as diary entries to be shared with her brother and possibly other members of the household, the journals

> WE TALKED with each other about each other
> Though neither of us spoke
> We were listening to the seconds' races
> And the hoofs of the clock.
>
> Pausing in front of our palsied faces,
> Time compassion took;
> Arks of reprieve he offered to us,
> Ararats we took.

Figure 4.2: Emily Dickinson, "We talked with each other about each other," in *Bolts of Melody: New Poems of Emily Dickinson* (New York: Harper Row, 1945), p. 146.

are difficult to decipher, using shorthand names to refer to individuals and places that needed little explanation for her brother. Although some of her writing had a wider public in mind, the journals did not. To print them raises a host of potential questions and concerns. The regularizing form of print elides **cancels** (i.e., where Wordsworth has crossed out words), as we have seen, and also the quality of the handwriting, which, as scholars like Pamela Woof have shown, seems to speed up, becoming messier, and slow down, becoming neater, at various points. As a result, information embedded in the handwriting and in the paper notebooks she used is lost when the text is rendered in print. Contextual information, corrections to spelling, and expansion of abbreviations are also generally considered necessary for modern readers, distancing its remediation from the original. Yet simply providing a facsimile of the original is hardly a solution, given how difficult it is for an inexperienced reader to decipher Dorothy's handwriting in the journals. The conundrums expand when we move beyond the practical and theoretical to the ethical. Do scholars have the right to reproduce private journals, never intended for print? Does the fact that Dorothy preserved them, and allowed some of her entries to be printed in the memoirs of her brother, authorize us to print and read them? We know that her first Victorian editors reacted with prudishness to her many references to bodily illness and functions, and even to the details she records about her daily household chores, excising these elements entirely from the first editions of the journals. Yet even with these restored (as they are by modern editors like Woof), the translation from script to print is necessarily inadequate, and subject to ethical debate.

When one medium (script) is translated into another (print), we can understand not only the gains and losses of each medium but also their distinctive features. Just as we have come to recognize that the movement between orality and print involves mediation, so too do we see the process of give and take between manuscript and print. Furthermore, we can recognize the cultural attitudes that shape the contact zone between media. Wordsworth's first editors found the content of her journals objectionable and censored them, whereas Dickinson's first editors believed that her poems had to be reshaped for a readership accustomed to printed poetry. Today, however, editors are unwilling to engage in similar editorial practices, allowing Wordsworth's words to stand as originally written and preferring not to separate Dickinson's poetic texts from their material instantiations. With respect to editors of Dickinson, however, this approach has its limits, since we all can't view Dickinson's original manuscripts, which are fragile and have already been subject to much handling by scholars. Nor can all of her manuscripts be reproduced to the exact specifications of the original. However, we can appreciate the specific relationship of Wordsworth's and Dickinson's chosen media to their artistic practices, just as we recognize how as users of various media, we regularly move between their contact zones.

Text and Image

In the final section of this chapter, we explore another division that has permeated the history of the book: that between text and image. Here, we're presented with a different set of issues, as we are not dealing with two media for communicating written words (like letterpress print and script), or even two communication systems (like orality and writing). Rather, we're presented with the more fundamental difference between words and images. Historically, the book has often been an intermedial space, incorporating both words and images. We have seen how print and script can be combined within a book, for example, by the addition of handwritten **marginalia** to a printed volume. Similarly, we have seen how oral and written culture can be combined, either within a book, as when a written book purports to record oral tradition, or within actual practices, as when a written document is read aloud. Text and image also have a unique history of enmeshment and separation, which we examine in this section.

The history of book illustration has often been told as a story of the fall and rise of images. Medieval manuscripts provide an example of the experimentation and artistry with which text and image were integrated prior to the invention of print. With the arrival of print, however, it became much harder to integrate text and image on the same **page**, because different techniques and equipment were required to print text and images during the handpress period. So the book entered a long "monochromatic" phase, in which images were much less common in books. When images did appear, they were not integrated with the text to the same extent as they had been in earlier periods. It was only with the invention of new image-reproduction technologies in the nineteenth century, followed by the digital revolution, that the book (in both its print and digital incarnations) returned to the visual sumptuousness of the pre-print era.

This story is helpful as a general outline of the history of book illustration, but we can also complicate some aspects of it. This history tends to understand the presence (or absence) of images within the book largely as a function of existing technology. This approach can be limited, in that it doesn't explain why certain technologies were developed and used at various times. We agree that the affordances and limitations of technologies play an important role in the history of the book, but we also want to emphasize that the use of technologies is embedded in social and historical contexts.

Manuscript books offered optimal flexibility for the integration of image and text. The tasks of writing and illustrating **illuminated manuscripts** were usually divided between individuals with different skills, although the same basic instruments (i.e., pen and brush and ink) could be used both to write and draw. Thus the manuscript page offered enormous scope not only for combining words and images but also for thinking of letters as images, as in the case of ornate decorative capital letters.

Early print attempted to emulate the manuscript book, but copying all of its design elements was difficult for **printers**. Several surviving copies of **Gutenberg's** 42-line bible (1454–56) were printed in two colours (red and black), "in imitation of the rubrication of manuscript books."[58] But this required a level of effort and technical difficulty that was difficult to sustain. Soon colour was added by hand: room was left for the **scribe** or illustrator to add decorated capitals, colour illustrations, and other embellishments. As Michael Twyman notes, "[s]ince early printed books were to a very large degree based on manuscript books and existed alongside of them, it would not have seemed strange for the two methods of production to be combined."[59]

As printed books became more common, early printers gradually discontinued the use of hand-colouring and decoration, and the visual appearance of the printed book began to diverge from that of the illuminated manuscripts it first sought to imitate. Printed books became largely monochromatic, and publishers and printers preferred "unillustrated books, or at the very least books with token illustrations only" (*BRBH* 44). Instead of using colour and images, printers developed typographical innovations to render complex texts both readable and visually appealing, for example through the development of specialized fonts, printers' ornaments, spacing, and italics.[60]

The separation of text and image in print has been often attributed to different technological methods of reproduction. To understand the place of images in the printed book, we have to go back for a moment to the processes of printing. There are basically three kinds of printing: **relief printing**, **intaglio printing**, and **planographic printing**, as Twyman explains (*BRBH* 39). The kind of printing we've mostly been discussing so far—printing with **moveable type**—is a form of relief printing. In relief printing, the raised sections of the printing surface are covered with ink, which then transfers to the paper in the press. The shapes of the letters are higher than the rest of the little stick of lead that is each piece of type, so they hold the ink and imprint their shapes on the paper. Printed images can also be made by relief printing, using wood blocks. Taking a piece of wood, a craftsman cuts away all the areas that he doesn't want to print, leaving the raised outline of an image. The image is cut in reverse, so that it will print the right way round. This wood block can then be locked into the chase with the type and printed along with it. **Woodcut** images were very widely used in early printing, especially in cheap **chapbooks** and **broadsides**. But there are some problems associated with them: they tend to produce fairly crude images, with no shading; they are usually fairly small; the wood is physically hard to work; and the sharp edges of the image get blunted from the force of the press, so the image loses definition over time.

These problems can mostly be avoided by **engraving** or **etching** the image, but these techniques require intaglio printing, which needs a different kind of press. An engraver uses a tool called a burin to scratch lines into a copper plate to make an image—again, in reverse. He then covers the plate with ink and wipes the surface clean, leaving only the ink that has seeped into all the little furrows he's scratched into the plate. Laying a sheet of dampened paper on the plate, he passes the plate and the paper through a rolling press, which compresses them between two rollers. The pressure of the rollers squeezes the ink out of its furrows and onto the paper, producing the image. Although shading is not possible, skilled engravers can achieve sophisticated effects by using cross-hatching and by varying the depth of the lines they scratch into the plate. Etching is a variation on the same technique. To prepare an etching, the artist covers the plate with wax, and then scrapes off the wax using a pin or stylus to expose the plate. He then immerses the plate in a bath of acid, which eats away at the exposed copper, leaving the areas covered in wax untouched. The plate can be printed once it's been removed from the acid and the wax has been cleaned off.

Both these techniques allow for larger, more detailed images that can be printed in greater numbers. (Once print **runs** became really large, in the nineteenth century, copper plates were increasingly replaced with steel, which lasts longer.) But since this process uses a different kind of printing press for the required intaglio printing method, combining text and images in the same book was complicated. Printed books containing images were usually expensive, because of the extra work involved in making them. Engraved images rarely appeared on the same page as text, because that meant passing the same sheet of paper through two different presses. As a result, images featured mostly in relatively high-status books or were confined to the front of the book as a **frontispiece** or decorative **title page**. We saw an example of the combination of image and word in the frontispiece of the First Folio (Figure 1.1). In this case, two separate printing processes were needed to produce the engraving and the surrounding text (title, subtitle, and **imprint**). Illustrations could also be distributed throughout the book. Maps and other illustrations could be tipped in as fold-outs (a tipped-in page is one that is printed separately from the main text of the book, but attached to it in some way, either by gluing it to or binding it with other pages). Other books, such as books of maps or views, could be made entirely from engravings. As in the cases Robert Darnton examines (*BRBH* 93–110), text and images work together to produce a book's effects. These effects aren't necessarily intended by any one individual: because of the different processes and technologies employed, several people are usually involved in the production of an illustrated book. Book producers thus innovated to find ways to combine print and image as best they could.

Readers also found their own ways to integrate word and image. They could add drawings and sketches to margins and **endpapers**. They could also extra-illustrate printed books, a process that came to be known as grangerizing (after James Granger, whose *Biographical History of England*, first published in 1769, was frequently unbound to allow for the addition of drawings, prints, and other visual materials, which were interleaved with the text). Grangerized texts could swell to many times their original size: for example, the Houghton Library at Harvard University holds an extra-illustrated collection of James Boswell's *Life of Johnson*, which was expanded by the collector Robert Borthwick Adam from the original six volumes to thirty-one in the late nineteenth century.[61]

Beginning a century earlier, new techniques emerged that allowed image and text to be printed on the same press and on the same page. One of these techniques was wood engraving, developed by Thomas Bewick (1753–1828). Unlike engraving on metal plates, wood engraving is a relief method, so

Bewick's wood blocks could be used alongside moveable type, locked into the same chase, and printed on the same press. Instead of typical wood-carving tools such as knives, Bewick used an engraver's burin to carve into wood blocks, which allowed him to create thin delicate lines. Second, traditional woodcuts used the softer side of the wood grain, whereas wood engraving used the harder end grain of the wood block, which made more durable and detailed images possible. Bewick developed his techniques for his book *A History of British Birds*, which first appeared between 1787 and 1804 and was reprinted continually throughout the nineteenth century. His innovations were driven by the needs of his project: high-quality, detailed images were necessary for this field guide for non-specialists (see Figure 4.3).

Lithography was another printing technique developed in the late eighteenth century that enabled the merger of print and image. It was developed by Alois Senefelder, a German playwright who sought an inexpensive

Figure 4.3: Thomas Bewick, "The Great Bustard," *A History of British Birds* (1787–1804).

method for reproducing his own plays. Senefelder invented a chemical process in which the printing and non-printing surfaces of a printing block (originally made of stone) are the same height, resulting in a "planographic" form of printing, as Twyman describes (*BRBH* 38). Using the well-known fact that oil and water do not mix but actually repel one another, Senefelder experimented with writing directly onto a stone with an oily substance; the stone was then treated with gum arabic, which stuck only to the parts of the stone that did not hold the oil-based image. When the stone was subsequently moistened, these areas retained water, and an oil-based ink could be applied that repelled water, so that only the original drawing on the stone would retain the ink and be printed.

Techniques such as wood engraving and lithography, as well as the later development of photomechanical processes for printing photographs in books and newspapers, ensured that, by the second half of the nineteenth century, images had become much more common in printed books. Not only did more books contain images, but the images were also more tightly integrated with the words, frequently appearing on the same page. Books often contained larger numbers of images than in earlier periods, and they were typically spread throughout the book instead of being confined to the frontispiece. Nevertheless, the story we have been narrating is not simply that of the rise and fall of the image. We have seen how technologies such as Bewick's wood engraving were developed throughout the print period in order to combine printed text and printed images, and how readers devised strategies to re-introduce the image into the book. The book has always been an intermedial site of negotiation between words and pictures.

As we have seen throughout this chapter, the book has long been a meeting ground for text and image, for script and print, and for oral and written communication. We have emphasized the intertwined nature of media, both over time and within any given artefact or practice. We have seen how technological and human factors could drive a wedge between manuscript and print (since it was difficult for print to emulate manuscript in many respects) and between image and text (because it was challenging to combine the two in the handpress era). In the next chapter we add another element to the mix, as we explore more fully the impact that the introduction of digital media has had on the book. Once again, our emphasis will be on influence and adaptation, understanding that the arrival of a new medium does not supplant the old but rather provides new opportunities for remediation and interaction.

Notes

1. Sven Birkerts, *The Gutenberg Elegies: The Fate of Reading in an Electronic Age* (London: Faber, 1994).
2. Alexandra Alter, "The Plot Twist: E-book Sales Slip, and Print Is Far from Dead," *New York Times* 22 September 2015, http://www.nytimes.com/2015/09/23/business/media/the-plot-twist-e-book-sales-slip-and-print-is-far-from-dead.html?_r=0.
3. Paul Duguid, "Material Matters: The Past and Futurology of the Book," *The Future of the Book*, ed. Geoffrey Nunberg (Berkeley and Los Angeles: U of California P, 1996), 65.
4. Roger Chartier, "*The Order of Books* Revisited," *Modern Intellectual History* 4.3 (2007): 511.
5. Peter Stallybrass, "Printing and the Manuscript Revolution," *Explorations in Communication and History*, ed. Barbie Zelizer (London: Routledge, 2008), 111; emphasis in original.
6. Stallybrass 111.
7. Stallybrass 112; emphasis in original.
8. Thomas Astle, *The Origin and Progress of Writing* (London, 1784), i.
9. Astle xxi.
10. Allan McEachern, Reasons for Judgment: *Delgamuukw v. BC* (Smithers, BC: Supreme Court of British Columbia, 1991), 19.
11. *Delgamuukw v. British Columbia* [1997] 3 S.C.R. 1010.
12. Christine Nystrom, "What Is Media Ecology?," Media Ecology Association, http://www.media-ecology.org/media_ecology/.
13. Marshall McLuhan and Quentin Fiore, *The Medium Is the Massage: An Inventory of Effects* (New York: Bantam, 1967), 26. In fact, the title was supposed to be McLuhan's well-known phrase, *The Medium Is the Message*, but when the typesetter made the error, McLuhan allowed it to persist.
14. Mark B.N. Hansen, "New Media," *Critical Terms for Media Studies*, ed. W.J.T. Mitchell and Mark B.N. Hansen (Chicago: U of Chicago P, 2010), 177.
15. Hansen 177.
16. Hansen 174.
17. Adam Fox and Daniel Woolf, *The Spoken Word: Oral Culture in Britain, 1500–1850* (Manchester: Manchester UP, 2002), 1.
18. Plato, *Phaedrus*, The Internet Classics Archive, http://classics.mit.edu/Plato/phaedrus.html.
19. John Durham Peters, "Mass Media," Mitchell and Hanson 271.
20. As Walter Ong put it in *Orality and Literacy: The Technologizing of the Word* (London: Methuen, 1982), "Today, parents and others fear that pocket calculators provide an external resource for what ought to be the internal resource of memorized multiplication tables" (78).

21　Leon Nayfakh, "Do Our Brains Pay a Price for GPS?," *Boston Globe* 18 August 2013, https://www.bostonglobe.com/ideas/2013/08/17/our-brains-pay-price-for-gps/d2Tnvo4hiWjuybid5UhQVO/story.html.
22　Ong 76.
23　Ong 81.
24　Ong 8.
25　Harold Innis, *Empire and Communications* (Oxford: Clarendon, 1950), 68–69.
26　Ong 11.
27　Ong 79.
28　Fox and Woolf 9.
29　Fox and Woolf 4.
30　Samuel Taylor Coleridge and William Wordsworth, *Lyrical Ballads: 1798 and 1800*, ed. Michael Gamer and Dahlia Porter (Peterborough, ON: Broadview P, 2008), Preface (1800), 171.
31　See Mason I. Lowance Jr., Ellen E. Westbrook, and R.C. De Prospo, eds., *The Stowe Debate: Rhetorical Strategies in Uncle Tom's Cabin* (Amherst: U of Massachusetts P, 1994) and Eric Sundquist, ed., *New Essays on Uncle Tom's Cabin* (Cambridge: Cambridge UP, 1986). As Susan Egenolf writes about Maria Edgeworth's *Castle Rackrent*, "Despite the fictional Editor's claims of authenticity, Maria Edgeworth in fact appropriates the voice of the native Irish Thady, and thus performs linguistic blackface for her English and Anglo-Irish readers." See "Maria Edgeworth in Blackface: *Castle Rackrent* and the Irish Rebellion of 1798," *ELH* 72.4 (2005): 846.
32　Fox and Woolf 19.
33　Fox and Woolf 21.
34　Fox and Woolf 21.
35　Fox and Woolf 28.
36　"What Is Intangible Cultural Heritage?" *UNESCO*, http://www.unesco.org/culture/ich/index.php?pg=00002.
37　"The Oral Heritage of Humanity," Res. No. 23, 12 Nov. 1997, *Records of the General Conference, Twenty-Ninth Session, Paris, 21 October to 12 November 1997*, Vol. 1, *Resolutions* (Paris: UNESCO, 1998), http://unesdoc.unesco.org/images/0011/001102/110220e.pdf.
38　Robinson Meyer, "To Remember a Lecture, Take Notes by Hand," *The Atlantic* 1 May 2014, http://www.theatlantic.com/technology/archive/2014/05/to-remember-a-lecture-better-take-notes-by-hand/361478/.
39　David Sax, "Why Startups Love Moleskines," *The New Yorker* 14 June 2015, http://www.newyorker.com/business/currency/why-startups-love-moleskines.
40　Ernest De Selincourt, ed., *Journals of Dorothy Wordsworth*, 2 vols. (London: Archon, 1970), quotation on flyleaf.
41　Wendy Martin, "Introduction," *The Cambridge Companion to Emily Dickinson*, ed. Wendy Martin (Cambridge: Cambridge UP, 2002), 1.

42 Harold Love, *The Culture and Commerce of Texts: Scribal Publication in Seventeenth-Century England* (Oxford: Clarendon, 1998), 288. For similar arguments that suggest the demise of manuscript culture, see Moyra Haslett, *Pope to Burney, 1714–1779: Scriblerians to Bluestockings* (Basingstoke: Palgrave Macmillan, 2003); George L. Justice and Nathan Tinker, *Women's Writing and the Circulation of Ideas: Manuscript Publication in England, 1550–1800* (Cambridge: Cambridge UP, 2002); and Linda Zionkowski, *Men's Work: Gender, Class, and the Professionalization of Poetry, 1660–1784* (New York: Palgrave, 2001).
43 Alexandra Socarides, *Dickinson Unbound: Paper, Process, Poetics* (Oxford: Oxford UP, 2012), 55–56.
44 Socarides 56. See p. 57 for an account of the multiple ways in which Dickinson circulated her poems to different individuals.
45 Mary Ellen Bellanca, "After-Life-Writing: Dorothy Wordsworth's Journals in the *Memoirs of William Wordsworth*," *European Romantic Review* 25 (2014): 201–18.
46 See Martin, *Cambridge Companion* 111, and "Publications in Dickinson's Lifetime," *Emily Dickinson Museum: The Homestead and the Evergreens*, https://www.emilydickinsonmuseum.org/publications_lifetime.
47 Taken from biology, the term "fascicles" means "a cluster of leaves or flowers with very short stalks growing closely together at the base." See Martin, *Cambridge Companion* 118.
48 Martin, *Cambridge Companion* 2.
49 Martha Nell Smith, "Dickinson's Manuscripts," *The Emily Dickinson Handbook*, ed. Gudrun Grabher, Roland Hagenbüchle, and Cristanne Miller (Amherst: U of Massachusetts P, 1998), 115.
50 Smith 115–16.
51 Martin, *Cambridge Companion* 117.
52 Martin, *Cambridge Companion* 118.
53 Sharon Cameron, *Choosing Not Choosing: Dickinson's Fascicles* (Chicago: U of Chicago P, 1993).
54 "Home," *Emily Dickinson Archive: An Open-Access Website for the Manuscripts of Emily Dickinson*, http://www.edickinson.org.
55 R.W. Franklin, *The Manuscript Books of Emily Dickinson: A Facsimile Edition* (Cambridge, MA: Belknap, 1981).
56 Martin, *Cambridge Companion* 120.
57 Qtd. in Martin, *Cambridge Companion* 120.
58 Michael Twyman, *The British Library Guide to Printing: History and Techniques* (Toronto: U of Toronto P, 1999), 26.
59 Twyman 29.
60 Twyman 30–31.
61 James Boswell, *Boswell's Life of Johnson*, ed. George Birkbeck Hill, extra-illustrated, MS Hyde 76, Houghton Library, Harvard College Library, Harvard U.

CHAPTER 5

REMEDIATING

Over two decades ago, as we mentioned briefly at the start of Chapter 4, Sven Birkerts penned a paean for the death of the printed book and the literary culture it sustained. Since then, David Ulin has fretted that we no longer know how to read, and Nicholas Carr has worried that the Internet is changing how we read, and not for the better. The titles of their books—*The Gutenberg Elegies* (Birkerts), *The Lost Art of Reading* (Ulin), *The Shallows* (Carr)—reflect the wistful tone the debate can often take.[1] Many people are obviously disquieted by the current migration from printed to digital forms, a migration that is uneven but apparently unstoppable. On the other hand, it's over 20 years since Birkerts published *The Gutenberg Elegies*, and new paper books are still published every day. Before we close the covers on the printed book in general, then, and this book in particular, we should look more closely at our current moment of media change and what it means for books. In this chapter, we return to the concerns of the first four—materiality, textuality, printing and reading, and **intermediality**—and ask how they are re-inflected by the digital turn.

New Media, New Materiality

The disquiet felt by many commentators reflects their concern that what's distinctive about the paper **codex**—its particular physicality, its feel, its smell, its heft—will be lost in a digital world where the words of the book will be absolutely identical, at the level of electronic storage, with everything else. For the digital, everything is data. Not only is the text of *Paradise Lost* functionally equivalent to the text of the End User License Agreement that no one ever reads, but it's also equivalent to the photos of your holiday, to the sex tape of a minor celebrity, to a million videos of cats. Everything is zeros and ones. In several important ways, e-books don't function like physical books, as Ted Striphas points out (*BRBH* 541–54). You can't so easily give them as gifts, display them on your shelves, share them with your friends, pass them on when you're finished with them, or buy and sell them second-hand. And while a physical book will survive for a long time if protected from fire and water, an e-book survives only as long as you have a working device that will allow you to read it. Since e-book formats are proprietary and specific to particular devices and distributors, if the company that produces a device decides to discontinue it, the books on that device might be lost.

It's easy to imagine that things were different with printed books. Each printed codex contained only one text, and the material form of the book could be adapted to reflect the nature, status, and intended uses of the text it contained. Art books could be large and heavy, full of colour reproductions. Prayer books could be small and light, easy to carry to church. In Oscar Wilde's novel *The Picture of Dorian Gray*, Dorian becomes so enamoured of a book that he "procured from Paris no less than nine large-paper copies of the first **edition**, and had them bound in different colours, so that they might suit his various moods."[2] He tailors the material form of the book not only to its contents but also to his own requirements. Now your Kindle looks and feels just the same whatever you use it to read (and whatever your mood), and it contains a whole shelf of books, all of which are practically indistinguishable. If you read on a tablet like an iPad, or a Kindle Fire, your device not only contains a shelf of books but also allows you instantly to turn aside from the book and attend to your email, social networks, shopping, or the myriad distractions of the Internet. And while you can read many books on one device, you can also read the same book on many devices, picking up your laptop to resume reading where you left off on your smartphone. *Fifty Shades of Grey* reportedly owed some of its runaway success to this new mismatch between the functional grey case of the e-reader and the purple prose it conveyed. People who wouldn't be seen dead clutching a paperback copy on the bus could read the book on their e-reader without a blush. Turning from *Dorian Gray* to *Fifty Shades of Grey* reveals how new technology is changing the relationship between the bibliographical and linguistic codes of the book.

The narrative of the "death" of the book has often been repeated in newspapers, which—not coincidentally—have been struggling with their own transition from a printed to an online existence and the change in business models it requires. But, for the sake of an eye-catching headline (or a click-baited one), this story drastically oversimplifies the situation. For a start, stories about the death of the book tend to assume a simple opposition between the "real" book and something else. On the one hand sits the printed codex, with all the memories, affection, and respect it inspires. On the other, somewhere in the cloud, is a new mutation that has nothing to do with books as we know them. This opposition overlooks the fact that books have been through media shifts in the past and that the printed codex is only one form the book has taken historically. Some of the current rhetoric about the future of books reprises concerns that were voiced in moments of past media change. Those moments show us that "new" media don't simply supersede "old" media. And just as "book" didn't always mean "printed book" in the past, nor does it always have to mean that in the future. Paying attention to the history of the book won't allow us to predict the future of the book, but it will certainly place us in a better position to understand that future as we enter it.

People who mourn the passing of the paper book—however prematurely—often behave as though what's being lost is not one material form of the book, but materiality itself. On this account, the book dematerializes—it goes from being a thing made of paper, card, glue, and so on, comfortingly ready to hand, to being something without a physical existence, conjured out of computer code. This overlooks the fact that e-books are just as material as physical books and that their materiality must be understood in terms of specific versions, platforms, systems, and devices.[3] They need hardware—e-readers, tablets, phones, or computers—often made by cheap labour in Asia and containing components that can be hazardous if not disposed of correctly at the end of the device's life. They also rely on an infrastructure of data centres, which is largely invisible to the end user but which requires large amounts of power (sometimes generated by burning fossil fuels). Shifting from paper books to e-books, then, does not mean moving from a material medium to an immaterial one. Instead, it means rearranging the relationship between material and immaterial elements. This is an important point for book historians or bibliographers, because it means the e-book is just as much their business as the paper book. If **bibliography** is the discipline that pays attention to the material form of the book, then it can have no purchase on an immaterial book. But e-books are not immaterial, and so bibliographical approaches can be brought to bear on them no less than on paper books.[4] Indeed, media archaeology attempts to study the material history of hardware and software, recognizing that production is tied to technology. For example, writing with a quill pen and liquid ink offers a very different writerly interface from writing using a typewriter or a word processor. Matthew Kirschenbaum, one of the leaders in this field, has conducted an in-depth study of the effects of the introduction of word processing in the early 1980s, a tool that has had important consequences for writers and editors. He finds that while some embraced the new technology, others lamented its coming as portending the death of writing, a familiar story in the history of media change, as we have seen.[5]

Those of us who have grown up with printed books have often made considerable emotional investments in them, turning them into privileged objects in our lives. This is perhaps especially true for those of us who study books or make our livings by reading, writing, and talking about them. If you look at the offices or the homes of literature or history professors, librarians or **publishers**, journalists or authors, there's not much doubt that books are important to us. They line our shelves and weigh down our suitcases when we go away. We take them to bed with us and give them to our friends for their birthdays. In many cases, this affection for the paper book is acquired early, with the ability to read or even before. Our identities are bound up in our books. And the books we choose to display reflect how we'd like to be seen by others. As Leah Price neatly puts it, "to expose a bookshelf is to compose a self."[6] Living with and among paper books, we are reminded of earlier moments in our lives when particular books were acquired or read.[7] It is difficult for us to imagine that people will ever lose their affection for the distinctive sensory experience that books offer. But it's entirely possible that new generations may transfer their emotional investments into new forms. You probably already know many people who love their smartphones with an intensity that, in other times and places, might have been directed at a book. Children who have grown up with tablets alongside paper books may one day feel the same sense of fondness and nostalgia for books read on the screen as some of us now feel for books read on the page. Our emotional investment in the paper book as a medium is historically and culturally constructed, and it could be constructed differently in the future.

In our current moment of media change, e-books often imitate paper books in their presentation. They still typically appear as pages, for example, although these are usually single pages rather than the diptych of **recto** and **verso** offered by the codex. In 2014, Amazon introduced new versions of its Kindle e-reader, the seventh generation of that product. The flagship model, the Kindle Voyage, which Amazon calls "our most advanced e-reader ever," features "reimagined page turns" and "delivers tactile feedback from a haptic actuator."[8] The Kindle is trying to mimic more closely some of the physical, sensory experience of reading a paper book. When in "sleep mode," the device shows various images, some of which are based on engravings from eighteenth- and nineteenth-century books. The short video Amazon produced to introduce the original Kindle to the world in 2007 showed an image of Johannes **Gutenberg** on the device's screen, connecting it with the invention of printing in the West, even as it suggested that it represented the next great epochal shift in the history of the book.⁹

Jesse England, a Pittsburgh-based conceptual artist, found an ingenious way to prompt discussions of the relationships between printed books and e-books. England took his Amazon Kindle edition of George Orwell's novel *Nineteen Eighty-Four*, put the e-reader on the glass bed of a photocopier, and photocopied each screen. Then he had the paper copies from the photocopier bound into a hardback book. You can now handle, store, and read the paper codex created by photocopying the Kindle's "pages." England selected that book because it was the subject of a 2009 recall by Amazon that saw copies of the novel unexpectedly removed from some Kindles because of **copyright** issues (the book has also been subjected to many censorship bans). This recall is not only deeply ironic, in the light of the novel's depiction of a regime that exercises total control over information; it also reminds us that there are aspects of the content on our devices that are beyond our control. "Re-versioning" the Kindle edition as a paper codex highlights the affordances and limitations of reading in different media, as well as of creating an object with sedimented layers of mediation. A paper copy of *Nineteen Eighty-Four*, first issued as a printed codex in 1949, was likely scanned and run through optical character recognition (OCR) software to create an electronic file, which was displayed on an e-reader, which was scanned again using a photocopier, printed out, and bound to make a new printed codex. In a final twist, England also uploaded a digital version of his paper backup to his Kindle.¹⁰

The e-book and the e-reader, then, are currently trying to mimic things that the paper book has been doing, and doing very well, for a very long time. But, in some respects, the paper book has also been trying hard for a very long time to do things that the e-book can do effortlessly. Take **hypertext**, for example. Hypertext is a network of textual nodes connected by links, which can be navigated in a non-linear, multi-sequential fashion by the reader. By this definition, there can be print hypertexts as well as digital ones. Gamebooks—of which the most popular are books in the *Choose Your Own Adventure* series published by Bantam from 1979—offer a crude version of hypertext's dendritic, or branching, structure. Avant-garde novelists like B.S. Johnson, as we mentioned in Chapter 1, experimented with non-linear organization, presenting textual nodes that the reader could move through at will. In the case of Johnson's *The Unfortunates* (1969), this meant printing the novel on a stack of cards rather than as a codex. Dictionaries and encyclopedias, with their multiple entries cross-referenced among themselves, also have a hypertext structure, so it's no surprise that they have easily migrated to digital formats. Even the most bookish person would probably prefer consulting the *Oxford English Dictionary* (*OED*) online from their computer, with enhanced search and hyperlinking functionality, to leafing through any of the 20 heavy and cumbersome printed volumes it occupies on a library shelf. The *OED* works well on a digital platform because, in a sense, it has wanted to be hypertext all along. The "Print Wikipedia" project by the artist Michael Mandiberg underlined the extent to which we now feel that the natural home of an encyclopaedia is online. He printed the entire text of Wikipedia as it existed on 7 April 2015 and had it bound in 7,473 volumes.[11] Whether Wikipedia is a good encyclopedia is debatable, but it clearly *is* an encyclopedia. That is to say, the encyclopedia, which was pioneered in paper form at the end of the eighteenth century, is now embracing the functionality of digital media to facilitate search, cross-referencing, and collaboration.

Our current media moment, then, which makes some people anxious about books dematerializing, should actually prompt us to think more carefully about the materiality of books and the materiality of digital culture. As Andrew Piper suggests (*BRBH* 511–24), reading in electronic times can throw into sharp relief the embodied practices of reading the printed page produces. Meanwhile, born-digital texts explore the affordances of the digital environment to incorporate multimedia content, network structures, and interactive functionality. We might have an entirely different experience reading the identical words in print form or on a cellphone. And digital devices create new opportunities for new forms of writing. Just as the innovations of **periodicals** and newspapers drove the invention of new journalistic genres, hand-held devices and immersive platforms are inciting new born-digital forms of writing. As we live through a period where people can turn repeatedly in the same day from reading on the page to reading on the screen, we have an historic opportunity to see the distinctive characteristics of both media and the wide variations that occur within each. Each medium and every device, in its own particular materiality, offers a specific kind of experience.

(Hyper)Textuality

Scholarly **editing** might seem like a very bookish pursuit, but **editors** have eagerly embraced the possibilities of digital media in ways that have transformed their practice. In Chapter 2, we discussed the idea of "textual pluralism," or a versioning model of textuality. This is the idea that where a **work** exists in several **texts**, we should view them as different versions embodying the author's shifting intentions (as well as those of other people in some cases). Instead of choosing one version as the **copy-text** for a new edition, textual pluralists argue, editors should present different versions alongside one another. Where there are two versions, it is simple enough to print them on facing pages of a paper book. But things quickly become tricky where there are multiple versions of a work. In some respects, at least, digital editions seem to offer a solution to this problem of the proliferation of versions.

Digital editions of works by Geoffrey Chaucer, William Blake, Walt Whitman, and Dante Gabriel Rossetti, for example, allow readers to choose which texts of a work interest them and to collate them dynamically in the browser window. The Blake Archive (www.blakearchive.org) was a pioneer in this respect. William Blake produced "illuminated books" that include both verbal and visual elements, printed them himself in small numbers, and coloured each one individually by hand, sometimes with the help of his wife. As a result, every copy of each work differs from all the other copies. When Blake's books are reprinted in modern editions, the images are often removed. When the images *are* reproduced, they make the book more expensive, so usually only an image of one copy of an illustration is provided. The Blake Archive revolutionizes access to Blake's verbal and visual art by attempting to digitize every known copy of every work he made, and to make it easy to search and compare them. The digital medium allows for images to be reproduced plentifully, something that is next to impossible in the realm of print. Thus the Blake Archive gives the modern reader the ability to compare side-by-side images of Blake's books that might be held in libraries thousands of miles apart. This is especially useful for studying a writer like Blake, whose production methods mean that any serious attempt to understand his work has to include looking at multiple copies. The William Blake Archive even offers users the ability to conduct highly specific image searches, based on their tagging of individual elements in Blake's visual works.

Digital archives can also be helpful for studying the textual transmission of works. When the **manuscript** in the author's own handwriting has been lost or destroyed, scholars attempt to reconstruct how the work was transmitted over time by examining the early manuscript copies made by others and printed texts of the work that do survive. In particular, they try to figure out which later texts might have been copied from which earlier ones, and they examine how variants were introduced in the process of transmission. Printed scholarly editions present this information in their critical apparatus at the foot of the page or gathered together at the back of the volume, but they cannot reproduce all the early texts of the work. A digital archive can, as it operates without the same constraints of print and the codex. The "multitext edition" of Chaucer's *Canterbury Tales*, for example, puts into electronic form the eight surviving manuscripts of the *Tales* (http://www.chaucermss.org/multitext). Still in progress, this edition allows users to browse, search, and compare multiple versions of each tale. The multitext edition thus allows its users to build their own editions tailored to their interests and preferences, instead of presenting them with the choices of the editors. This makes it relatively simple for users to examine in detail the textual tradition of this famous medieval work. There may also be reasons for viewing the original manuscripts of an author, as we discussed in relation to the writing of Dorothy Wordsworth and Emily Dickinson in the previous chapter.

Compared to the printed edition, then, digital technology enables editors to assemble and remediate an entire **archive**, creating resources with a number of advantages. It is not constrained by the space limitations of the codex, so digital editions can include much more material. A complete critical edition of T.S. Eliot's collected, uncollected, and unpublished prose works is now in progress and includes over 900 essays and other items. It will be a digital edition; it is unlikely that it would have been economically viable to publish it as set of paper volumes.[12] Digital editions can also include material that a paper book cannot easily incorporate due to cost constraints, like full-colour images, or at all due to the nature of the medium, such as audio and video. A digital edition of Robert Burns's songs, for example, could include recordings of them being performed. A digital edition of Samuel Beckett's plays could include video of productions the playwright himself directed.

A digital archive can also include a lot of information about the material forms in which the works it contains previously circulated. Jerome McGann argues that printed editions are limited in the ways they can present this material, because their own physical form is the same as that in which the works they contain first circulated (*BRBH* 459–74). When you use a book to study books, McGann suggests, you have to make difficult decisions. Either you can present a **facsimile** of one earlier text of the work or you can draw on the evidence of several texts to produce an "eclectic" edition. The first kind of edition will include a lot of information about the physical form of one early text, but it can't present much detail about how it differs from other texts. The second will present a lot of detail about textual differences among the early texts, but little information about their material forms. A digital archive can do both. It can include facsimile page-images of many texts, not just one, and it can present the textual differences between versions in a readily understandable way, as part of an interface that allows the user to search and compare different texts of the work.

In some respects, digital archives turn every reader into his or her own editor. The new technology puts pressure on the categories of editorial work that emerged in a print environment. Where editors previously had to choose between different versions and settle on one way of presenting them in print, now they can make all the relevant versions available and allow the user to navigate among them. Online collation tools also make it possible for people without specialist training to upload and compare different texts of a work.[13] A journalist, for example, can use these tools to compare the pre-released version of a politician's speech with a transcript of what he or she actually said. The same type of program, running on a large scale, is used to detect **plagiarism** in students' essays. New tools for online collaboration also make it possible to crowd-source some aspects of large editorial projects, such as **transcription**. The "Transcribe Bentham" project engages volunteers to help transcribe the vast archive of materials by the philosopher and reformer Jeremy Bentham held at University College London. These transcriptions will then form the basis of a printed edition of Bentham's collected works and an online repository of texts.[14] No longer only the end users of editions, readers can now be engaged in the process of producing them, blurring the boundaries between the roles of editor and reader.

Ray Siemens and his team at the Electronic Textual Cultures Laboratory at the University of Victoria are pushing the idea of collaboration in digital textual scholarship even further (*BRBH* 475–89). They urge editors to embrace the potential of social media and the interactive functionality of Web 2.0 to enhance their work on editions. Indeed, they think that these new digital tools will produce a profound rethinking of the nature of editions and editorial work. Beyond digital archives that transfer some of the practices of print editing online, they call for a new model of the "social edition," which they undertake for an early-sixteenth-century miscellany known as the *Devonshire Manuscript*. Their edition attempts to make the most of new software to promote and incorporate the efforts and ideas of its users. Editors working on this model would engage in collaborative annotation, locate or produce content that contextualized or elucidated the work(s), tag sections of text to improve the metadata that allow more sophisticated computer-assisted analysis of the work(s), supply bibliographical citations, and collaborate on textual analysis. Such an edition would never be finished, and could never be definitive. Instead, it would value the edition as a process of enquiry rather than a product, and the editors as facilitators of others' textual explorations.

For some, the new digital editions might seem unsatisfactory. Returning to the previous chapter, we might ask whether a digital edition of the works of Emily Dickinson's poetry or Dorothy Wordsworth's writing will solve all problems, since such a project would involve remediating complex, three-dimensional material objects into digital forms. Digital editions are also expensive to produce and maintain, requiring software developers and server storage. Although they can be corrected or added to more easily than printed books, they require regular maintenance, as the software and hardware on which they rely rapidly becomes obsolete. Digital editions offer unprecedented possibilities to present multiple texts of a work, but some readers will want the number of versions they have to engage with curtailed rather than increased. Students, non-specialists, and general readers will ask, quite understandably, which is the best version, or the most authoritative, or the most interesting. As we saw in Chapter 2, those questions don't have easy answers, but that doesn't necessarily mean that editors should simply decline to answer them at all, passing the difficult decisions of editorial work on to the reader or user. Whether in print or on screen, then, editions that offer a single clean reading text of a work will still be in demand. Traditionalists might feel that digital archives, when they present many versions of a work, risk shirking the editor's responsibilities rather than democratically sharing them.

Once editing moves into digital media, however, received understandings of the editor's "responsibilities" begin to break down. New digital archives de-mystify some of the otherwise arcane practices of scholarly editors. They provide the tools and resources that allow readers or users of the edition to make some editorial decisions for themselves. They can even make the reader part of the edition's creation. In these conditions, the roles of editor and user begin to blur, and other fundamental concepts in textual scholarship, such as the reading text, copy-text, and work begin to seem outmoded. Where there are multiple versions of a work, users can explore the differences between them, without viewing them as either stages in a progression toward a finished work or faulty witnesses to an immaterial original. In a new medium, a new conception of textuality itself becomes possible.

Digital Printing and Screen Reading

How has digital technology transformed the ways in which texts are both produced and read? Let's begin with production. The vast majority of print books are produced today using offset printing, a method of production, based upon **lithographic** principles, that has been in use since the late nineteenth century. Digital printing, which combines a computer-driven high-speed copying machine with computer-driven **bindery** equipment, is a growing form of book production, particularly for print on demand. Some fine books continue to be produced using traditional letterpress. Nevertheless, *print* production remains, as it has been for some time, dominated by offset production. The back-office workflows of publishers have been transformed by digital technologies, but the production of paper books is only just starting to be transformed.

What has grown exponentially in the past two decades is the publication of books, periodicals, and newspapers in digital form (often, as we shall see, alongside print production). Digital publication takes a range of forms along a spectrum that moves further and further away from print. E-books and e-journals may replicate the forms of printed books and journals from which they derive, even if the print forms are no longer produced. Digital publication can take place alongside print publication of the same material, as in online newspapers, which often share many of the same elements as the print edition. Digital versions can also take advantage of the medium to include large numbers of detailed colour photographs, charts, or other features that might have been prohibitively expensive in print. And born-digital writing, in journalism or literature, can go beyond what is possible in print, for example by introducing interactive elements. Born-digital media, such as blogs or Twitter feeds, possess a distinctive appearance and structure unknown in print realms.[15] But digital publication has not supplanted print publication. Rather, print and digital media continue to circulate alongside one another in multiple forms.

One example of the complexity of the shifting media landscape is the recent history of *Newsweek* magazine. *Newsweek*, an American news weekly in print since 1933, announced in 2012 that it would become the first major magazine to go all-digital, at the end of that year. However, by the end of 2013 the magazine reversed course, saying that it would resurrect the print edition, apparently in response to the demands of loyal readers committed to print. *Newsweek* stated it would print 70,000 print copies—a huge decrease from its peak two decades before, when its print **circulation** was 3.3 million. Nevertheless, the return to print demonstrates the fluidity of the current media landscape and warns us, yet again, not to presume that print is dead.

In fact, many news outlets operate in this hybrid world: the *New York Times*, for example, offers an array of subscription options, as we see in Figure 5.1: web and smartphone, web and tablet, all digital access, and all digital access plus home delivery of the print edition. These offers document the range of ways in which news is now consumed, with the image in the top right corner of the advertisement featuring the wide variety of devices and surfaces we read upon: laptops, tablets and phones, and, enduringly, paper. Some of us have our preferred media, such as the dedicated *Newsweek* readers devoted to print, but many of us consume our news, and other reading material, in a range of media. The nature of the packages offered by the *New York Times* strongly implies that most individuals access their news in multiple ways.

If you look closely at the images of the *New York Times* in print and on a laptop in Figure 5.1, you will notice how the latter replicates the former to a great extent. Media scholars have observed this mimicking of the printed page and criticized digital technology for failing to re-imagine the way in which we consume text. The mundane translation of print media into PDFs (portable document format) and many e-book formats offer a case in point. They frequently attempt to do what the printed book does, but often with far less success. Navigating and even reading many e-books

CHAPTER 5 • REMEDIATING

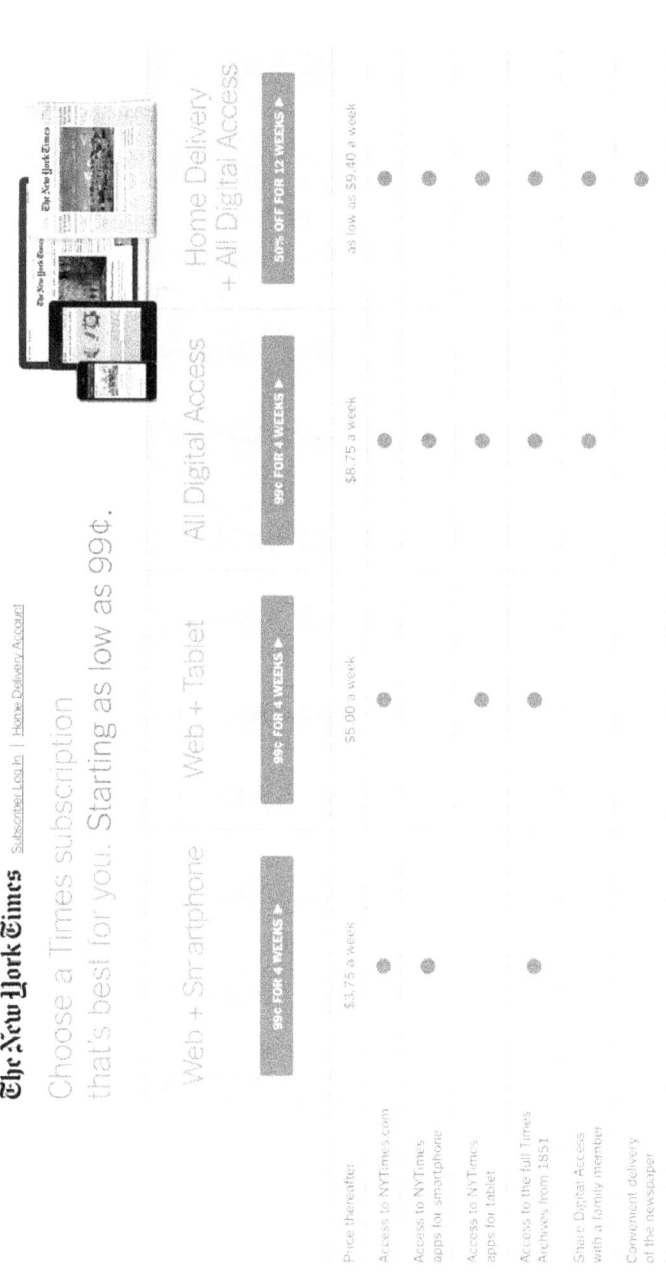

Figure 5.1: *New York Times* Subscription Plans, 21 January 2016.

can be a challenge. Screens can cut off full-page views, and clicking through pages that take seconds to load can produce a reading experience far more stilted than that of reading a physical book. Furthermore, the range of e-book formats can be daunting, with a user having to negotiate each new interface before reading can even begin.

Annotated and illustrated editions designed for e-book readers that take advantage of the affordances of digital media have emerged slowly. In part, this is because the developers of e-ink readers, in their efforts to reproduce the effects of reading a printed page, have produced monochromatic devices that cannot reproduce even the colour illustrations usually found on the covers of paperback and hardback books. Tablets and other full-colour devices, like the Kindle Fire, enable the reproduction of colour illustration as well as the integration of audio and video files. One recent example of an e-book edition that provides this multimodal functionality is the interactive edition of Jane Austen's novel *Pride and Prejudice*, published by Anchor Books in 2014. This version includes 2,500 notes and hundreds of illustrations, as well as interactive maps, audio clips, and videos.

Figure 5.2 provides an image of the first page of the novel in this edition. The buttons on the left-hand side allow one to access the multimedia content:

- the * allows access to annotations, as do the hyperlinked numbers;
- the play button, to videos (if there is one linked to the page in question);
- the Q, to study questions;
- the i, to a guide to how to use the interactive features;
- and the volume symbol, to audio-recordings of the novel, synced to the page.

With interactive maps and timelines, appendices that provide introductions to topics such as music and dancing in Austen's day, and image galleries on fashion and architecture, the volume comes to 675 pages, swelling the length of the novel to more than double its original size. In some respects, this annotated, interactive edition replicates the much older form of thickening books known as extra-illustration or grangerizing, discussed in the previous chapter. The e-book version of *Pride and Prejudice* enacts a similar process, but here the labour of extra-illustration has been done by the editor and publisher, not the reader. The social practices of book

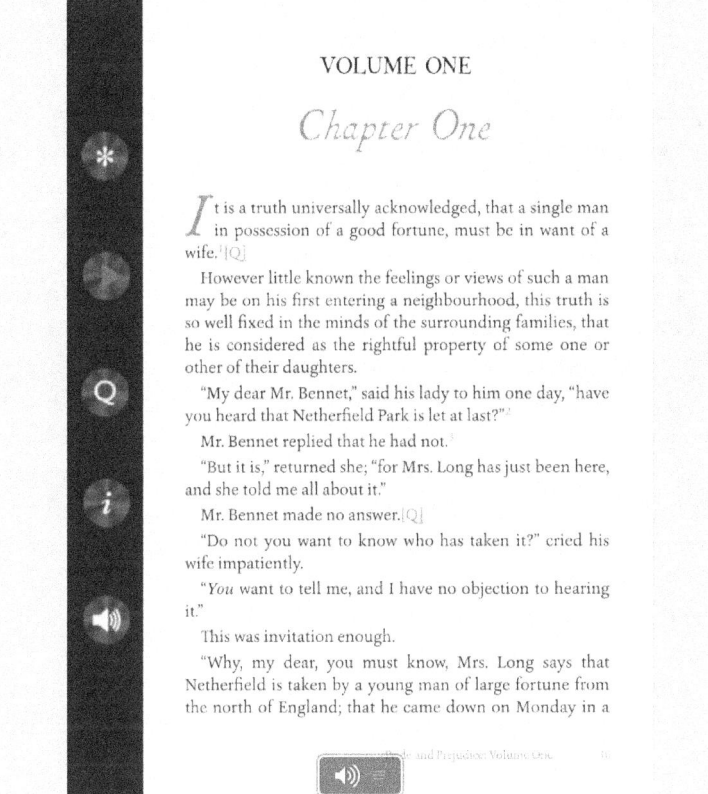

Figure 5.2: Jane Austen, *Pride and Prejudice*, Interactive Edition (Anchor Books, 2014).

breaking and remaking—as was done in the process of eighteenth-century extra-illustration—reappear here in a commodified product.[16]

The inclusion of interactive features within the book's contents raises a potentially deeper critique of how digitizing literature affects reading. Andrew Piper has imagined a future, now upon us, of

> "enhanced" e-books, every publisher's dream, [which] will soon consist of vast amounts of animation (sound tracks, pop-up windows, and moving images).... It may be that we should no longer even call this reading. Listening to music, watching movies, pointing, and clicking—these have nothing to do with reading. But we should also remember that reading has very often had

this "multimedia" quality about it, even if not in such an overpopulated sense. (*BRBH* 513)

Piper's suggestion that "we should no longer even call this reading" has emerged from studies of screen reading. In her survey of the evidence about how we read on screens, N. Katherine Hayles (*BRBH* 491–510) suggests that there may be profoundly different cognitive outcomes of reading within different environments. It may be that practices of immersive reading are more difficult in hyperlinked online texts, such as the interactive *Pride and Prejudice*, or on devices that allow for easy movement outside of the reading text. One way to describe this form of reading is "hyper-reading," defined by James Sosnoski as "reader-directed, screen-based, computer-assisted reading" (496). Hayles continues: "Examples include search queries (as in a Google search), filtering by keywords, skimming, hyperlinking, 'pecking' (pulling out a few items from a longer text), and fragmenting" (496). Hyperreading enables us to do different and arguably new things with texts, and may be considered to be one aspect of an emergent **digital literacy**; at the same time, the evidence suggests that it also impedes practices of attentive reading.

Although hand-held readers (such as the Kindle or Kobo) attempt to imitate the look and feel of reading print through the use of e-ink, students report issues with retention and concentration when using these devices.[17] In early 2015, Naomi Baron and her colleagues reported on their survey of over 300 university students in the US, Japan, Germany, and Slovakia, which found a near-universal preference for print. Ninety-two per cent of participants said they could concentrate best when reading in hard copy. This preference was stronger for serious reading; students reported that format poses less significant issues for lighter reading. When given a choice of various media—including hard copy, cellphone, tablet, e-reader, and laptop—the overwhelming majority chose a hard copy. Baron reports:

> When I asked [students] what they don't like about reading on a screen—they like to know how far they've gone in the book. You can read at the bottom of the screen what per cent you've finished, but it's a totally different feel to know you've read an inch worth and you have another inch and a half to go. Or students will

tell you about their visual memory of where something was on the page; that makes no sense on a screen.[18]

In addition to the disorienting features of reading on screens, students reading on non-purpose-built devices, such as smartphones, noted the problem of being "distracted, pulled away to other things."

As early as 1994, Sven Birkerts questioned whether reading on screens would enable readers to inhabit a text. Birkerts claimed, somewhat hyperbolically, that as a result of digital reading, our "[a]ttention spans have shrunk and fragmented." He asked, "Who has the time or will to read books the way people used to?"[19] Hypertext was originally lauded as a tool to supplement, extend, and enlarge our reading experience. But, two decades later, evidence is mounting that "contrary to the claims of early hypertext enthusiasts such as George Landow, hyperlinks tend to degrade comprehension rather than enhance it" (Hayles, *BRBH* 498).

While hyperlinks and other digital functionality can be detrimental to our understanding of traditional, linear texts, authors of electronic literature have turned these tools to their advantage. They create experimental, non-linear texts that use the functionality of digital media as an integral part of their artistry. Shelley Jackson's very early work of electronic literature, *Patchwork Girl* (1995), is a well-known example. Written in the proprietary Storyspace software, it consists of fragments of text and image that the reader can assemble as she navigates the interface. As the reader browses among the scraps and shards of text, a story begins to emerge that takes as its starting point the female creature stitched together from disjointed body parts by Victor Frankenstein in Mary Shelley's novel, but destroyed before she is brought to life. The collage structure of the text, as well as its reuse of material from its print precursors, thus reflects formally the creature's assembly from repurposed flesh. Jackson also uses both the fragmented form and the story it tells to reflect on the unstable nature of gender and its relation to the body. The broken-apart fiction compels the reader to actively remake it in order to make sense of it. The reader's efforts to assemble the text parallel Mary Shelley's efforts, in the story that emerges, to assemble the female creature.

While Jackson gives readers the tools to find their own way through the text, other creators of electronic literature use digital media to unsettle our habits of reading and making sense. In Judd Morrissey's *The Jew's Daughter* (2000), for example, the words on the screen shift and change as the user moves the cursor across the page with the mouse. The reader doesn't follow hyperlinks but simply moves the mouse over highlighted words, causing the text to reassemble itself, sometimes changing what's coming next and sometimes reconfiguring what has gone before. This thoroughly disrupts habits of linear reading that make us expect to move through the text from beginning to end, consuming a narrative as we go. Readers keen to "get to the end" may find the experience frustrating. Rather than racing ahead, readers are invited to dally, to dither, to loiter with the words on the screen, as the tesserae of the text unfold and interweave on a single, unstable "page." By combining poetic storytelling with accomplished programming, Morrissey aims to offer a reading experience that could not exist within the limits of a printed codex.

Beyond these differences in the cognitive experience of reading, reading on screens involves a physical shift in our embodied relationship to the objects we read. As Piper has noted:

> Reading isn't only a matter of our brains; it's something that we do with our bodies. Reading is an integral part of our lived experience, our sense of being in the world, even if at times this can mean feeling intensely apart from it. How we hold our reading materials, how we look at them, navigate them, take notes on them, share them, play with them, even where we read them—these are the categories that have mattered most to us as readers throughout the long and varied history of reading. They will no doubt continue to do so into the future.[20]

The revival of the printed book, discussed in Chapter 4, seems to endorse Birkerts's and Piper's claims about the power of reading print and its integration into our "lived experience." The return of the print book is also heralded by the opening, in November 2015, of Amazon's first ever physical store, in Seattle. Boasting a façade literally made of bricks and mortar, it sells thousands of printed books. Along with this revival of interest in printed books, there seems to be a renewed interest in the art of the book, with some publishers reviving high-end touches such as gilt edges, page-marking ribbons, and other features that had previously disappeared from most printed books.

Reading, Knowledge, and the Digital Turn

Alongside the new experience of reading individual books formatted for the e-reader, we can now encounter the printed books of the past through their remediation into large-scale databases. Since the emergence of the Internet, massive databases containing the full texts of thousands of works have been produced. Some of them are commercial products undertaken by corporations; others are pro-bono efforts managed by charitable trusts or educational institutions. Collectively, as we'll suggest in this section, these databases promise to revolutionize many fields of study, including literary and book history, leading us to re-think the category of "reading" itself. But they also throw up a number of problems that will need to be overcome if scholars are to realize the potential of these new textbases and the methods and tools that are being developed to query them.

Full-text databases allow users to search and read large numbers of works. One example is Literature Online, a database produced by ProQuest LLC that includes the full texts of more than 350,000 works of poetry, drama, and prose. These works have been re-keyed for the database by clerical workers who have copied their sources quite accurately. However, Literature Online does not attempt to compare different texts of a work to produce a new edition, and so it reproduces errors from the earlier editions it copies. While it initially relied on out-of-copyright editions, often with unreliable texts, in more recent years ProQuest has increasingly entered into agreements with other producers to license more authoritative editions. Another example is Project Gutenberg, a volunteer-led initiative that seeks to make out-of-copyright works available in electronic forms. Founded in 1971 by Michael Hart, it initially relied on hand-keyed texts produced by volunteers in generic ASCII-formatted text. The transcriptions appeared in a pared-down style that can be read by different configurations of software and hardware. The encoded texts are not tied to proprietary formats and so are likely to remain readable in future. (More recently, Project Gutenberg has increasingly relied on automated processes for scanning books and has introduced other formats that can include page images alongside texts.) These databases, and others like them, make possible new kinds of reading experiences and allow us to ask new questions about the history of literature and publishing. But because they rely (at least in part) on re-keyed texts, they tend to detach the words of a book from the material forms in which that book circulated in the past. In this respect, they participate in the disentangling of a book's textual content from its material form, which book historians oppose.

Other databases do a better job of including information about the material form of the books they remediate. The standard practice for full-text databases is now to offer page images, backed up by a machine-readable text created with the help of OCR software. Databases such as Early English Books Online (EEBO), Eighteenth-Century Collections (ECCO), Google Books, and the Hathi Trust all use this dual format, as do many of the books added to Project Gutenberg since roughly 1990. Alongside these large-scale databases, many researchers have created digital resources that include smaller, curated collections of books, or even just one work digitized to a high standard. Where page images are available, moving to digital media has actually fostered a renewed interest in the material forms taken by books in the past. A student in New Delhi—provided she has Internet access—can browse through an early **quarto** edition of a Shakespeare play held in the British Library in London.[21] Not only can she read an early-modern play but she can also read it in an early-modern book, or at least a digital version of one. High-resolution page images, of course, are not a perfect substitute for encountering the book itself, as they fail to capture many aspects of the material page and the book of which it is a part. But they encourage us to reflect on the physical form in which the text circulated in the past, as well as on how new technologies mediate it to us in the present. If researchers can use a digital surrogate instead of a rare and fragile book, that also helps to preserve that book for future generations by reducing how much it is moved and handled.

But while these new digital resources have great value, we should also be aware of their problems and limitations, in order to be critical users of them and of the research that depends on them. Even the best attempts to remediate the books of the past have limitations inherent to the digital media in which they operate. It's almost impossible to study **watermarks** in digital versions, for example. Digital surrogates rarely include images of the **binding** of a book, or its edges and spine, all of which contain valuable bibliographical information. And they seldom record in any systematic way the evidence of **endpapers**, which are often made from discarded parts of other books and manuscripts that may be interesting in their own right.

Much of the underlying text on which these resources rely is produced by OCR software and has not been corrected by human readers. This "dirty OCR" text is often hidden from view in proprietary databases, but it contains a significant number of errors. Although it is continually improving, OCR software still has difficulty with early-modern printing and regularly misreads the long s as an f. The problem is especially acute in EEBO, which was produced not by scanning the books themselves but by scanning earlier microfilm copies of them. The TypeWright project is an experiment in crowd-sourcing the correction of OCR text in ECCO (http://www.18thconnect.org/typewright). Large databases include "metadata" about the books they contain, such as details of the author, publisher, and date of publication. This information is sometimes faulty, especially in Google Books, where it has been derived algorithmically from the scanned books rather than being entered by hand or imported from an authoritative source. As a result, many books are misdated or misattributed, which creates errors when using the database for research.

Even when a digital surrogate is produced to a high standard, it represents only one copy of the book, while book historians will often be interested in comparing several copies to look for copy-specific information and textual variants. The booktraces project (www.booktraces.org), mentioned in Chapter 1, provides one attempt to record and preserve what "readers wrote in their books, and . . . [the] pictures, letters, flowers, locks of hair, and other things [left] between their pages." The project was begun as "many books [particularly those printed between 1820 and 1923] are in danger of being discarded as libraries go digital." The site captures images of hundreds of books that have been written and drawn in, with attached postcards and bookplates, surveying the rich history of how we inhabit books. In addition to preserving records of uniquely marked books, the booktraces project hopes to raise awareness about the risk of losing an important part of our cultural heritage, given that books tell us not only about the history of their making but also about their use. Books that are out of copyright, but not scarce enough to be very valuable, are sometimes discarded or removed to off-site storage by librarians who reason that they are available in digital form. But a digital surrogate reproduces only one copy of a book, so when other copies of the book are discarded, much copy-specific information is lost. This practice offers yet another example of the limitations of the supersessional model of media change and of its implications for the preservation of old media.[22]

In 2004, when Google announced it would begin digitizing the collections of five major research libraries in the US and the UK, the project was met with what Robert Darnton has described as "utopian enthusiasm."[23] Kevin Kelly expressed this view, imagining, in 2006, that "all the books in the world" would "become a single liquid fabric of interconnected words and ideas," realizing the ancient dream of a universal **library**.[24] Such projects seemed to offer the possibility that, with improved access to knowledge, its production and dissemination could be both democratized and accelerated. However, the Internet, as Anthony Grafton reminds us (*BRBH* 555–73), will not bring us anything like a universal library. Several kinds of books are underrepresented in Google Books: very valuable early books, which would be expensive and difficult to scan; books published beyond the West and in languages other than English; books subject to copyright; as well as anything that could be considered pornographic. This makes it hard to use the Google Books database to research certain topics. In addition, because Google Books and other databases like it are proprietary, the policies and practices that produced them are not made public, so assessing their accuracy, reliability, and scope is difficult. For all these reasons, according to Grafton, large-scale digitization projects "will result not in the infotopia that the prophets conjure up, but in one more in a series of new information ecologies, all of them challenging, in which readers, writers, and producers of text have learned to survive and flourish" (559).

Computer-Assisted Reading

For all their flaws, these digital resources provide very powerful tools for research, and they are transforming our ways of reading. In some respects, large full-text databases speed up traditional modes of reading and research without fundamentally altering them. For example, databases allow queries about the origin of a quotation to be answered in seconds using keyword searching, where they might previously have demanded hours in the library looking through printed books. They make it possible to find all the occasions on which a poet used a particular word. In the past, this would have required using a printed **concordance**, but concordances were compiled only for major poets. In these ways, then, databases make some of the tasks of traditional scholarship much easier.

Machine-assisted reading is not, however, just a faster version of regular reading. Instead, it makes it possible to detect patterns in texts that unassisted readers would not notice. Stephen Ramsay has pioneered what he calls "algorithmic criticism": a form of hermeneutics that uses computational tools, in his words, to "enable critical engagement, interpretation, conversation, and contemplation."[25] Stylometry is another machine-assisted method of reading which uses computation and statistics to attribute texts whose authorship is contested or unknown by comparing linguistic features in the text in question to a **corpus** of texts by a known author. Using these techniques, scholars have attempted to attribute works to Shakespeare, and to attribute certain numbers of the federalist papers to one, or more, of the American Founding Fathers known to have authored some of the papers.[26] Stylometry's findings have rarely been definitive, however, and are often subject to dispute, a reminder that computational methods supply results that must then be interpreted, not ready-made conclusions.[27]

Another application of machine-assisted reading is a field called corpus stylistics, which uses the tools of corpus linguistics to study literature. A classic example is J.F. Burrows's 1987 analysis of the speech patterns of Jane Austen's characters, *Computation into Criticism: A Study of Jane Austen's Novels*.[28] By using statistical methods to analyse the speech patterns using only the frequency with which characters use the most common words in the language—words such as "the," "of," "it," and "I"—Burrows demonstrates that Austen's characters use highly distinctive idiolects. His computational analysis of these words reveals patterns not obvious to most readers, as these patterns of usage lie below the threshold of what even an attentive reader can perceive. Burrow's findings present strong evidence for Austen's stylistic mastery in creating character speech. They also uncover patterns by comparing the idiolects of characters across the novels, which, when supplemented by Burrows's skillful close reading, provide rich insights into the meaning of the six novels.

These techniques offer new ways to approach a corpus of text—such as the works of Shakespeare, or the federalist papers, or the novels of Jane Austen—that a researcher has already read in the traditional way. But large full-text databases also offer the possibility of "reading" far more books than any individual or team of researchers could possibly read. Some scholars are now using computational methods borrowed from other disciplines to "read" and analyze large corpora of textual material, including thousands or tens of thousands of volumes. One such method is topic modelling, a technique that automatically identifies groups of words that tend to occur together ("collocate") in a large collection of documents.[29] Other methods include basic keyword searches (to track the emergence and disappearance of certain words over time), searches for the most distinctive words (that is, words that are distinctive to a given corpus); and analysis of the most common words, which is typically used in author attribution but also successfully deployed in literary analysis.

Employing these techniques calls into question what counts as "reading" in the humanities. Franco Moretti has been at the forefront of a movement to abandon the practices of literary "close reading"—at least temporarily—in favour of what he terms "distant reading." By using quantitative and statistical methods drawn from the social sciences, as well as other practices for visualizing large amounts of data, Moretti and others have initiated a "quantitative turn" in the humanities. In *Graphs, Maps, Trees: Abstract Models for Literary History* (2005), Moretti claims that the problem with literary history lies with its methods of close reading, described as "detailed and precise attention to rhetoric, style, language choice, and so forth through a word-by-word examination of a text's linguistic techniques" (Hayles, *BRBH* 494). Close reading, Moretti implies, necessitates a very small **canon** of literary works that is in no way representative of what was actually written and read during a given period. His examination of national bibliographies reinforced for him

> what a minimal fraction of the literary field we all work on: a canon of two hundred novels, for instance, sounds very large for nineteenth-century Britain (and *is* much larger than the current one), but is still less than one per cent of the novels that were actually published: twenty thousand, thirty, more, no one really knows—and close reading won't help here, a novel a day every day of the year would take a century or so... And it is not even a matter of time, but of method: a field this large cannot be understood by stitching together separate bits of knowledge about individual cases, because it *isn't* a sum of individual cases: it's a collective system, that should be grasped as a such, as a whole....[30]

Moretti suggests that humanists adopt models from the natural and social sciences—graphs from quantitative history, maps from geography, and trees from evolutionary theory—in order to grasp what he calls the "collective system . . . as a whole."[31]

In his essay "Style, Inc. Reflections on Seven Thousand Titles (British Novels, 1740–1850)" (*BRBH* 525–40), Moretti examines the titles of 7,000 novels published in Britain between 1740 and 1850. Such a large dataset allows him "to see a larger literary field" (530). In his analysis, Moretti detects certain patterns: for example, as the market for novels increased over the period he studies, the length of most titles (as measured by the number of words) dropped dramatically, whereas the number of titles with only one, two, or three words increased rapidly. He proceeds: "That titles became short is interesting, yes, but in the end, So what?" (534). This is one of the key questions that pervades quantitative and computational approaches to literary scholarship. Moretti's answer is that titles moved away from summarizing a book's contents to labelling it with an abstraction. This move signifies "a perceptual shift which has persisted for 200 years" (534). That titles went from very long descriptions of the contents to distillations of them was a development that, Moretti claims, reflects the commodification of the novel itself: titles "compress meaning; and as they do that, they develop special 'signals' to place books in the right market niche" (535).

Images present their own set of problems for any method of distant reading. Lev Manovich addresses this issue when he considers "How to Compare One Million Images?" Here, he confronts the problem of analysing visual cultural data, such as photographs, designs, or video, which may number in the hundreds of thousands, millions, or billions.[32] Manovich and his team use computational methods to help detect patterns and relations within huge data sets, such as the corpus of over one million page images taken from Manga comics. Like Moretti, Manovich questions traditional methods in the humanities: "The fact that using tiny samples has been a default method of humanities until now does not mean that we should keep using it forever."[33] Manovich uses computational methods to process and interpret visual data, by combining automatic digital-image analysis to measure a number of visual characteristics with media visualization. Manovich claims that we no longer have to choose "one scale of analysis" but rather are "able to easily traverse between all of them at will, observing patterns at any scale."[34]

These techniques are often advertised as "new" and "revolutionary" by their advocates, and they sometimes provoke anxiety and suspicion among traditional humanists, who fear that something valuable is being lost. But perhaps computer-enhanced forms of reading are better understood as the latest and most technologically advanced in a long line of practices for breaking apart texts and reassembling them in new forms. What digital humanists do with their software may be a new, computer-assisted version of what fifteenth-century humanists did with the bookwheel, a machine that allowed you to have several books open before you at once, moving between them by turning the wheel to read "across" several books as well as "within" any one of them. Or we might see topic modelling as a new version of what seventeenth-century thinkers did with **commonplace books**, into which they copied excerpts from the books they read and arrayed them under a variety of topical headings. Or we might see parallels between the snippet view that Google Books offers of some copyrighted books and the slips of paper that eighteenth-century readers often cut out of books and magazines with their scissors and pasted into scrapbooks. In all these ways, the history of books and reading provides us with a long historical perspective on the new digital techniques for reading and interpreting books.

Notes

1. Sven Birkerts, *The Gutenberg Elegies: The Fate of Reading in an Electronic Age* (London: Faber, 1994); David Ulin, *The Lost Art of Reading: Why Books Matter in a Distracted Time* (Seattle: Sasquatch, 2010); Nicholas Carr, *The Shallows: How the Internet Is Changing the Way We Read, Think, and Remember* (London: Atlantic, 2011).
2. Oscar Wilde, *The Picture of Dorian Gray*, ed. Norman Page (Peterborough, ON: Broadview P, 1998), 161.
3. Matthew G. Kirschenbaum, *Mechanisms: New Media and the Forensic Imagination* (Cambridge, MA: MIT P, 2008).
4. Alan Galey, "The Enkindling Reciter: E-Books in the Bibliographical Imagination," *Book History* 15 (2012): 210–47.
5. Kirschenbaum, *passim*.
6. Leah Price, ed., *Unpacking My Library: Writers and Their Books* (New Haven, CT: Yale UP, 2011), 1.
7. Walter Benjamin discusses this in his essay "'On Unpacking My Library': A Talk about Book Collecting," *Illuminations*, ed. Hannah Arendt, trans. Harry Zohn (New York: Schocken, 1978), 59–68.
8. "Amazon Introduces Two New Kindles," *Businesswire* 17 September 2014, http://www.businesswire.com/news/home/20140917006456/en/Amazon-Introduces-All-New-Kindles.

CHAPTER 5 • REMEDIATING

9   See the original Kindle announcement, "Kindle: Amazon's Original Wireless Reading Device," http://www.amazon.com/Kindle-Amazons-Wireless-Reading-Device/dp/B000FI73MA.
10 For more information about this art project, see Jesse England, "Project: E-book backup," http://jesseengland.net/index.php?/project/e-book-backup/.
11 The project was shown at Denny Gallery in New York City in the summer of 2015. For more information, see "Print Wikipedia," *Wikipedia*, https://en.wikipedia.org/wiki/Print_Wikipedia.
12 See "The Complete Prose Edition of T.S. Eliot: The Critical Edition," *Project Muse*, http://muse.jhu.edu/about/reference/eliot/.
13 See, for example, Juxta, a collation tool that exists in an older, downloadable version (http://www.juxtasoftware.org/download/) and an online version (http://juxtacommons.org/).
14 *Transcribe Bentham: A Participatory Initiative*, University College London, http://www.ucl.ac.uk/transcribe-bentham.
15 Blogs have been published in print editions, however, as have Twitter novels.
16 This edition, moreover, has been designed for use on Apple products—iPads, iPhones, and Mac computers—thus limiting its accessibility.
17 See Alice Robb, "92 Percent of College Students Prefer Reading Print Books to E-Readers," *New Republic* 14 January 2015, https://newrepublic.com/article/120765/naomi-barons-words-onscreen-fate-reading-digital-world.
18 Qtd. in Robb.
19 Birkerts xiv.
20 See Andrew Piper, "Out of Touch: E-reading Isn't Reading," *Slate* 15 November 2012, http://www.slate.com/articles/arts/culturebox/2012/11/reading_on_a_kindle_is_not_the_same_as_reading_a_book.html.
21 See the digital versions of Shakespeare quartos at *Treasures in Full: Shakespeare in Quarto*, British Library, http://www.bl.uk/treasures/shakespeare/homepage.html.
22 Nicholson Baker, in *Double Fold: Libraries and the Assault on Paper* (London: Vintage, 2002), reported on the sale, donation, and destruction of large quantities of vintage newspapers by UK libraries.
23 Robert Darnton, *The Case for Books: Past, Present, and Future* (New York: Public Affairs, 2009), 15.
24 Qtd. in Darnton 17.
25 Stephen Ramsay, *Reading Machines: Toward an Algorithmic Criticism* (Chicago: U of Illinois P, 2011), x.
26 For a survey of some of these examples, see MacDonald Pairman Jackson, *Defining Shakespeare: Pericles as Test Case* (Oxford: Oxford UP, 2003), 107–09, and Joseph Rudman, "The Twelve Disputed 'Federalist' Papers: A Case for Collaboration," DH2012, http://www.dh2012.uni-hamburg.de/conference/programme/abstracts/the-twelve-disputed-federalist-papers-a-case-for-collaboration.1.html.

27 See Leighton Evans and Sian Rees, "An Interpretation of Digital Humanities," *Understanding Digital Humanities*, ed. David Berry (Basingstoke: Palgrave Macmillan, 2012), 27.
28 J.F. Burrows, *Computation into Criticism: A Study of Jane Austen's Novels* (Oxford: Clarendon, 1987).
29 See Ted Underwood, "Topic Modeling Made Just Simple Enough," *The Stone and the Shell: Using Large Digital Libraries to Advance Literary History*, 7 April 2012, http://tedunderwood.com/2012/04/07/topic-modeling-made-just-simple-enough/.
30 Franco Moretti, *Graphs, Maps, Trees: Abstract Models for Literary History* (London: Verso, 2005), 3–4; emphasis and ellipsis in original.
31 Moretti 4.
32 Lev Manovich, "How to Compare One Million Images?," Berry 249–78.
33 Manovich 252.
34 Manovich 253.

CONCLUSION

This is a book about books. But books, as we've tried to show, take lots of forms: rolls of papyrus inscribed with hieroglyphics or hieratic script on the banks of the Nile, in the shadow of half-built pyramids, over four thousand years ago; scrolls of parchment written in Hebrew and Aramaic two thousand years ago and hidden in desert caves at Qumran on the shores of the Dead Sea; a Buddhist sutra printed with carved wooden blocks in China twelve hundred years ago; books of hours inscribed by monks on vellum and illuminated with gold in Europe seven hundred years ago; a bible printed on paper made from rags and bound into a folio codex in the fifteenth century by Johann Gutenberg; a poor-quality quarto of one of Shakespeare's plays, published without its author's permission in London in the 1590s; a chapbook carried by a pedlar crossing the country on foot in the eighteenth century; a three-volume novel in octavo, printed on paper made from wood pulp in the nineteenth century and shipped from London to British India; a paperback detective novel in a pocket-sized format, sold in a nineteenth-century railway station or a twentieth-century airport; an e-book read on a smartphone in a twenty-first-century café. The book can be all of these and more, and book history can study it in whatever form it takes. The book is not one thing: it's a shape-shifter that adapts with alacrity to new technologies, new markets, and new consumer demands.

But whatever form books take—and whatever form they may take in the future—they live a double life. They circulate, promulgate, and preserve words and images by giving them a particular material existence. Book historians pay attention to the duality of the book, regarding it as at once material and immaterial. On the one hand, books are material things. Made with papyrus, vellum or paper, with glue, leather, and ink, with microchips, circuit boards, and moulded plastic, they exist in the world and are subject to the ravages of time. They take up space. They can be attacked by worms, burnt in house fires, or dropped in the bath. On the other hand, books contain texts, and these texts can migrate from one vehicle and one medium to another. The works that books circulate can be recited, memorized, copied by hand, reprinted, and now digitized, and all of these acts can enable the survival of a written work far beyond the existence of a single material book. Book history insists that these two dimensions of the book—the material and the linguistic—are entwined. It asserts that the material form of the book is an integral part of how the book constructs its meanings. It refuses to treat the text simply as "content" and the book that contains it simply as "vehicle." Instead, it invests its efforts in understanding their unique entwinement. This double life of books explains in large part their unique history and our long fascination with them.

Books need readers, and studying the production, circulation, and reception of books also means thinking about reading. Just like books, reading takes many forms and serves many purposes. A monk in his cell might practice *lectio divina*, a form of devotional reading. A scholar preparing an edition might read two texts of a work side by side to collate the variants between them, or use a collation machine to mechanize the process. A pupil cramming for an exam might skim-read a textbook in search of information. A novel-reader might weep over the fate of a favourite character. The reader of a political tract might scribble agreement or disagreement in its margins. A student might copy passages into a Google doc to share with a classmate. A parent might read aloud to her children, or a lover to his betrothed. A digital humanist might convert a text into a machine-readable format to allow for word searching and topic modelling. And reading isn't the only thing we do with books. Given as gifts, displayed on shelves, used to screen ourselves from other people when we don't want to talk, repurposed to decorate pubs, taken apart to wrap food, or cut up to make book sculptures, books have a complex social and aesthetic life quite apart from how they are read.

Questions about reading are also inseparable from questions about who owns books and who has access to them. Children writing their names in the front of their schoolbooks know this, as they declare their ownership over this particular copy. So do librarians, as they decide which books to purchase (a particularly fraught task in an era of shrinking budgets) and how best to make them available to the library's users. So do religious or political censors, as they produce lists of books to be banned or restricted. Book history, then, also entails studying the circulation of books. The ledgers of a publisher, recording sales figures and advertising costs, can tell us something about the popularity of different books and their marketing. The archive of a library, recording purchases and borrowings, can inform us about the circulation of books in a particular community. The catalogue of an auction house selling someone's private library can reveal what books that person owned and, sometimes, who bought those books next. The proceedings of a court, recording actions brought for libel or injunctions sought against copyright infringement, can provide evidence of efforts to restrict the circulation of certain texts. Understanding the material infrastructure, social codes, professional protocols, and legal frameworks that enabled or restricted the distribution, storage, classification, and circulation of books gives us insights into who read what and when.

Books, we have argued, are produced, circulated, and consumed alongside other media. We have attempted to situate the book within this much broader media ecology. Now—especially if we're reading on an Internet-enabled device—we commonly turn aside from our books to look at images, videos, or news reports. We're used to the versioning of works, for example when the novel that appeared in the UK as *Harry Potter and the Philosopher's Stone* was retitled *Harry Potter and the Sorcerer's Stone* for the US market, with many textual differences designed to make the book suitable for these different audiences, or when, in both markets, it was published simultaneously in editions aimed at children and at adult readers. And we're accustomed to seeing works remediated into different media, for example when that novel was adapted for the big screen. We debate the movement of texts and images between media all the time—as they migrate from a book to a film, from a comic book to a videogame (or the reverse)—even though we don't always recognize that these are precisely the kinds of questions raised by an attentiveness to the affordances of different media. These practices of intermediality, versioning, and remediation have a long history. Cultural consumers in earlier times and in a variety of places consumed books omnivorously among a range of media. They turned freely from their books to printed, painted, and drawn images; to the theatre, concert hall, ballet, and opera, and later the radio, cinema, and television; to conducting conversations and writing letters. And this range of media, in turn, reappeared in their books, as the book became an important medium for discussions of art and performance, as well as for discussions of the concept of media itself. The book has always been produced and consumed in relation to other media.

Understanding the place of the book in the media ecology also helps us to situate it in the history of media change. Rejecting an earlier model of media supersession—in which print replaced manuscript and is now being replaced in turn by digital text—we have drawn attention to the ways in which media co-exist. When print first arrived, it did not kill off manuscript; in fact, early print emulated manuscript and stimulated more of its production. Similarly, the latest and most expensive version of Amazon's

CONCLUSION

Kindle e-reader, called the Kindle Oasis, attempts to mimic many of the features of a printed codex and is specifically targeted at book lovers.[1] "New" media don't simply supersede "old" media, although changes in the media ecology do give new inflections to the cultural significance of existing media. Claims about the "death" of the book in the digital age miss this point. Once we consider how the book has navigated moments of media change in the past, we can develop a more sophisticated understanding of our current moment of media change. We now live in an interactive, multimodal, networked mediascape. In order to engage with it critically, we need to understand its genealogy in the history of the book. Opera-goers who followed printed libretti and young women who copied poems from printed books into manuscript albums made print an interactive medium. Gallery visitors who sketched in their printed catalogues and readers who cut printed images from books, pasted them into scrapbooks, and wrote poems underneath created multimedia hybrids of script and print, image and text. Members of salons who used a printed text to structure their conversations and then turned those conversations into print, or courting couples who annotated books for one another—as John Keats did for Fanny Brawne—made the printed codex into a social-media object. The history of the book is more compelling now than ever because it illuminates the genealogy of our contemporary media disruptions. The history of the book is the history of the present.

This is, therefore, a particularly good time to study book history. We hope that, in our attempt to distil many of the key ideas and synthesize some of the central questions that animate the field, we have conveyed our enthusiasm for the exciting work that has been and is being done, by book historians but also in the intersecting fields of media theory, digital humanities, and textual scholarship. The history of the book continues to offer new and unexpected discoveries. In just the last few years, previously unknown copies of the First Folio of Shakespeare's plays have turned up. In 2014, a copy missing its title page was identified in a library in Saint-Omer, France, where it had lain unknown for centuries.[2] In 2016 another copy was identified in an aristocratic house on the Isle of Bute, off the western coast of Scotland. This one had been split into three and bound in separate volumes for tragedies, comedies, and histories, making the volumes easier to handle.[3] No doubt other surprises from the past lie in wait for the book historians of the future. An introduction like this cannot offer a comprehensive guidebook tracing all the byways of book history and the many interesting sights you can take in along the way, but we have aimed to provide a map for the journey. As we survey our current moment of media change, we can see that book history offers not only a journey into the past, but one that takes us into the future as well.

Notes

1   Will Oremus, "Amazon's Quixotic Quest," *Slate* 13 April 2016, http://www.slate.com/articles/technology/technology/2016/04/amazon_says_the_kindle_oasis_is_an_e_reader_for_book_lovers_is_it.html.
2   Kim Willsher, "Shakespeare First Folio Found in French Library," *Guardian* 25 November 2014, http://www.theguardian.com/culture/2014/nov/25/shakespeare-first-folio-found-in-french-library.
3   Russell Cheyne, "Rare Shakespeare First Folio Found on Scottish Island," *CBC News*, 7 April 2016, http://www.cbc.ca/news/arts/shakespeare-first-folio-scotland-1.3524723.

The History of the Book: A Brief Chronology

BCE

c. 3500	Sumerians use cuneiform alphabet, pressed in clay with a triangular stylus.
c. 2500	Animal skins are used for scrolls in Western Asia.
c. 2400	**Earliest surviving papyrus scrolls with writing.**
c. 650	Papyrus scroll introduced into Greece from Egypt.
c. 250	Chinese shift from writing on bamboo to writing on silk.
c. 300	**Library of Alexandria, the largest library known to have existed, was founded.**
c. 196	Rosetta Stone is cut; it contains same text in Egyptian hieroglyphic, Egyptian demotic, and Greek.
c. 150	**The first paper is made in China from hemp and water.**
c. 150 BCE– 40 CE	Creation of the "Dead Sea Scrolls," Hebrew and Aramaic documents, biblical and non-biblical, found near the Dead Sea in 1957.

CE

39	First public library established in Rome at the Libertas Temple.
47	The Library of Alexandria was damaged by fire when the city was besieged by Julius Caesar.
c. 150–450	**Manuscript book gradually shifts from scroll to codex.**
c. 300–700	Shift in West from papyrus to parchment.
391	Library of Alexandria destroyed under the direction of Archbishop Theophilus of Antioch.
c. 400–600	In the West, many manuscripts are destroyed and the production of new manuscripts slows dramatically.
610	Papermaking introduced into Japan from China.
c. 750–800	Papermaking reaches Central Asia and Middle East.
868	**First dated book made by block-printing is the *Diamond Sutra* published in China; it also includes one of the oldest colophons.**

896		Oldest known manuscript colophon, in Books of the Prophets written by Moses ben Asher in Tibet.
1041		**First book printed in China from moveable type.**
1119		Printing in clay using stamped individual carved wooden Roman square capitals into clay on the Prüfening dedicatory inscription, possibly the first use of the typographic principle in Europe.
c. 13th		In Italy, the production of books moved from monastic scriptoria to civilian professional scribes in cities.
1276		Watermarked paper introduced in Tuscany at Fabriano Mills, also the first paper mill in Italy.
1338		Oldest known paper mill in France.
1373		Bibliothèque nationale founded in Lyons, France.
1377		*Jikji, Selected Teachings of Buddhist Sages and Seon Masters*, the world's earliest-known book printed with moveable metal type, was printed in Korea.
1403		Guild of Stationers founded in London.
1418		Earliest extant example of woodblock printing in Europe.
1454		**Gutenberg prints indulgences on lead-based moveable type in Mainz, the earliest known European book printed by moveable type.**
1456		Gutenberg prints 42-line Bible.
1457		Mainz Psalter published by Fust and Schoffer: first extant book printed with moveable type with colophon and color printing.
1465		Cicero's *De oratore*, believed to be the first printed book, published in Subiaco, Italy.
1465		First drypoint engravings made in Germany by the Master of the Housebook.
1470		Ulrich Gering establishes first printing press in Paris.
1477		First book with intaglio illustrations, *Il Monte Sancto di Dio*, published in Florence.
1486		Caxton prints his first book in Westminster, England.
1493		First books with etchings published in Germany and Switzerland.
1495		John Tate establishes first English paper mill in Hertfordshire.

1498	Ottaviano Petrucci of Venice develops types for printing music.
1534	Cambridge University Press founded; first book printed 1583.
1536–41	**Henry VIII disbands the monasteries and seizes the books and manuscripts, many of which are lost or destroyed.**
1539	First North American Press established in Mexico City; and first North American book, *La escala espiritual de San Juan Clímaco*, is published.
1557	London Stationers' Company granted royal charter.
1575	First North American paper mill, in Mexico City.
1605	German-language *Relation aller Fürnemmen und gedenckwürdigen Historien* recognized as the first newspaper; over the next few decades, newspapers quickly followed in other European and British cities.
1626	First facsimile edition by Plantin, sixteenth-century *Martyrologium Hieronymianum* (engraved on copper plates).
1640	First printed book in British North America, *Bay Psalm Book*, published in Cambridge, Massachusetts.
c. 1660	First known mezzotint, "The Grand Executioner," by Prince Rupert, c. 1660; process invented c. 1640 by Ludwig von Siegen.
1653	First North American public library founded in Boston.
1662	**Licensing Act establishes legal copyright and codifies practice of deposit library in England.**
1683–84	Joseph Moxon publishes *Mechanick Exercises on the Whole Art of Printing*, the earliest printing manual.
1690	First Paper mill in America, near Germantown, Pennsylvania.
1694	Licensing Act of 1662 expires.
1702	***The Daily Courant**, the first British daily newspaper, published in London.*
1705	***The Boston News-Letter**, the first continuously published newspaper in British North America.*
1710	**The Statute of Anne, the first copyright law in England and the world, limits the terms of copyright protection in England to 14 years, with the possibility of extending another 14 years.**

1725	William Ged invents the stereotype in London.	
1734	Aquatint process invented by Jean-Baptiste Le Prince.	
c. 1740	James Whatman makes first-known wove paper in Maidstone, England.	
1746–73	Johnson's *Dictionary of the English Language* published.	
1752	Publication of the first Canadian newspaper, *Halifax Gazette*.	
1753	British Library founded.	
1774	*Donaldson v. Beckett*, a decision of the British House of Lords, denies the existence of perpetual copyright and holds it to be a creation of statute.	
1788	First press imported to Australia.	
1790	The first US federal Copyright Act grants copyright for a term of 14 years with the possibility of another 14 years renewal.	
1793	France sets copyright protection for ten years after author's death.	
1798–99	Louis-Nicolas Robert patents the first paper-making machine.	
1798	Alois Senefelder invents lithography.	
1799	Rosetta Stone discovered near the mouth of the Nile and is used to break the code for deciphering ancient Egyptian works.	
1800	Library of Congress founded.	
1800	**Charles Stanhope, third Earl Stanhope, builds the first cast-iron press; they quickly replace wood presses.**	
1803	**Henry and Sealy Fourdrinier buy patent for Robert paper-making machine, the basis for the Fourdrinier machine.**	
1802–18	Friedrich Koenig develops the first steam-powered cylinder press.	
1814	*The Times* (of London) uses the Koenig cylindrical press for the first time; it is capable of printing 1,000 impressions per hour.	
1822	William Church patents the first typesetting machine.	
1829	William Austin Burt invents the typographer, a predecessor to the modern typewriter.	
1833	**Daguerreotype, the earliest photographic process, invented by Louis Jacques-Mandé Daguerre.**	

THE HISTORY OF THE BOOK: A BRIEF CHRONOLOGY

1837	Chromolithography, a process allowing multi-color printing, is developed by Godefroy Engelmann in France.
1838	Moritz von Jacobi develops an electrotype process, first used for reproducing illustrations and later for moveable type and illustrations.
1841	Tauchnitz Verlag publishes the first paperback editions in Germany.
1840s	**The use of wood to make pulp for paper begins in Germany.**
1851	Microphotography first suggested as a means of document preservation.
1853	Mechanically processed wood pulp used for paper making in England.
1860s	Pencils and erasers began to be mass-produced.
1863	The rotary perfecting press, invented by William Bullock, is capable of printing 10,000 double-sided sheets per hour.
1867	**The first commercially successful typewriter is invented in Milwaukee.**
1874	Chemically produced wood pulp (using sulfite) is introduced for paper making in Sweden.
1878	Remington introduces typewriter featuring shift key for upper-case letters.
1886	Ottmar Mergenthaler invents Linotype hot metal composing machine, used by the *New York Tribune*.
1886	**Berne Convention establishes international reciprocity of copyright protection.**
1890	Edinburgh Bibliographical Society founded, followed by the Bibliographical Society of London (1892) and of America, founded in New York in 1904.
1935	**IBM markets Electromatic, first successful electric typewriter.**
1938	Chester F. Carlson invents xerography.
1940	**Laszlo Biro invents the ballpoint pen.**
1942	The first electronic digital computing device, Atanasoff-Berry Computer (ABC), used to solve linear equations.
1946	ENIAC (Electronic Numerical Integrator and Computer) was the first general-purpose electronic computer.

1951	First inkjet printers sold by Siemens.
1955	Universal Copyright Convention establishes another system of international copyright protection than the Berne for signatory nations.
1959	Xerox markets first xerographic photocopier.
1967	OCLC (Online Computer Library Center, Inc.) produces Worldcat, the largest public access catalogue (now online).
1969	MARC (Machine-Readable Cataloging), is the first known use of metadata.
1969	ARPANET, the precursor to the Internet, was developed in Southern California.
1972	Stephen Dorsey, of Automatic Electronic Systems (AES), introduces the world's first programmable word processor with a video screen.
1976	IBM introduces the first commercial laser printer, the IBM 3800.
1977	**First commercial sales of personal computers (Commodore PET and Apple II).**
1991	**The World Wide Web, invented and developed by Tim Berners-Lee, is publicly launched.**
1993	Adobe launches the PDF (portable document format), a file format that represents a document independent of hardware, software, and operating systems.
1994	Jeff Bezos founds Amazon.com.
1996	**XML (Extensible Markup Language) is developed.**
1998	**Google, now the world's most widely used web-based search engine, uses the PageRank algorithm.**
2001	Wikipedia, an online, open-source, crowd-sourced encyclopedia is launched; by 2014, it is estimated that if Wikipedia were printed, it would comprise over one million pages.
2003	3D printing machines, the process of making three-dimensional objects from a digital file, begin to be used and sold.
2003	*Deep Love*, the first cell-phone novel, is published by a Japanese man, writing under the pen-name "Yoshi."
2004	Google announces Google Print project, now known as Google Books.

2004	Sony Librie, the first modern e-reader, is released.
2005	More than 300,000,000 copies of J.K. Rowling's *Harry Potter* series are printed worldwide.
2007	Amazon's Kindle is released.
2009	According to Amazon.com, sales of Kindle e-books surpass print books for the first time during the Christmas season.
2009	Apple introduces ibookstore; one year later, they announce that over 100,000,000 ibooks (Apple's name for ebooks) have been downloaded in the previous year.
2010	Apple introduces the iPad.
2010	The University of Texas at San Antonio's Applied Engineering and Technology Library is possibly the first library to contain no physical books.
2010	Google books has scanned more than 15 million books since its inception, six years earlier.
2012	After 80 years in print as one of the world's most recognizable magazines, *Newsweek* issues its last print edition.
2013	*Newsweek* announces it will continue to produce its print edition, in response to demands from loyal print readers.

Glossary

This glossary is designed to help you understand specialist terms used in this book, but it is by no means a comprehensive guide to terminology used in bibliography, printing history, or textual scholarship. For fuller information, please consult the following reference works:

- John Carter and Nicolas Barker, *ABC for Book Collectors*, 8th ed. (New Castle, DE: Oak Knoll P, 2004).
- Geoffrey Ashall Glaister, *Encyclopedia of the Book*, 2nd ed. (New Castle, DE: Oak Knoll P, 2001).
- *OED* Online (Oxford University Press).
- Philip Gaskell, *A New Introduction to Bibliography* (New Castle, DE: Oak Knoll P, 2000).
- Elizabeth H. Thompson, *A.L.A. Glossary of Library Terms* (Chicago: American Library Association, 1943).

Accidentals / Substantives

W.W. Greg describes these two types of variants that can exist between two texts of a work. Accidentals are details that don't affect the meaning of the text, such as variant spellings. Substantives are details that do affect the meaning, such as variant words. Punctuation and capitalization may or may not be substantive, depending on whether they change the meaning. Where an author's manuscript is lost, Greg suggests that editors should choose an early text of the work as their copy-text and follow it in accidentals, since these are likely to follow the manuscript. He thinks editors should consider emending the text to include substantive variants in later editions, where these are likely to reflect the author's revisions. In each case, editors must distinguish between variants that arise from the author's revisions and those that arise from mistakes made in the process of printing.

Analytical bibliography (see **Bibliography**)

Anthology
A published collection of writings (which may be excerpts, or short works in their entirety) by multiple authors.

Archive
A collection of historical or public documents, or the building in which these are housed; also used as a term for scientific or academic periodicals from the early eighteenth century.

Authorial intention
Texts of any kind don't simply mean what their authors intended them to mean. In 1946, literary critics W.K. Wimsatt and Monroe Beardsley inaugurated the modern era of skepticism about the relevance of authorial intent for literary interpretation in their article "The Intentional Fallacy." Authorial intent is, however, a key concept for some methods of textual editing. Some editors want to identify the words that the author intended to write, and to distinguish them from errors that have crept into the text and/or modifications introduced by others without the author's consent. Thomas Tanselle distinguishes between three kinds of authorial intention; the most important for textual editors is "active intention," or the intention formed in the process of writing to write one word rather than another. Authorial intentions are seldom stable or straightforward, so this concept remains a vexed one for textual scholars and literary critics alike.

Bibliography
Broadly, the study of books as material objects. **Descriptive bibliography** is primarily concerned with discerning and recording in detail the material properties of a document, including its size, format, collation (the arrangement of leaves that make up the book), and the presence or absence of title pages, errata slips, advertisement leaves, and other paratexts. Bibliographers record these details using a system of symbols and abbreviations. **Analytical (or critical) bibliography** uses this study, combined with knowledge of the history of printing, to establish the order in which editions were printed, the order in which pages within a book were printed, and the number of compositors and pressmen who worked on it. This information helps to resolve textual cruces, where editors need to decide which of two variant readings is more likely to reflect

the author's intentions. The use of bibliographical procedures to address textual or editorial problems is sometimes called "**New Bibliography**" to distinguish it from the older tradition of treating bibliography primarily as something of interest to collectors of rare books.

Bibliometry
The statistical study of books or other publications. Examples include counts of the titles issued by a publisher, the number of books published on different topics in a given period, and the number of times a given book or scholarly article has been cited by others.

Binder; Bindery; Binding (see **Bookbinding**)

Blackletter
The group of scripts that emerged in Europe in the twelfth century and formed the design for early printing types. (See also **Typography**.)

Bookbinding
The process through which printed or manuscript sheets are fastened together and enclosed in a cover, which may be made of materials such as leather, board, or cloth. A process distinct from printing, binding was undertaken by binders (their workshops being known as binderies), although some early printers either were also binders or worked systematically with specific binders. In England from about the sixteenth to the late eighteenth century, arranging for binding seems to have become the purview of booksellers who received works in sheets and then often offered both bound and unbound versions to customers; individualized and often decorative bindings could be a way for book purchasers to customize their books, and they may have purchased works in sheets and then worked with a preferred binder, especially in order to assure the uniformity of a collection. Different bindings could significantly affect the total cost of a book. Only from the nineteenth century on were books routinely sold in their bindings.

Bookseller (as opposed to publisher and printer)
The individual responsible for selling books to the public through a retail bookshop; some booksellers also sold books wholesale to other

GLOSSARY

booksellers. Until roughly the eighteenth century in England the roles of printer, publisher, and bookseller were not always clearly differentiated.

Broadside

A document printed on one side only of a single sheet of paper. Originally associated with political proclamations, they also became a mode of transmission for poetry and ballads, and can also be known as **broadsheets, street or stall ballads,** or **blackletter ballads** (due to the predominant use of blackletter type).

Cancel (n.)

A part of a book that is substituted for an original part with the aim of modification. Cancels can range in size from a square containing a single letter to several sheets; perhaps most common is the leaf inserted where another leaf containing errors has been cut out. Motivations for inserting a cancel may include the rectification of printer's errors as well as last-minute changes, additions, and deletions.

Canon (adj. canonical)

A body of texts agreed, by general consensus, to have merit and to be worthy of regard and respect; also sometimes used to mean a group of texts firmly attributed to one author. In its non-literary implications, the term may also refer to ecclesiastical authority (for example, canon law, which is the category of rules and regulations governing Christian churches).

Catalogue

A listing (either digital or physical) of books available for a given purpose; in the case of a library's catalogue, this purpose will be consultation and possibly circulation via lending, whereas in the case of a publisher's catalogue, the purpose will be sales.

Censorship

Censorship is the suppression of work that is deemed to be objectionable on political, religious, moral or other grounds, or on the grounds that its publication would compromise national security or endanger the safety of individuals. It may take the form of pre-publication censorship, in regimes that require works to be submitted for review before permitting their publication, or post-publication censorship, where authorities may require published works deemed objectionable to be withdrawn from circulation. Authors and publishers may also engage in self-censorship, moderating or changing their works to avoid adverse reactions.

Chapbook
Small, cheap, paperbound pamphlet or book containing a popular tale, legend, poem, ballad, often of moral or educational character, usually illustrated with a woodcut and distributed by hawkers or chapmen, not booksellers. Since about 1830, the term has been used as a conscious anachronism.

Circulating library
Established in the latter part of the seventeenth century and most likely originating with booksellers in London, circulating libraries were privately owned, commercial libraries; readers paid a subscription, and in some cases also a small fee, for each book borrowed. Circulating libraries carried a variety of works but were especially important in the circulation of three-volume novels. In the nineteenth century, Mudie's circulating library routinely purchased a large proportion of the total print run of new novels. (See also **Library**.)

Circulation
Describes the process by which manuscript, print, or oral texts are disseminated. Circulation can take place in more or less conventional ways; it can be narrow or broad; and it can take place across media (e.g., an orally recited poem might be remembered, and then hand-copied and distributed; a printed work could be read aloud; a manuscript could be printed; etc.). All forms of circulation involve the passing of texts between individuals.

Codex (pl. codices)
A document, either printed or in manuscript, in which multiple sheets are stacked, bound along a spine, and generally enclosed by a cover; i.e., the format of most modern books, as opposed to scrolls.

Collation

The physical makeup of a book, or a description of it for the purposes of comparison with other books. The description may be more or less detailed, but will typically contain information about the end-papers, title page(s), and the sheets from which the book is made, including how they are folded and stitched together to make the book. Collation also refers to the comparison and classification of the variant forms of a given text (these may be print or manuscript versions, or a combination of the two). The aim is to identify differences between the texts in which the work appears so as to clarify problems of interpretation, authentication, and textual history.

Colophon

Frequently used in early printed works, a colophon is a statement at the end of the main text giving particulars such as the title, subject of the work, the author, the publisher, the printer, and the date and place of publication. Sometimes found with the device, or imprint, of the printer or publisher and information about the typeface. Since the sixteenth century in England the colophon has been replaced by the title page; however, during the transition period the colophon and the title page were both in use, sometimes in contradiction with one another, when, for instance, a new title page was printed with an out-of-date colophon. The colophon is occasionally used in the present day, mostly in fine-press printing.

Commonplace book

A handwritten collection of extracts, usually compiled in a small notebook, chosen at the discretion of an individual, either as an aid to study or primarily on the basis of personal interest and pleasure, and transcribed by that same individual; may also include original compositions or other material.

Communications circuit

A model tracing the production and reception of books through various stages, first introduced by book historian Robert Darnton in 1982 (see Figure 3.2, p. 75).

Composition
The setting up of type. A compositor takes individual pieces of type from a type case and arranges them in a composing stick to form words and lines of text. The type is then transferred from the composing stick to a metal tray, where the lines of type form a page. Several pages are arranged ("imposed") and assembled into a type forme ready for printing on the handpress. (See also **Compositor**.)

Compositor
Craftsman who set up type by hand or machine, corrected machine-set compositions, made up and imposed pages, and assembled the type forme. (See also **Composition**.)

Concordance
An alphabetical index of the principal words in a work or group of works, showing their location in the text, usually giving context, and sometimes supplying a definition.

Copper engraving (see **Engraving**)

Copyright
Copyright is a legal right to reproduce in some form (print, performance, film, or record) a written, artistic, or musical work, within a defined geographical area. The first copyright law was the Statute of Anne, enacted in England in 1710. The first **international copyright** agreement, the Berne Convention, was passed in 1886; it protected the rights of creators in all countries who had signed the convention. Copyright initially rests with the creator of the work, but it can be transferred to a third party such as a publisher. Subsidiary rights, such as the right to publish translations or to adapt the work for film or television, may be governed by other legal agreements.

Copy-text (see **Edition**)

Corpus (pl. corpora)
Usually used to describe a large set of texts. A corpus of texts may now be stored in digital form and used in computational analysis.

GLOSSARY

Corruption
The introduction of errors into the text in the process of transmission, for example when a scribe copies a word incorrectly, or when a compositor misreads a manuscript when setting it in type.

Coterie
A small, select group of individuals, usually organized with social and/or intellectual aims. Coterie members often wrote texts for, and exchanged them with, other members of the group.

Critical bibliography (see **Bibliography**)

Descriptive bibliography (see **Bibliography**)

Digital literacy
The ability to find, navigate, evaluate, use, share, and create content using a range of digital technologies.

Diplomatic transcription (see **Edition**)

Duodecimo
A book printed on sheets folded to make twelve leaves or twenty-four pages. Commonly called a **twelvemo** (12mo, 12o). The size of the book will depend on the size of the sheets, but the large number of folds means that most duodecimos are small books, easily carried in a pocket. For this reason, duodecimo is a common format for prayer books. (See also **Format**.)

Eclectic edition (see **Edition**)

Edition
1) all the copies of a book printed from a single setting of type. In hand-press printing, the type is set to produce a book and then broken up and returned to the typecase for use in the next printing job. If the type is reset to print more copies (usually at a later date), then those copies form a new edition of the work. The number of copies of each edition printed is known as that edition's print run. The title page often includes the number of the edition, or words such as "a new edition."

These indicators, however, are not always reliable, since booksellers, printers, or publishers sometimes added a new title page to an existing edition, or deliberately misnumbered editions to give the impression that a work was selling very well.

2) a later printing, usually of a canonical work or historical document, prepared by an editor. These editions may be of several kinds. Most editions begin by identifying an early text of the work to use as the **copy-text** for the new edition. The editor may then choose to produce a **facsimile reprint** or **diplomatic transcription** of a copy-text, an **eclectic edition** that emends the copy-text to include variant readings found in other texts, a **variorum edition** that includes details of readings from all significant texts of the work, a **parallel text edition** that allows readers to compare two versions on facing pages, or another kind of edition. These choices will depend on the editor's understanding of editorial theory, the textual history of the work under consideration, and the intended audience of the edition.

Editor/Editing

Editing divides into pre- and post-publication editing. An **editor** is anyone who undertakes the editing of a text. The editor's role could be formal or informal; she might be a friend, relative, teacher, colleague, or a professional editor. Pre-publication **editing** involves making suggestions to the author for additions, excisions, revisions, and corrections. This can be done in any medium; for example, an editor might revise a text in manuscript; an author or editor might correct print proofs of a text prior to it being published in print; a compositor might make further corrections when setting type; and an author or reader might further revise a text after it is published, by adding revisions in handwriting to a copy of a printed text and/or issuing a new edition. Post-publication editing involves emending a text for a new edition of the work. The aim of such editing is usually (but not always) to reflect the author's intentions more precisely than earlier texts of the work have done.

Emendation

A correction or revision in a text, or the process of correcting/revising (i.e., making an emendation to a text).

Endpapers

The endpapers are sheets of paper that appear at the front and end of a bound book. The front endpaper consists of one half of the sheet pasted against an inside cover (the pastedown), and the other serving as the first free page (the flyleaf). Endpapers could be made with plain or decorated paper.

Engraving

Engraving is one of several techniques for producing printed images (and the chief reproductive method before the introduction of photography in the second half of the nineteenth century). The engraver scrapes lines into a copper plate with a sharp instrument called a burin, and then spreads ink over the plate and wipes the plate clean. Some ink remains in the grooves made by the burin. A sheet of paper is then laid on the plate and the whole thing is passed through a rotary press, which applies pressure and squeezes some of the ink out of the grooves and onto the paper. This process was used in Europe at least as early as the fourteenth century, and possibly even earlier, for playing cards and religious pictures. It produces high-quality images, but there are three limitations associated with it. First, the printing process is different from that used for letterpress text, which makes it difficult to combine text and image on a single page. Using woodcuts, where the image is cut into the end of a block of wood, allows images to be reproduced alongside text, as woodcuts and letterpress are both printed on the same kind of press. Second, the effort required to work the plate with the burin is considerable, and only the most highly accomplished engravers can produce a wide range of effects, such as shading. **Etching** reduces the effort involved in producing the plate and allows a wider range of effects: in etching, the plate is covered with wax or a similar material, and this wax is scraped away to reveal some areas of the surface of the plate. The plate is then immersed in acid, which eats into the exposed areas. It is then cleaned, inked, and printed in the same way as an engraving. Thirdly, since copper is fairly soft, the plate becomes damaged in the process of printing, which means that only a limited number of images can be produced from each plate. The use of steel plates in place of copper from the mid-nineteenth century onwards allowed larger numbers of impressions from each plate. In some discussions of printed images, "engraving" is used as an umbrella term for all these techniques, as well as a specific term for one of them.

Enumerative bibliography (see **Bibliography**)

Ephemera
Printed material of a transitory kind, not intended for preservation. Examples include tickets, labels, posters, and playbills.

Epistle
1) a letter from an apostle, for example St Paul, forming part of the New Testament.

2) letters regarded as literary works because of their elegant composition, sometimes written in poetry; collections of letters were made into manuals in the Middle Ages and had become a popular branch of rhetoric by the tenth century.

Errata
A list of typographical errors occurring in a book, along with corrections, also called corrigenda. If the prelims have not yet been completed, the errata are sometimes added to a spare page; otherwise they are printed on a slip or extra leaf and tipped in. When multi-volume books are published at intervals, later volumes sometimes contain lists of errata for the earlier. When errors are not detected until after publishing, only later copies may contain an errata slip or leaf, but since errata slips are prone to accidental detachment or omission, this makes it difficult to verify and poses a problem for collectors. In most cases the book is considered complete with an errata slip if the majority of copies have an errata slip, and vice versa.

Etching
The application of chemicals to a surface so as to either dissolve part of the material, creating a design (the other parts having been previously treated so as to be protected), or create different properties on that surface. (See also **Engraving**.)

Glossary

Extensive/Intensive reading

Whereas extensive reading involves reading widely among a larger body of texts with less sustained attention to any given one, intensive reading confines itself to a smaller body of texts that are the subject of careful study and repeated attention. Some historians of reading postulate a shift from intensive to extensive reading as books became cheaper and more widely available.

Facsimile

A copy or reproduction of a manuscript, printed book, map, etc. that attempts to replicate the original as closely as possible.

Fair Copy

A clear or legible manuscript copy, often one that incorporates revisions made on a previous copy.

Folio

A book printed on full-size sheets folded medially once, making two leaves or four pages. (See also **Format**.)

Format

The way in which printed sheets are folded and gathered together to form the leaves of a book. In a folio (Fo, 1o) each sheet has been folded once, making two leaves (four pages), where the leaf is half of the original sheet. In a quarto (Qto, 4to, 4o) each sheet is folded twice, making four leaves (eight pages), where the leaves are a quarter of the original sheet. In an octavo (oct., 8vo, 8o) the sheets have been folded to make eight leaves (sixteen pages). In a duodecimo (12mo) each sheet is folded to make twelve leaves (twenty-four pages). Smaller formats are possible and are usually designated 16mo, etc., but these are uncommon.

If the folded sheets are simply stacked on top of each other for sewing, then the format is indicated by a single term. If the sheets are nestled inside each other to form gatherings, the format of the completed book is expressed as, e.g., quarto in eights. The exact size of books in different formats depended on the size of the sheets, which varied according to the manufacturer. For this reason, leaf measurements are normally used when more precision is necessary.

Forme
A Body of type that has been arranged into pages and prepared for printing; the frame containing this type.

Frontispiece
An illustration preceding the title page of the book, normally printed on the verso of the front free endpaper facing the title page. A volume is considered to have multiple frontispieces if two or more such leaves precede the title page. It is important to note, as well, that when plates are numbered in an illustrated book, the frontispiece is rarely included in this numbered sequence.

Galleys
Galleys is short for galley proofs, which are preliminary printed copies of a work that the printer sends to the author (or his/her designate), editor, or proofreader for corrections. Galley proofs are named for the galleys, or metal trays, in which a printer (in the days of the handpress) laid and tightened type into place. Galley proofs represent an earlier stage of print production than page proofs, and extensive editing was often expected at the galley stage. Page proofs represent a later part of the prepublication process, when most of the corrections and edits are expected to have already been done. Making corrections at the page-proof stage is generally discouraged as it involves more expense.

Gathering
A number of sheets folded together for binding. (See also **Format**.)

Gloss
Explanations inserted into a manuscript or printed text for the sake of clarification, either in the case of foreign phrases or difficult meaning. May appear either in the margin or directly in the text, often as footnotes or endnotes.

Gutenberg
Johannes Gutenberg (1398–1468) was a German printer and publisher who used previous technologies in addition to his own inventions to create moveable type and the handpress around 1440.

Handpress

A printing press powered by hand, invented around 1440 by Johannes Gutenberg and based on existing presses used for making wine or olive oil. The handpress, along with moveable type, made it possible to produce books much more quickly, reliably, and cheaply than copying by hand. It was replaced by steam-powered rotary presses in the nineteenth century.

Holograph

A manuscript written entirely in the hand of the author.

Hypertext

Digital text that is displayed on the screens of computers or other digital devices and that offers access, commonly through a mouse click, key sequence, or, in the case of touch screens, pressure, at designated points (hyperlinks) to additional text, as well as images and other graphics. Its most familiar application is the World Wide Web.

Illuminated manuscripts

Manuscripts that contain hand-painted decorations, often adorning initial letters, single words, or first lines, but also included in the margins or as full-page illustrations. Illuminations may feature gold, silver, or coloured designs.

Imprint

Written formula that specifies the individuals responsible for the production of a book, generally including a name, place of publication, and date; may refer to either a printer's imprint or the publisher's imprint, or to a combination of the two. Most commonly located either on the title page or at the end of the book.

Intaglio printing

A form of printing where the ink sits in incised areas of the printing surface and is then squeezed out as the printing surface passes through the press. Its most common application in the production of books is to produce engravings or etchings using the rotary press. (See also **Engraving**; **Planographic printing**; **Relief printing**.)

Intensive reading (see **Extensive/Intensive reading**)

Intermediality
The study of the interactions between various media, and the acceptance that various media always exist alongside each other.

Job printing
Printing, usually commercial, that produces documents not catalogued as books, periodicals, or newspapers; examples may include menus, invitation cards, and posters. Most printing houses took on jobbing work, which was done in between printing books and represented a significant portion of the press's income.

Leaf/Leaves
A leaf is one of the units into which the original sheet is folded to make a book. Each leaf consists of two pages, one on its front side (recto, obverse) and one on its back (verso, reverse). Leaf, leaves are abbreviated as l., ll., or f., ff. (See also **Format**.)

Libel
Libel is a legal term used to describe published statements that are considered to be false, dangerous, or otherwise defamatory. Historically, in Britain, a libel could be directed against an individual or an institution (such as a government); thus there were both private libels (against individuals) and public ones (against the public, for publishing seditious, obscene or blasphemous writing).

Library
A collection of resources (which may include printed or handwritten texts, as well as digital resources). The collection may be made available to a community of individuals for consultation and/or borrowing. Criteria for belonging to the community of users varies and may include relationships (**family library**, which refers to the collection of books owned by a particular family and thus available to its members and other individuals to whom it chooses to grant access), geography (many **public libraries** are funded through the taxation of the population of a given area), membership in a larger institution that funds the collection (**university libraries**), or paid subscription (**circulating libraries**).

Libraries may vary widely in size and degree of specialization and often evolve complex systems of organization and categorization so as to render their resources available. Increasingly, libraries may offer digital, rather than physical, access to resources (e.g., online journals, e-texts).

Licensing Act

A British Act of Parliament in effect between 1662 and 1695. It granted significant authority to the Stationers' Company, allowing for the imposition of restrictions on the number of printers and presses, and enabling works to be censored prior to publication. Under the Act, a member of the Company could register a given book and then have the exclusive right to print, copy, and publish it. The Act was controversial, and when it was allowed to lapse permanently in 1695 there followed a long series of unsuccessful attempts to introduce replacement legislation.

Linotype

Linotype is a process developed in the late nineteenth century by German-American Ottmar Mergenthaler (1854–99) to facilitate typesetting and casting: after an operator enters text with a keyboard, the machine assembles the matrices (that is, the molds from which type is produced) and casts an entire line of type at once, rather than on a letter-by-letter basis, therefore greatly increasing the speed of typesetting and facilitating, in particular, the publication of newspapers and journals. (See also **Typography**.)

Literacy

Generally, the ability to read and write (as well as the extent of this ability in a given time period or geographic location), though it may also be used more generally to refer to competence in a given field (for example, **digital literacy**). Historically, the ability to read and write did not always go together, since the two skills were taught separately.

Lithography

A planographic printing process developed at the end of the eighteenth century in Germany that relies on the use of a flat plate (neither incised nor raised) that may be either metal or stone: the image is marked on the plate with an oily substance and the remaining area is treated to render it water-attracting: thus, when inked, the ink is attracted only to the image to be impressed. Widely used in cartography, commercial stationery, and other non-book printed matter, it greatly facilitated the production of colour illustrations.

Manuscript
A work written by hand, abbreviated as ms/MS or pluralized as mss/MSS.

Marginalia (adj. marginal)
Material, separate from the main content of a document, which is either written or printed into the margins, often by readers. May include notes, comments, and illustrations, and often (but not always) relates or responds to the main content.

Monograph
A systematic treatise on a particular subject.

Moveable type
Single-letter pieces of type, which are arranged to make words for printing. Once printed, they can be reused to make new words. (See also **Compositor**.)

Octavo
A book made by folding the printed sheet to form eight leaves (sixteen pages). Octavos were one of the most common formats in the eighteenth and nineteenth centuries. (See also **Format**.)

Oral culture (see **Orality/Oralism**)

Orality/Oralism
Transmission of information through vocal mechanisms (primarily speech and song) rather than written symbols. **Oral culture** refers to this being the predominant mode of transmission amongst a given group, or in a given time or historical period. **Oral works** are those shared by oral means, sometimes through formalized recitations; as such, they often possess features to aid with memorization and recitation.

Page
One side of a leaf. (See also **Format**.)

Page proofs (see **Galleys**)

Pamphlet
A short complete work, usually polemical in nature, printed unbound, and making use of either staples or sewn pages instead, occasionally utilizing paper wrappers, and designed for wide circulation.

Papyrus
Writing material made from a large variety of rushes by the ancient Egyptians. In use in Egypt in the eleventh century BCE and in Greece and Rome by the fourth century BCE.

Paratext (adj. paratextual)
Any of the textual elements that surround the main body of a printed book, including but not limited to title pages, half-titles, advertisement leaves, prefaces, errata slips, blurbs, dedications, epigraphs, annotations, appendices, and indices.

Parchment
Used primarily as a writing surface (although sometimes also for binding), parchment is formed from the untanned, split portion of an animal's skin, usually a sheep or goat. It is prepared through a process of stretching and scraping so as to produce an even writing surface.

Periodical
A magazine or newspaper published at various intervals, commonly daily, weekly, monthly, quarterly, or annually.

Piracy
Publishing an edition of a work without the permission of the copyright owner. (See also **Copyright**.)

Plagiarism
Literary theft; the action or practice of taking the work of someone else and presenting it as one's own.

Planographic printing
A family of printing techniques (**lithography** being one example) in which designs are created using a level surface rather than one in which designs are raised (**relief**), or incised (**intaglio**). The surface is prepared so that the design accepts ink (in the case of lithography, through the application of an oil-based substance) and the remainder of the surface is prepared so as to repel it. Thus, when ink is applied, it deposits only on the design, and the rest of the surface appears as white space on the printed page. (See also **Relief printing**; **Intaglio printing**.)

Playbook
A printed version of the text of a theatrical drama made commercially available; playbooks could be intended for use by actors in the process of staging the play, or for reading as literary material. Playbooks could originate from a number of manuscript sources: a manuscript written by the playwright himself; a transcribed manuscript offered by, or solicited from, a players' company; a manuscript made available by unauthorized means; or from manuscript versions of performance texts.

Preface
A note preceding the main body of text of a book, which may state the origin, purpose, and scope of the work as well as acknowledgements of assistance. It is distinguished from the introduction, which deals more with the subject of the book.

Pressmark
A mark, sometimes a letter or number and sometimes found in the bottom margin of a printed book, thought to indicate which employee of the printing house typeset or printed certain sheets. Such marks are difficult to decipher, but they were probably used to calculate the wages of pressmen. (See also **Signature**.)

Presswork
The work undertaken to print a text of images using the printing press, and the arrangement of this work in the printing house. More especially, the work of operating the press, as distinct from pre-press work of composition and imposition, and post-press work of folding, collating, and stitching.

Printer

The individual or company responsible for the physical manufacture of a book through the process of setting text and producing impressions of ink; a given printer would own type and a press and would use these to print the texts brought to him, but would generally have no responsibility for obtaining texts for printing or for ensuring sales of the printed book.

Proofs

Printed versions of an unpublished document made available, to the author and/or other individuals, for the sake of corrections or changes. May include a number of stages (first proofs, revised proofs, final proofs). **Proofing**: the activity of examining and correcting proofs. (See also **Galleys**.)

Publisher

The individual or company who makes a financial investment in the publication of a given work. Publishers acquired the rights to texts, financed their printing, and stood to gain or lose a profit based on how well the text sold. In some cases, publishers shared the financial risks of publication either with other publishers, or with the author, through a variety of arrangements. Before the eighteenth century, the role of publisher was not always clearly distinguished from that of printer or bookseller.

Quarto

A book made by folding the printed sheet twice, producing four leaves (eight pages). In the sixteenth and seventeenth centuries, this format was commonly used; many of Shakespeare's plays, for example, appeared in quarto format. In the eighteenth and nineteenth centuries, this format tended to be reserved for more expensive books. (See also **Format**.)

Recto

The front side of a leaf (also known as the obverse). In an open codex, it appears as the right hand page. (See also **Verso**.)

Relief printing
Family of printing techniques (including woodcut, metalcut, and relief etching) in which portions of a surface (which may be wood or metal) are cut away, leaving a design that remains at the original height of the surface (and is then said to be in relief). When ink is applied to the surface, it deposits only on these raised portions, which then appear as the inked portions of the design, while the portions of lower height do not receive ink and appear as the white portions of the design. Along with **intaglio** and **planographic** techniques, relief forms one of the three main groupings of printing techniques. Since printing from moveable type is technically a form of relief printing, other forms of relief printing are relatively easy to incorporate alongside it and this has contributed to their widespread use. (See also **Intaglio printing**; **Planographic printing**.)

Roll (see **Scroll**)

Run (see **Edition**)

Scribal culture
A culture in which writing with the hand constitutes the dominant mode of communication. Scribal culture refers principally to the period between the invention of writing and the invention of printing. Literacy was largely confined to small groups of individuals (scribes, though the term denotes more specifically individuals responsible for transcribing texts, either from dictation or from another written source) who therefore mediated most forms of written communication. Scribal culture was not destroyed by the invention of printing, but continued in modified forms.

Scribal publication
A term developed by Harold Love to describe a mode of circulating texts (primarily in the seventeenth and eighteenth centuries in England) that relies on private and commercial manuscript production for circulating texts, rather than making them available in print. Importantly, Love has shown that commercial (or paid) scribes continued to prepare copies of manuscripts long after the advent of printing. (See also **Scribal culture**.)

Scribe (see **Scribal culture**)

GLOSSARY

Scriptorium (pl. scriptoria)
The room in a monastery or other religious house devoted to the copying of manuscripts.

Scroll
An early form of book that was written on a strip of papyrus or other material and rolled on one or more rods, also called a rolled book or roll. Papyrus sheets were overlapped and pasted together to form a roll, normally no more than twenty sheets long, or about fifteen feet. The inside of the roll was written on and the outside of the roll was usually left blank. Book rolls, or volumen, could be as long or as short as needed, but were usually about thirty to thirty-five feet. Scrolls were read by unrolling with the right hand, while rewinding the read portion with the left hand. Papyrus rolls generally had eight- to ten-inch columns, containing twenty-five to forty-five lines each, with half inch margins and larger margins at the top and bottom.

Sheets
Pieces of paper that, after printing, may be folded into two, four, or eight pages to generate respectively a folio, quarto, or octavo volume. (See also **Format**.)

Stationers' Company
Composed of booksellers, printers, and bookbinders based in London, the Company was formed by Royal Charter in 1557 with the aim of regulating and organizing printing and the book trade. It issued strict rules controlling most aspects of the book trade and also established a Register intended to record the books that a given printer had the right to print.

Statute of Anne
The Statute of Anne, enacted in Britain in 1710, also known as the Copyright Act, was the first statute to provide for copyright regulated by the government and courts. It specified a copyright period of 14 years, with one further extension of an additional 14 years if the author was still alive at the expiration of the first 14-year term. After that, the copyright would end and the work would enter the public domain.

Subscription

A method of publication, particularly prevalent in eighteenth-century England, where the printing of a text was financed by contributions from individuals who offered advance payment for their copies. Subscribers were often wealthy and influential; in return for their contributions, texts often included lists acknowledging their subscribers.

Technological determinism

A theory that locates the advent of new technologies as the driving force for social changes and the evolution of cultural values. It posits technology as largely separate from other realms of human activity, and in fact directing the course of those activities, rather than as part of a larger cultural ecology.

Text/Work

A literary work (such as *King Lear*) may exist in multiple texts (such as those published in quarto in 1608 and 1619 and in the First Folio of 1623). In some cases, the differences between texts reflect changes in the **authorial intentions** for the work. In other cases, they reflect imperfections in the production of the text. Where several texts of a work exist, scholars debate whether they should be treated as different witnesses to the same work, or as different versions of the work, or as different works. In the first case, an **eclectic edition** could combine evidence from several texts to produce a new and better text of the work than any existing text. In the second case, an editor might edit two or more versions and present them on facing pages for comparison. In the third case, two different editions might be required.

Title page

A page at the beginning of a book or work, bearing its full title, and often the author's name, as well as the editor's, etc., and the imprint. The leaf that includes the title page is commonly called the title page, though technically it is the title leaf. The half-title is the title of a book printed on the leaf before the title page.

Transcript

A handwritten or typed copy of an original that attempts to reproduce the original; a **diplomatic transcription** attempts to reproduce the original exactly.

Typecase

A wooden box with compartments to hold the different pieces of moveable type used in letterpress printing. Traditionally, capital letters would be stored and sorted in an upper case; this is the origin of the term uppercase to describe capital letters and lowercase to describe minuscules.

Typeface/Type

A set of characters for printing that share a common appearance; also known as a **font family**. Typefaces in common use today include Times New Roman and Helvetica. In non-specialist use, "typeface" is often used interchangeably with "font"; however, a font is in fact a specific subset of a typeface. Thus Times New Roman is a typeface, while Times New Roman ten point italic is a font.

Typescript

A typed copy of a text.

Typesetter (see **Compositor**)

Typography

The design and process of producing type, as well as the study of this process. Aspects of typography include choice of **typeface** (the design of how characters will appear), size, line length, and questions of spacing between lines (**leading**), words (**justification**), and individual characters (**kerning**).

Vellum

Used first as a writing surface for manuscripts, and later as binding and covering, vellum is made from untanned animal skin (usually calf, but sometimes lamb, goat, or deer) stretched so as to generate an even surface. Unlike parchment, which is generally formed from split skin, vellum is usually made using the whole skin. Vellum may also indicate finer quality of parchment. (See also **Parchment**.)

Verso

The backside (or reverse side) of a leaf; in an open codex it appears as the left hand page. (See also **Recto**.)

Watermark

A distinguishing mark or device contained within the wire mesh of the tray in which the pulp settles in the process of papermaking. The subsequent watermark, also called a **papermark**, can be seen when the finished product is held against the light. Since watermarks are often dated, they can help to date books, by providing the earliest date the paper could have been in use. Watermarks also provide evidence for the makeup of the book, because their location in the book will be determined by the number of times the sheet has been folded. They can therefore help to determine format when this is difficult to determine by examining the binding or by other means. Some sheets also included a **countermark**, a smaller unit introduced in the seventeenth century that was usually placed on the opposite half of the sheet to the watermark.

Woodcut

An illustration generated by the impression of an inked piece of wood into which a design has been cut (specifically, the non-design portions are cut away, leaving the image in relief). Woodcuts represent the earliest form of printed illustration, appearing in Europe in the fifteenth century, though more ancient examples of the technology are available from Asia.

Work (see **Text**)

Further Reading

This book is designed as a companion volume to *The Broadview Reader in Book History*, and we encourage you to turn to that book to continue your exploration of the field. In this guide to further reading, we have mostly omitted books and articles that are excerpted in the *Broadview Reader*. Here, instead, we list some of the many other useful books and articles that address different aspects of the field, paying particular attention to those that offer an introductory approach.

Useful Collections

The Cambridge History of the Book in Britain. Cambridge: Cambridge UP, 1999–. 7 vols. Gen. eds. John Barnard, D.F. McKenzie, David McKitterick, I.R. Willison.
> A monumental, seven-volume survey of the history of the book in Britain offers a detailed account of the creation, material production, dissemination, and reception of texts from the Roman period to present.

Eliot, Simon, and Jonathan Rose, eds. *A Companion to the History of the Book*. Oxford: Blackwell, 2009.
> A landmark collection of commissioned essays providing a wide survey of book history as it existed in 2009.

Howsam, Leslie, ed. *The Cambridge Companion to the History of the Book*. Cambridge: Cambridge UP, 2014.
> A wide-ranging collection of essays from leading scholars aimed at readers new to the field, which provides an excellent grounding in book history.

Levy, Michelle, and Tom Mole, eds. *The Broadview Reader in Book History*. Peterborough, ON: Broadview, 2014.
> A collection of seminal essays from the last thirty years and more, showing the growth and shaping of the field and connecting it to recent thinking about the history of media.

The Oxford History of Popular Print Culture. Oxford: Oxford UP, 2011–. 9 vols. Gen. ed. Gary Kelly.
> The first comprehensive survey of popular print, currently in production.

Suarez, Michael F., S.J., and H.R. Woudhuysen, eds. *The Book: A Global History.* Oxford: Oxford UP, 2013.
> An ambitious collection aimed at producing the first truly global approach to book history, based on the editors' two-volume *Oxford Companion to the Book.*

General Introductions

Bland, Mark. *A Guide to Early Printed Books and Manuscripts.* Malden, MA: Wiley-Blackwell, 2013.
> An introduction to bibliographical studies and textual scholarship as they pertain to early modern manuscripts and printed texts.

Dane, Joseph A. *What Is a Book?: The Study of Early Printed Books.* Notre Dame, IN: U of Notre Dame P, 2012.
> An introduction to the study of books produced in the handpress era, between 1450 and 1800, and the history of book-copies.

Darnton, Robert. *The Case for Books: Past, Present, and Future.* New York: Public Affairs, 2009.
> Darnton has been a defining figure for book history. This collection of his essays offers an insight into the range of his recent work in the field, including his leadership of the Digital Public Library of America project.

Houston, Keith. *The Book: A Cover-to-Cover Exploration of the Most Powerful Object of Our Time.* New York: Norton, 2016.
> This book offers a learned but accessible introduction to the history of the book, written for non-specialists.

Howsam, Leslie. *Old Books and New Histories: An Orientation to Studies in Book and Print Culture*. Toronto: U of Toronto P, 2006.
> This is an accessible introduction, written in an engaging style from the perspective of an historian and aimed at students starting to study book history.

Lyons, Martyn. *Books: A Living History*. London: Thames and Hudson, 2011.
> A lavishly illustrated volume exploring the variety of forms that books have taken over a long historical range, from cuneiform tablets to electronic texts.

Commentaries on the Field

Kirschenbaum, Matthew, and Sarah Werner. "Digital Scholarship and Digital Studies: The State of the Discipline." *Book History* 17.1 (2014): 406–58.
> A review essay that addresses the intertwining of print and digital book technologies, surveying the digital tools and resources available to book historians and the need for book historians to study computer software, platforms, and codes.

Lerer, Seth. "Epilogue: Falling Asleep Over the History of the Book." *PMLA* 121.1 (2006): 229–34.
> A witty and provocative take on the relationship between book history and other academic trends of the recent past.

Price, Leah. "Introduction: Reading Matter." *PMLA* 121.1 (2006): 9–15.
> An overview of the emergence of book history in relation to other academic trends—in particular the rise of Theory—and a survey of the current state of the field in 2006.

———. "Reading: The State of the Discipline." *Book History* 7.1 (2004): 303–20.
> A survey of the diversity of methods used to study the history of reading.

Print Culture

Hammill, Faye, and Mark Hussey, ed. *Modernism's Print Cultures*. London: Bloomsbury Academic, 2016.
> A guide to periodical publishing and the material history of early-twentieth-century publishing—covering topics including small presses, typography, illustration, and book design.

Patten, Eve, and Jason McElligott. *The Perils of Print Culture: Book, Print and Publishing History in Theory and Practice*. Houndsmill: Palgrave, 2014.
> A collection of essays that explore recent methods for, and perils in, the study of print culture.

Robertson, Frances. *Print Culture: From Steam Press to Ebook*. New York: Routledge, 2013.
> A theoretically informed introduction to the concept of print culture, and an overview of the work that concept might do in our historical understanding.

Robinson, Solveig C. *The Book in Society: An Introduction to Print Culture*. Peterborough, ON: Broadview, 2013.
> A sociological approach to the circulation of printed books and the various structures and institutions that shape their trajectories through culture and society.

History of Reading

Cavallo, Guglielmo, and Roger Chartier. *The History of Reading in the West*. Amherst: U of Massachusetts P, 2003.
> A wide-ranging survey of the changing practices of reading in Western culture from antiquity to the present.

Jackson, Heather. *Marginalia: Readers Writing in Books*. New Haven, CT: Yale UP, 2002.
> A lively study of how the history of reading may be traced in the history of marginalia and annotations.

Manguel, Alberto. *A History of Reading*. London: Flamingo, 1997.
> A beautifully written, learned, and non-chronological approach to the history of reading aimed at the general reader.

Price, Leah. *How to Do Things with Books in Victorian Britain*. Princeton, NJ: Princeton UP, 2012.
> An engaging and wide-ranging account of how books were used in the Victorian period for purposes other than reading.

Radway, Janice. *Reading the Romance*. Chapel Hill: U of North Carolina P, 1984.
> A landmark study exploring the responses of women readers to romance genre fiction.

Raven, James, Helen Small, and Naomi Tadmor. *The Practice and Representation of Reading in England*. Cambridge: Cambridge UP, 2007.
> A wide-ranging collection of essays that was a landmark in the emergence of the history of reading as a distinct field of study.

Towheed, Shafquat, Rosalind Crone, and Katie Halsey, eds. *The History of Reading*. London: Routledge, 2010.
> A collection of previously published essays giving a thorough overview of this field.

History of the Book Trade

Raven, James. *The Business of Books: Booksellers and the English Book Trade, 1450–1850*. New Haven, CT: Yale UP, 2007.
> The four-hundred-year history of the English book trade, told in impressive detail. This book is particularly notable for the attention it pays to the shifting historical geographies of book production.

Thompson, John. *Merchants of Culture: The Publishing Business in the Twenty-First Century*. Cambridge: Polity, 2010.
> A sociological approach to trade publishing, based on extensive interviews with key figures in the industry.

Women and Book History

Ezell, Margaret. *Social Authorship and the Advent of Print*. Baltimore: Johns Hopkins UP, 2003.
> An influential account of the collaborative practices of social authorship, the private production, and circulation of manuscripts in the seventeenth and eighteenth centuries that was an especially important means of literary transmission for women and those living away from large cities.

Hackel, Heidi Brayman, and Catherine E. Kelly, eds. *Reading Women: Literacy, Authorship, and Culture in the Atlantic World, 1500–1800*. Philadelphia: U of Pennsylvania P, 2008.
> A collection of essays that demonstrates women's growing literacy and engagement with reading over the first three centuries of print and describes women's active involvement in the print market and literary genres.

Ingrassia, Catherine, ed. *The Cambridge Companion to Women's Writing in Britain, 1660–1789*. Cambridge: Cambridge UP, 2015.
> Several essays in this compilation focus on women's involvement in print culture during the Restoration and eighteenth century.

Levy, Michelle. "Do Women Have a Book History?." *Studies in Romanticism* 53.3 (2014): 297–317.
> A challenge to scholars working in the field to consider its relationship to women's history and feminist scholarship.

McDowell, Paula. *The Women of Grub Street: Press, Politics, and Gender in the London Literary Marketplace, 1678–1730*. Oxford: Clarendon, 1998.
> A ground-breaking study of the women's extensive participation in the production and transmission of print culture and, with it, public life.

Smith, Helen. *"Grossly Material Things": Women and Book Production in Early Modern England.* Oxford: Oxford UP, 2012.
> A comprehensive study of women's roles in writing, making, and using early modern books.

Bibliography

Carter, John. *ABC for Book Collectors.* 9th ed. Ed. Nicolas Barker and Simarn Thadani. New Castle, DE: Oak Knoll, 2016.
> A new, illustrated edition of this classic reference book, containing over 450 alphabetical entries. Not just for book collectors, but for anyone interested in the history of the codex.

Gaskell, Philip. *A New Introduction to Bibliography.* New Castle, DE: Oak Knoll, 1995.
> The classic manual of bibliography, examining every aspect of the subject in rigorous detail.

Tanselle, G. Thomas. *Bibliographical Analysis: A Historical Introduction.* Cambridge: Cambridge UP, 2009.
> A well-informed historical overview of what bibliography entails and how it has developed.

Textual Scholarship

Fraistat, Neil, and Julia Flanders, eds. *The Cambridge Companion to Textual Scholarship.* Cambridge: Cambridge University Press, 2013.
> A wide-ranging collection of new essays surveying both Anglo-American and Continental traditions of textual scholarship, as well as the uses of digital technologies in scholarly editing.

Greetham, David C. *Textual Scholarship: An Introduction.* London: Routledge, 1994.
> A thorough textbook of textual scholarship and scholarly editing, offering a wide-ranging introduction to the field.

———. *Theories of the Text*. Oxford: Oxford UP, 1999.
> A comprehensive account of how textual criticism and scholarly editing have responded to the challenges of contemporary critical theory.

Kelemen, Erick. *Textual Editing and Criticism: An Introduction*. New York: Norton, 2009.
> A useful, practical textbook aimed at graduate students in the humanities, providing a good introduction to textual scholarship and a set of practical examples to work through.

Tanselle, G. Thomas. *Textual Criticism since Greg: A Chronicle, 1950–2000*. Charlottesville: Bibliographical Society of the U of Virginia, 2005.
> An historical account of developments in the field over this period, providing an excellent grounding in the evolution of debates, but mostly stopping short of the digital revolution in editing.

Remediation / Media History

Bolter, J. David, and Richard Grusin. *Remediation: Understanding New Media*. Boston: MIT P, 1999.
> A pioneering study that examines how "new" media rely on conventions and connotations of existing media to foster cultural legitimacy.

Drucker, Joanna. *Graphesis: Visual Forms of Knowledge Production*. Cambridge, MA: Harvard UP, 2014.
> Drucker presents a critical survey of the visual interfaces through which most of our knowledge is mediated, the most significant of which is the graphical user interface (GUI), the dominant feature of the screens of nearly all consumer electronic devices.

Emerson, Lori. *Reading Writing Interfaces: From the Digital to the Bookbound*. Minneapolis: U of Minnesota P, 2014.
> A study of how interfaces mediate between writer and text as well as between writer and reader; Emerson moves backwards

chronologically, from today's handheld devices to yesterday's desktops, from typewriters to Emily Dickinson's self-bound fascicles.

Gitelman, Lisa. *Always Already New: Media, History and the Data of Culture.* Boston: MIT P, 2006.
: A seminal work of media history that examines the cultural significance of media in their historical contexts.

———. *Paper Knowledge: Toward a Media History of Documents.* Durham, NC: Duke UP, 2014.
: A media history of documents over the last 150 years, examining various technologies for creating, copying, and storing documents, including mechanical, chemical, and digital forms.

Kirschenbaum, Matthew. *Track Changes: A Literary History of Word Processing.* Cambridge, MA: Belknap, 2016.
: A history of how writing was transformed by the introduction of word-processing software, describing how the act of writing always arises from particular instruments and media, from quills to keyboards.

Kittler, Friedrich A. *Gramophone, Film, Typewriter.* Trans. Geoffrey Winthrop-Young and Michael Wutz. Stanford, CA: Stanford UP, 1999.
: Kittler's influential account of how the emergence of new media technologies in the late nineteenth century, particularly phonography, photography, and cinematography, restructured our relationship to referentiality and to the technology of print.

Permissions Acknowledgements

p. 68: Copy of one of Gutenberg's 1454 indulgences. Copyright © the University of Manchester.

p. 75: Darnton, Robert. "The Communications Circuit," Figure 7.1 from *Kiss of Lamourette*. Copyright © 1990 by Robert Darnton. Used by permission of W.W. Norton & Company, Inc., and Faber and Faber Ltd.

p. 75 ebook: Darnton, Robert. "The Communications Circuit," Figure 7.1 from *Kiss of Lamourette*. Copyright © 1990 by Robert Darnton. Used by permission of W.W. Norton & Company, Inc.

p. 76: Adams, Thomas R., and Nicolas Barker. "The Whole Socio-Economic Conjuncture," from "A New Model for the Study of the Book," in *A Potencie of Life: Books in Society: The Clark Lectures 1986–1987*, edited by Nicolas Barker. London: British Library Studies in the History of the Book, 1993. Reprinted with the permission of the British Library, Oak Knoll Press, and the authors.

p. 93: Crowd of unemployed men reading newspapers, 1928. Chicago History Museum, DN-0085379; Chicago Daily News, Inc., photographer.

p. 120: Dickinson, Emily. "We talked with each other about each other," c. 1879, Amherst Manuscript #514. The Emily Dickinson Collection, Amherst College Archives & Special Collections.

p. 147: Subscription Options, screenshot from the New York Times website, 2016. Copyright © 2016, the New York Times. All rights reserved. Used by permission and protected by the Copyright Laws of the United States. The printing, copying, redistribution, or retransmission of this content without express written permission is prohibited.

p. 149: *The Annotated Pride and Prejudice* (screenshot), based on *Pride and Prejudice* by Jane Austen; annotated and edited by David Shapard. Anchor Books/Knopf Doubleday, 2014.

Index

accidentals, 40
Adam, Robert Borthwick, 126
Adams, Thomas R., 76–77
advertisements, xv, 67, 69, 81, 85
Albert Angelo (Johnson), 14
algorithmic criticism, 157
Alter, Alexandra, 101–02
Amazon, 80, 138, 152
American Library Association, 89
analytical bibliography, 10
Annales school, xiv
Annals of the Fine Arts, 32, 39
anthology, 7, 32
archival methods, 91
archives, 56, 81, 142–45. *See also* publishers' archives
Arthurian legends, 111
Astle, Thomas, 103
Auden, W.H., 46
    Collected Shorter Poems, 54
    Selected Poems, 54
    "Spain, 1937," 54
    "Spain," 54
Augustine, Saint, Bishop of Hippo, *Confessions*, xiii
Austen, Jane, 157
    Pride and Prejudice, 148–50
author attribution, 157–58
authorial intention, 40–41, 45–55, 59, 141
authoritative versions, 33
authors, 13, 75
    author and reader relationship, 94
    circulation of writings in handwritten form, 114, 116
    control over physical production of work, 7
    history of authorship, ix
    paying for costs of printing, 21
    reprinted in America without payment, 83–84
    use of both script and print, 116–17
author's revisions, 21–22, 33, 37, 46, 48–49

Barker, Nicolas, 76–77
Barnard, John, 32
Baron, Naomi, 150
Barthes, Roland, "The Death of the Author," 93
Beethoven, Ludwig van
    "Moonlight" Sonata, 33
Bentham, Jeremy, 143
Benton, Megan, 24
Berliner format, 93
Berne Convention (1886), 83
Bewick, Thomas, 126, 128
    A History of British Birds, 127
Bezos, Jeff, 80
Bible, 36
bibles, 94
biblical criticism, 36
bibliographic code, xv, 4, 6–7, 12, 15–17, 25, 118, 120, 136
    literary and bibliographic codes diverge, 16
    type as part of, 22–23
    used to smuggle radical ideas, 16
bibliography, xiv, 10–17, 77, 137
    Greg's approach, 11–12

McKenzie's approach, 12–13
  as sociology of texts, 13
  status of a science, 12
bibliometry, 10
binding, 9, 21, 26, 66–67, 81, 90, 154
  computer-driven bindery
    equipment, 145
Biographical History of England
  (Granger), 126
Birkerts, Sven, 151–52
  The Gutenberg Elegies, 135
blackletter, 24
Blake, William, 91, 141
Blast magazine, 24
Blayney, Peter, 43
Blithedale Romance (Hawthorne), 42–43
book history, xiii–xv, 69
  chronology, 171–77
  interdisciplinary study, 11
  models for, 74–77
  what it excludes, 69
book illustration. *See* text and image
bookplates, 8–9, 26, 90
books, 67. *See also* codex; e-books
  access to, 78, 80, 85, 114, 166
  affection for the paper book, 138
  banned and challenged books, 89
    (*See also* censorship)
  bound printed book, 66
  business model for new titles, 78–79
  business model for titles being reprinted, 79
  death of (*See* death of the book)
  duality, 165–66
  life cycle of, 76
  materiality, 3–26, 140
  recovery of the book, 101

booksellers, 13, 17, 75, 81, 87, 102
booktraces project, 8, 155
"The Boscombe Valley Mystery," 94
Boswell, James, *Life of Johnson*, 126
Bourdieu, Pierre, 104
Bowdler, Thomas, 89
bowdlerization, 89
Bowers, Fredson, 37, 42–43
Brawne, Fanny, 168
broadsheet, 92–93
broadsides, 67–68, 79, 125
Broadview Reader in Book History (or BRBH), xix
Brontë, Charlotte, *Jane Eyre*, 4
Buchwissenschaft, xiv
Burrows, J.F., *Computation into Criticism*, 157
Byron, George Gordon, Baron, 50–51, 115
  Don Juan, 16, 87, 91

Cambridge Edition of the Complete Fiction of Henry James, 49
Cameron, Sharon, 119
cancels, 122
canon, 90–91, 158
Canterbury Tales (Chaucer), 142
capitalization, 31–32, 40, 119–20
Carr, Nicholas, *The Shallows*, 135
Carver, Raymond, 34–35
catalogues, 5, 81, 90, 166, 168
Catholic Church, 67–68
censorship, 49–50, 52, 87, 89
chapbooks, 16, 79, 125
Charlie Hebdo, 89
Chartier, Roger, 22, 73–74, 90–92
"chase," 19

INDEX

Chaucer, Geoffrey
  Canterbury Tales, 142
  digital editions, 141–42
Chen, Anna, 92
Chesterfield, Philip Dormer Stanhope, Earl of, 3
Children's and Household Tales, 109
Choose Your Own Adventure series, 139
circulating libraries, 79–80
circulation of books, 10, 52, 166–67
  religious and state control over, 81–89 (*See also* censorship)
Citizen Kane, 13
Clare, John, 51
Cleland, John, *Fanny Hill*, 88
close reading, xvii, 157–58
codex, xv, xix, 14, 66–67, 135–36, 138. *See also* books
cognitive abilities, 107
cognitive experience of reading, 152
cognitive outcomes of reading within different environments, 150
Cohen, Matt, 112
  The Networked Wilderness, 111
Coleridge, Samuel Taylor, 8, 91, 110
  "The Rime of the Ancient Mariner," 55
collate, 35
Collected Poems (Moore), 53
Collected Shorter Poems (Auden), 54
collections, 90
colophon, 6
The Coming of the Book (Febvre and Martin), 71
commonplace books, 114, 160
commonplacing, 90
communication technologies, 73

communications circuit model, 74–76, 94, 103, 117
  inclusion of the reader, 75
compositors, 13, 18, 22, 43–44, 65, 113
Computation into Criticism (Burrows), 157
computer-assisted reading. *See* machine-assisted reading
concordances, 156
Confessions (Augustine), xvii
conjectural emendation, 44–45
"Continental" tradition of book history, 10–11
control of print and reading, 81–89
Copinger, W.A., 11
copy-specific information, 7, 9–10, 90, 155
copy-text, 38–41, 46, 56, 141
copyright, x, 79, 83–84, 91, 139, 156
  lack of international copyright, 83
  reprinting British books in America, 83–85
copyright law, xvi, 33, 94
  American copyright law, 84
  effect on price, 85
Cornell edition of Wordsworth's poetry, 48
corpus, 157
corpus stylistics, 157
corruption, 36
Crane, Ralph, 44
Crane, Stephen, 41
"critical apparatus," 35
critical bibliography, 10
critical theory, 13
cultural appropriation, 110
cultural production, 104

219

INDEX

Darnton, Robert, 74–77, 90, 94, 103, 126, 156
Darnton's communications circuit, 76–77, 94, 103, 117
Darwin, Charles, 8–9
    On the Origin of Species, 49–50
De Certeau, Michel, 94
De Selincourt, Ernest, 116
De Vinne, Theodore Low, 25
"The Death of the Author" (Barthes), 93
death of the book, xii, 101, 136, 168
Delgamuukw v. British Columbia, 103
descriptive bibliography, 66
Devonshire Manuscript, 144
dialect, 51, 110
diaries, 91
Dickens, Charles, 83–84
Dickinson, Emily, 116–19, 121, 142, 144
    "We talked to each other about each other," 121
Dickinson's fascicles, 117–18
dictionaries and encyclopedias, 140
digital archives, 142–44
digital editions, 141–42, 154
digital literacy, 150
digital media, xiii–xiv, 73, 140, 145, 151
digital publication alongside print publication, 145–46. *See also* intermediality
digital remediations, 121
digital technology, xvi–xvii
digital textual scholarship, 56, 143–45
diplomatic transcriptions, 58
Don Juan (Byron), 16, 87, 91
Don Quixote, 22
Douglass, Frederick, 86
Doyle, Sir Arthur Conan, 94
Droeshout, Martin, 15, 21

Drucker, Johanna, 24
Duguid, Paul, 102
duodecimo, 19, 87
dust jacket, 9

e-books, 135, 137, 145, 148–50
    imitation of paper books, 138, 156
    materiality, 137
    multimodal functionality, 148
    re-versioning as paper codex, 139
e-journals, 145
Early English Books Online (EEBO), 154
ECCO, 155
eclectic editing, 35, 38
economics of printing. *See* print economies
Edinburgh edition of Scott's Waverley novels, 49
editing, xiv, 35
edition, 7, 21, 35, 119, 136
    digital editions, 141–42, 154
    later editions, 36
    multitext, 142
    new editions produced by scholarly editors, 33, 38
    print runs, 125
    social edition, 144
edition sizes, 78
editors, 34, 51, 59, 109
    scholarly editors, 33, 35–36, 59
editors and readers, blurring roles of, 143
Eighteenth-Century Collections Online (ECCO), 154, 155
Eisenstein, Elizabeth, 71–73, 77
    The Printing Press as an Agent of Change, 70

INDEX

The Printing Revolution in Early Modern Europe, 72
Electronic Textual Cultures Laboratory, 143
Eliot, T.S., 142
emendation, 32
Emily Dickinson Archive, 119
endnotes, 6
endpapers, 8, 26, 126, 154
England, Jesse, 139
engravings, 9, 125–27
enumerative bibliography, 10
ephemera, 67–69, 81, 85
"Epistles to Several Persons" (Pope), 3
errata, 37
Essay on the Origin of Language (Rousseau), 109
etching, 125
expurgated versions, 52
extensive reading, xvii–xviii
extra-illustration, 9, 126, 148
extrinsic evidence, 41–42
Ezell, Margaret, 114, 116

facsimile, 121, 143
fair copies, 36
fair-copy manuscript, 39–40
Family Shakespeare (ed. Bowdler), 89
fan fiction, 94
Fanny Hill (Cleland), 88
fascicles, 117–18
Febvre, Lucien, 6, 72, 74
  The Coming of the Book, 71
federalist papers, 157
Fifty Shades of Grey, 136
First Folio of Shakespeare's plays, 14–15, 20–21, 43–45, 168
  bibliographic code, 15

image and word in, 126
price, 78–79
Folger Shakespeare Library in Washington, DC, 43
folio, 18, 78
format, 9, 18, 78–79
forme, 19
foul case, 18
Fox, Adam, 111
Fraktur, 25
Frankenstein (Shelley), 58
Franklin, Benjamin, 36, 68–69, 80
Franklin, R.W., 121
freedom of expression, 85, 87, 89
frontispiece, 126
full-text databases, 153–54, 157

galley, 18
Gamebooks, 139
gathering, 18
Genette, Gérard, 6
Geschichte des Buchwesens, xiv
glosses, 56
Godwin, William, 59
Google Books, 154–55, 156, 160
Google Books database, 156
government authorization to produce and trade printed books, 82
GPS systems, 107
Grafton, Anthony, 156
Granger, James, *Biographical History of England*, 126
grangerizing, 126, 148
Graphs, Maps, Trees (Moretti), 158
Grasmere Journals (Wordsworth), 121
Greg, Sir Walter Wilson, 12, 40, 77
  "What Is Bibliography?," 11
Grenby, M.O., 8

221

INDEX

Grimm brothers, 109
Gutenberg, Johannes, xi, 19, 67–70, 94, 138
Gutenberg Bible, 68, 78, 124
The Gutenberg Elegies (Bickerts), 101, 135
The Gutenberg Galaxy (McLuhan), 72
Gutjahr, Paul, 24
Guy Mannering (Scott), 91

Hancher, Michael, 46–47
hand-copying, 71, 81–82, 114–15
handpress period, 17, 19–20, 23, 65, 79, 114
handwriting. *See* scribal culture; writing
Hansen, Mark B.N., 105
Hart, Michael, 153
Hathi Trust, 154
Hawthorne, Nathaniel, *Blithedale Romance*, 42–43
Hayles, N. Katherine, 150
Heaney, Seamus, 52–53
Helvetica (2007), 25
Helvetica typeface, 25
Henry V (Shakespeare), 45
hermeneutics, 157
Higginson, Thomas Wentworth, 119
high-status books, 79, 126
histoire du livre, xiv, 10
historical bibliography. *See* analytical bibliography
A History of British Birds (Bewick), 127
history of reading, xiv–xv, 65, 73–74, 89–95
history of the book. *See* book history
Holmes, Sherlock, 94
holograph, 118
home computer and printer, 113

horizontal revision, 47
Hulu, 80
Hustwit, Gary, 25
hybrid readers, 101–02
hybrid world, 146
hyperlinked online texts, 150
hyperreading, xviii–xix, 150
hypertext, 139–40, 151

illuminated books, 141
illuminated manuscripts, 124
illustration. *See* text and image
imprint, 126
indulgences, 66–69, 94
information overload, xviii–xix
Innes, Harold, 108
inscriptions, 90
intaglio printing, 125–26
  planographic printing, 125
  relief printing, 125
Intangible Cultural Heritage (ICH), 112
The Intellectual Life of the British Working Class (Rose), 90
intellectual property, 84. *See also* copyright
intention. *See* authorial intention
intermediality, xx, 101–03, 111, 135, 167
  field of cultural production model, 104
  manuscript and print, 112–23
  new media theory, 104–05
  orality and writing, 105–12
  text and image, 123–28
Internet, 136, 153, 156
iPad, 136

Jackson, Shelley, *Patchwork Girl*, 151
James, Henry, 49

222

Jameson, Frederick, 13
Jane Eyre (Brontë), 4
The Jew's Daughter (Morrissey), 151–52
job printing, 67–69
Johns, Adrian, 71–72, 74, 77
Johnson, B.S.
    Albert Angelo, 14
    The Unfortunates, 14, 139
Johnson, Thomas, 119
Jonson, Ben, "To the Reader," 15
journals, 69
Joyce, James, 90
    Ulysses, 57–58
Judenlettern, 25

Kastan, David Scott, 15
Keats, George, 32
Keats, John, 51, 91, 168
    Lamia, Isabella, The Eve of St Agnes and Other Poems, 32, 39, 91
    "Ode on a Grecian Urn," 31–33, 39–40, 44
Kelly, Kevin, 156
Kerouac, Jack, *On the Road*, 57
keyword searches, 150, 156, 158
Kindle, 94, 136, 138, 148, 150, 168
Kirschenbaum, Matthew, 137
knowledge explosion, 71
Kobo, 150

Lackington, James, 80
Ladenson, Elizabeth, 86
Lady Chatterley's Lover (Lawrence), 52, 87, 89, 94
Lamia, Isabella, The Eve of St Agnes and Other Poems (Keats), 32, 39, 91
Landow, George, 151

Lawrence, D.H., *Lady Chatterley's Lover*, 52, 87
leaves, 8, 26, 58
letters, 91, 114
Lewis, Wyndham, 24
libel, 16, 83, 86–88
librarians, 5, 138, 155, 166
library stamps, 90
Licensing of the Press Act (1662), 83
Life of Johnson (Boswell), 126
linguistic code, 4, 7, 12, 14, 17, 120, 136, 160
Lish, Gordon, 34
literacy, xvi, 107, 113
literary merit as defence against censorship, 87
literary work, defining, 57
Literature Online (database), 153
lithography, 127–28, 145
The Lost Art of Reading (Ulin), 135
Lyrical Ballads (Wordsworth and Coleridge), 91, 110

machine-assisted reading, 156–60
machine-made paper, 78
magazines, 69
Mandiberg, Michael, 140
Manovich, Lev, 159
manuscript, 17, 32, 71, 102, 142
manuscript books
    alongside printed volumes, xvi, 113, 117
    flexibility for integration of image and text, 123–24
manuscript culture, 35, 113. *See also* scribal culture
marginalia, 8–9, 26, 90, 123
Martin, Henri-Jean, 6, 71–72, 74, 119

Martin, Wendy, 116
Marx, Karl, 90
The Master Letters of Emily Dickinson, 121
materiality, xiii, 3–25, 135, 137, 140, 165
    bibliography, 10–17
    typography, 22–25
materiality of digital culture, 140
Matthiessen, F.O., 42
McDowell, Paula, 110
McEachern, Allan, 103
McGann, Jerome, 4, 12, 14, 92, 120, 143
    "double helix of perceptual codes," 7
McGill, Meredith, 83
McKenzie, D.F., 12–13, 20, 66, 74, 76–77
McKerrow, R.B., 38–39
McLuhan, Marshall, 13, 73, 92, 103–04
    The Gutenberg Galaxy, 72
media change, xx, 72, 102, 137
media ecology, xvi, xx, 103, 116, 167
media history
    rise and fall model, 72, 102–03, 111, 167
medieval manuscripts. *See* manuscript books
"the medium is the message," 13, 73
medium theory, 71
Melville, Herman, *White-Jacket*, 42
Mendel, Gregor, 9
Mendelson, Edward, 54
metadata, 155
"Mickey Mouse Protection Act," 84
The Minstrelsy of the Scottish Border (Scott), 109
mise en page, 23
monographs, 4–5

"Moonlight" Sonata, 33
Moore, Marianne, 54
    Collected Poems, 53
Moretti, Franco, 158
    Graphs, Maps, Trees, 158
    "Style, Inc. Reflections on Seven Thousand Titles," 159
Morris, William, 25
Morrissey, Judd, *The Jew's Daughter*, 151–52
moveable type, xv, 19, 86, 125
multimedia content, 140
multimedia forms, 94
multimodal functionality, 148
multiple authorship, 51
Murray, John, 16, 50–51

Nashe, Thomas, 38
natural language, 110
Netflix, 80
The Networked Wilderness (Cohen), 111
new media theory, xvi, 104–05
New York Times, 146
newspapers, 67–69, 79, 85, 92–93, 140
Newsweek magazine, 146
Nineteen Eighty-Four (Orwell), 139
notices, 69
novels, 91

Obscene Publications Act (1959), 87
octavo, 19, 85
"Ode on a Grecian Urn" (Keats), 31–33, 39–40, 44
offset printing, 145
On the Origin of Species (Darwin), 49–50
On the Road (Kerouac), 57
The 120 Days of Sodom (de Sade), 34

INDEX

Ong, Walter, 73–74, 92, 108–09
   Orality and Literacy, 107
online collation tools, 143
online newspapers, 145
optical character recognition (OCR)
   software, 139, 154–55
oral culture, xvi, 70, 73, 103, 106–10
Orality and Literacy (Ong), 107
orality and writing, 105–12
   primary orality, 107–08
Orwell, George, *Nineteen Eighty-Four*, 139
ownership inscriptions, 9
Oxford English Dictionary (OED), 140

pages, 18, 78, 123, 126
Paget, Sidney, 94
pamphlets, 69, 79, 85
paper, 9, 71, 77–78, 85, 113
paratexts, 6–7, 22
parchment, 19, 71
"The Pargiters" (Woolf), 53
Parrish, Stephen, 48
Patchwork Girl (Jackson), 151
Penguin, 87
perceptual codes, 7, 12. *See also*
   bibliographic code, linguistic code
periodicals, 65, 67–69, 117, 140
Peters, John Durham, 107
Phaedrus (Plato), 106–07
physical form. *See* materiality
The Picture of Dorian Gray (Wilde), 136
Piper, Andrew, 140, 149–50, 152
piracies, 83–84, 87
planographic printing, 125, 128
Plato
   Phaedrus, 106–07
   written culture a threat to oral
      tradition, 108–09

playbooks, 79
Pope, Alexander, "Epistles to Several
   Persons," 3
posters, xvi, 65
Poulet, Georges, 3
prayer book, 4–5
The Prelude (Wordsworth), 47–48
Price, Leah, 138
Pride and Prejudice (Austen), 148–50
print, 70–74, 103, 109, 122
   as agent of change, 70
   history in China, 19, 72
   rapid advancement of learning, 71
   scholarly focus on, 114
print culture, xvi, 35
print economies, 77–81
print martyrs, 86
print runs, 125
"Print Wikipedia" project, 140
printed books, 17–22, 152. *See also*
   codex
printers, 13, 17, 21, 50, 68, 75, 81, 124
printer's devils, 37
printing, 65, 67, 73
   digital, 145
   history of, 65
   inexpensive self-printing, 113
   job printing, 68–69
   offset printing, 145
   planographic printing, 125
   relief printing, 125
   religious and political struggles
      intertwined with, 83
   stop-press corrections, 20, 44
"Printing-for-manuscript," 102
printing from woodblocks, 19
printing practices in colonial America,
   68

INDEX

printing press, xv, 113. *See also*
    Gutenberg, Johannes; handpress
*The Printing Press as an Agent of
    Change* (Eisenstein), 70
*The Printing Revolution in Early
    Modern Europe* (Eisenstein), 72
programmatic intentions, 47–48, 52
progressive narrative. *See* media
    history, rise and fall model
Project Gutenberg, 153–54
proofs, 20, 36, 42
ProQuest, 153
proscribed religious writing, 86
Protestant Reformation, 70
publishers, 7, 16–17, 21–22, 34, 50, 75,
    81, 109, 138
    strategies to lower costs of print
        production, 78–80
    symbiotic relation with circulating
        libraries, 80
publishers' archives, 12–13, 78, 90
publishers' catalogues, 81
publishing industry, 6, 76
punctuation, 31–32, 40, 51

quantitative and statistical methods,
    158–59
quarto, 19, 44, 85, 154
Queen Mab (Shelley), 16

Ramsay, Stephen, 157
Raven, James, 77, 81–82, 86
reading, xvii, xviii, 58, 73, 75, 91, 158, 166
    attempts to control, xvi, 86 (*See
        also* censorship)
    as creative act, 93–94
    history of, xiii–xiv, 65, 73–74,
        89–95

hyperreading, xviii–xix, 150
machine-assisted reading, 156–60
preference for print over screen, 150
readers as editors, 143
screen reading, xvii, 150–52
silent reading, xvii, 73
reading aloud, xvii
reading clubs, 80
*The Reading Experience Database
    (RED)*, 91
*The Reading Nation in the Romantic
    Period* (St. Clair), 90
recto, 138
relief printing, 125–26
religious censorship, 86
remediation, 111, 167
Renaissance, 70
"The Rime of the Ancient Mariner"
    (Coleridge), 55–56
Roberts, Jeanne Addison, 43
Robinson, Charles, 58
Romeo and Juliet (Shakespeare), 44
Rose, Jonathan, 86, 91
    *The Intellectual Life of the British
        Working Class*, 90
    "The Welsh Miners' Libraries," 90
Rossetti, Dante Gabriel, 141
Rousseau, Jean-Jacques, 110
    Essay on the Origin of Language, 109
    idealized oral culture in relation to
        print, 109–10
Rowe, Nicholas, 43

Said, Edward, 13
scholarly editions, 38
scholarly editors, 33, 35–36, 59, 145
    using digital technologies, 56, 141
Scientific Revolution, 70

INDEX

Scott, Walter
   Guy Mannering, 91
   "Magnum Opus" edition of his works, 49
   The Minstrelsy of the Scottish Border, 109
screen reading, xvii, 150–52
scribal culture, 70, 115–16. *See also* hand-copying; manuscript; writing
scribes (monastic scribes), 81, 124
scriptoria, 81–82
scroll, xv, 14, 67
Selected Poems (Auden), 54
self-censorship, 49–50, 52–53
Senefelder, Alois, 127–28
Shakespeare, William, 35–36
   attributing works to, 157
   expurgated versions, 89
   First Folio, 14–15, 20–21, 45, 78–79, 126, 168
   Henry V, 45
   Romeo and Juliet, 44
   The Tempest, 43–44
The Shallows (Carr), 135
sheet, 18, 66, 113
Shelley, Mary, 59, 151
   Frankenstein, 58
Shelley, Percy, 58, 91
   Queen Mab, 16
Shelley-Godwin Archive, 58
Siemens, Ray, 143
Silver, Brenda, 53–54
smartphones, 138, 151
Smith, Martha Nell, 117–18
sociology of texts, 13, 66, 74
song-sheets, xvi, 65
Sosnoski, James, 150
Southey, Robert, 87

"Spain, 1937" (Auden), 54
"Spain" (Auden), 54
St. Clair, William, 85, 91
   The Reading Nation in the Romantic Period, 90
Stallybrass, Peter, 67–69, 102
stamp duty on newspapers, 85
stamps, 80–81
standardization, 72
Stanhope Press, 19
state-sponsored censorship, 87
Stationers' Company, 82
Statute of Anne, 83–84
steam presses, 20
Sterne, Laurence, *Tristram Shandy*, 7
Stiegler, Bernard, 105
Stillinger, Jack, 51, 55–56
Strand magazine, 94
Striphas, Ted, 135
stylometry, 157
subscription, 21
substantives, 40–41
Supreme Court of Canada, 103

tablets, 148
tabloid, 93
Tanselle, G. Thomas, 47
taxation, 85
Taylor, John, 51
technological change, 70, 74
   impact on human consciousness, 73
technological determinism, 71, 103–04
technology, xvi, 65, 107, 136
The Tempest (Shakespeare), 43–44
Temple of the Muses, 80
text / work, 33–34, 57, 115, 141
text and image, 9, 123–28

227

cost of printed books with images, 126
in digital age, 123
early printed books, 123–24
handpress period, 123
illuminated books, 141
integration by readers, 126
in Medieval manuscripts, 123–24
textual bibliography, 10. *See also* critical bibliography
textual criticism, 33
textual crux, 43
textual history, 36
textual pluralism, 54–59, 141
textual scholars. *See* scholarly editors
textual transmission, 35–36, 39
textuality, ix, 145
Three Guineas (Woolf), 53
Times New Roman, 22
tipped-in pages, 126
title page, 6, 81, 126
"To the Reader" (Jonson), 15
Todd, Mabel Loomis, 119
topic modelling, 157
"Transcribe Bentham" project, 143
transcript, 32, 143
Treaty of Waitangi, 13
Tristram Shandy (Sterne), 7
Twitter feeds, 146
Twyman, Michael, 17, 124–25, 128
type / typeface, 9, 22–23, 65, 113
moveable type, xv, 19, 86, 125
reusing, 78
typecase, 18
typesetter. *See* compositor
TypeWright project, 155
typewriter, xvi, 112–13
typographical code, 118

typography, 22–25, 92
gendered and racialized, 25
political concerns and, 24

Ulin, David, *The Lost Art of Reading*, 135
Ulysses (Joyce), 57–58
uncut leaves, 8, 26
UNESCO, 112
The Unfortunates (Johnson), 14, 139
universal library, 156
university press, 5
US Supreme Court, 88

Valéry, Paul, 46
variants, xx, 35–36, 40–45, 119
vellum, 71
versions, 55–56, 141
verso, 138
vertical revision, 47–48

Warde, Beatrice, 24
watermarks, 154
"We talked to each other about each other" (Dickinson), 121
"The Welsh Miners' Libraries" (Rose), 90
Werner, Marta, 92
"What Is Bibliography?" (Greg), 11
White-Jacket (Melville), 42
Whitman, Walt, 141
Wilde, Oscar, *The Picture of Dorian Gray*, 136
William Blake Archive, 141
Wood, Henry, Mrs., 90
wood engraving, 126–28
woodcuts, 125
Woof, Pamela, 122

Woolf, Daniel, 111
Woolf, Virginia, 90
   "The Pargiters," 53
   Three Guineas, 53
   The Years, 53
word processing, 137
Wordsworth, Dorothy, 117, 122, 142, 144
   Grasmere Journals, 121
   use of print and scribal publication practices, 116
Wordsworth, William
   Lyrical Ballads, 91, 110
   The Prelude, 47–48
work. *See* text / work
writing, 56–57, 73, 92, 108, 113–15. *See also* scribal culture
   history of, 103
   impact on orality, 107
   as mediated communication, 107

The Years (Woolf), 53

www.ingramcontent.com/pod-product-compliance
Lightning Source LLC
Chambersburg PA
CBHW070443090526
44586CB00046B/1663